AF574632

AMERICAN GODDESS

JEAN PATCHETT

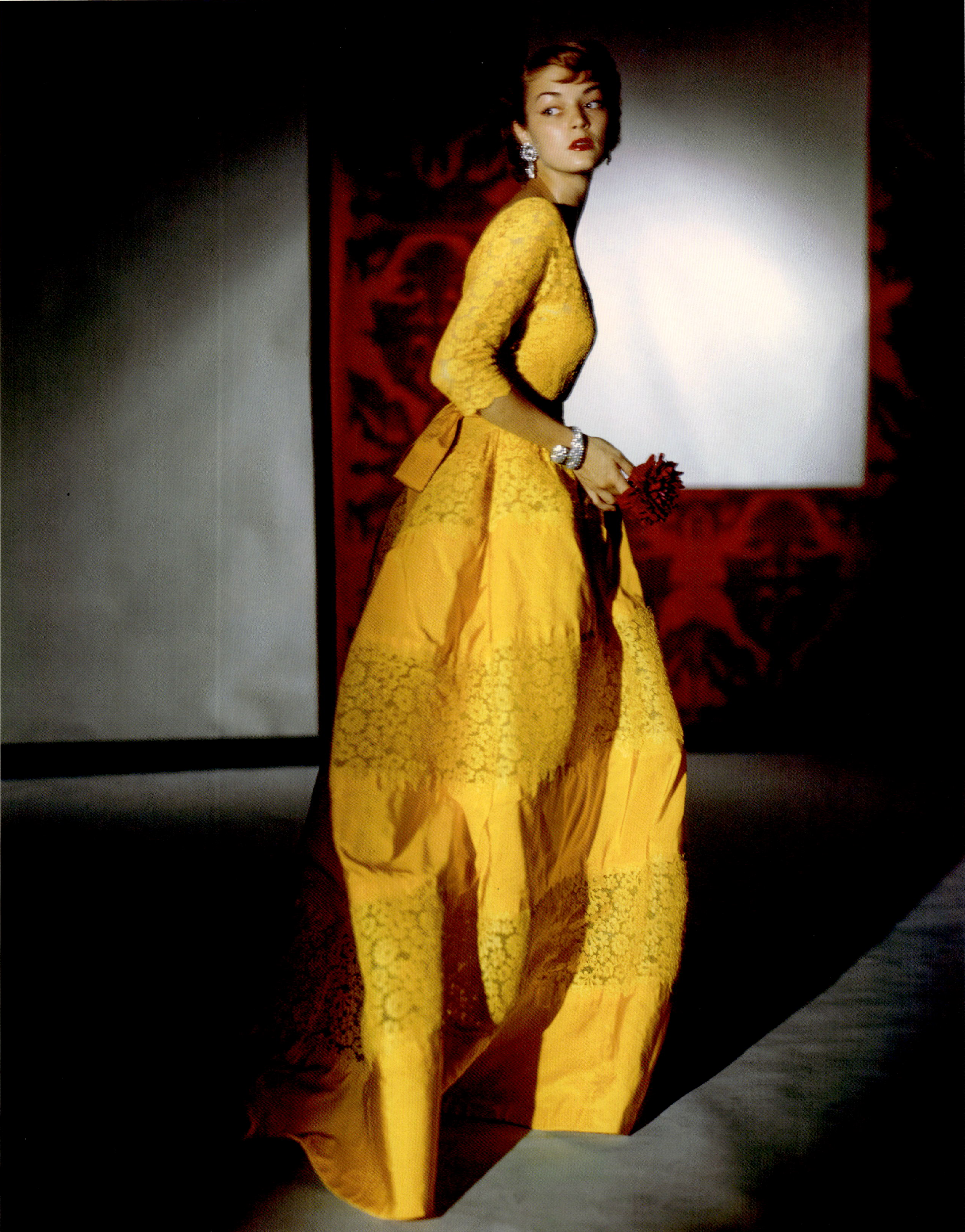

AMERICAN GODDESS
JEAN PATCHETT

by Robert Lilly and Lois Allen Lilly

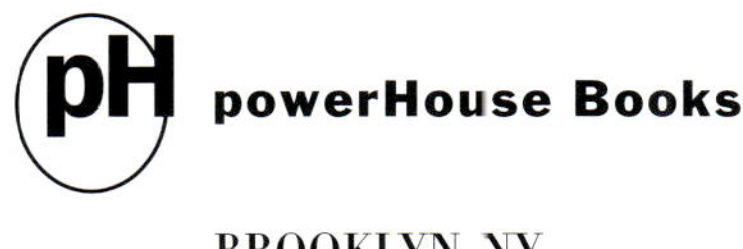

BROOKLYN, NY

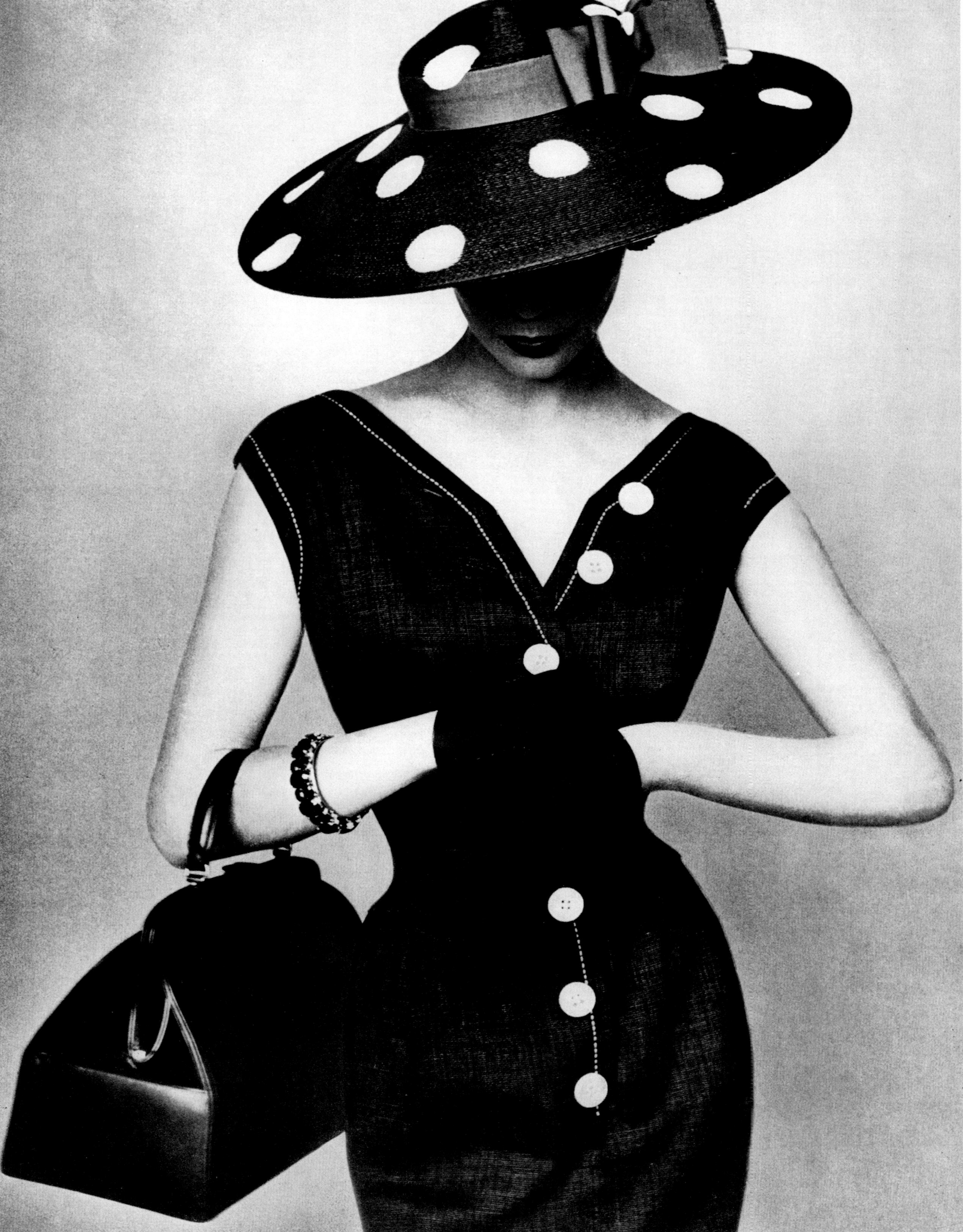

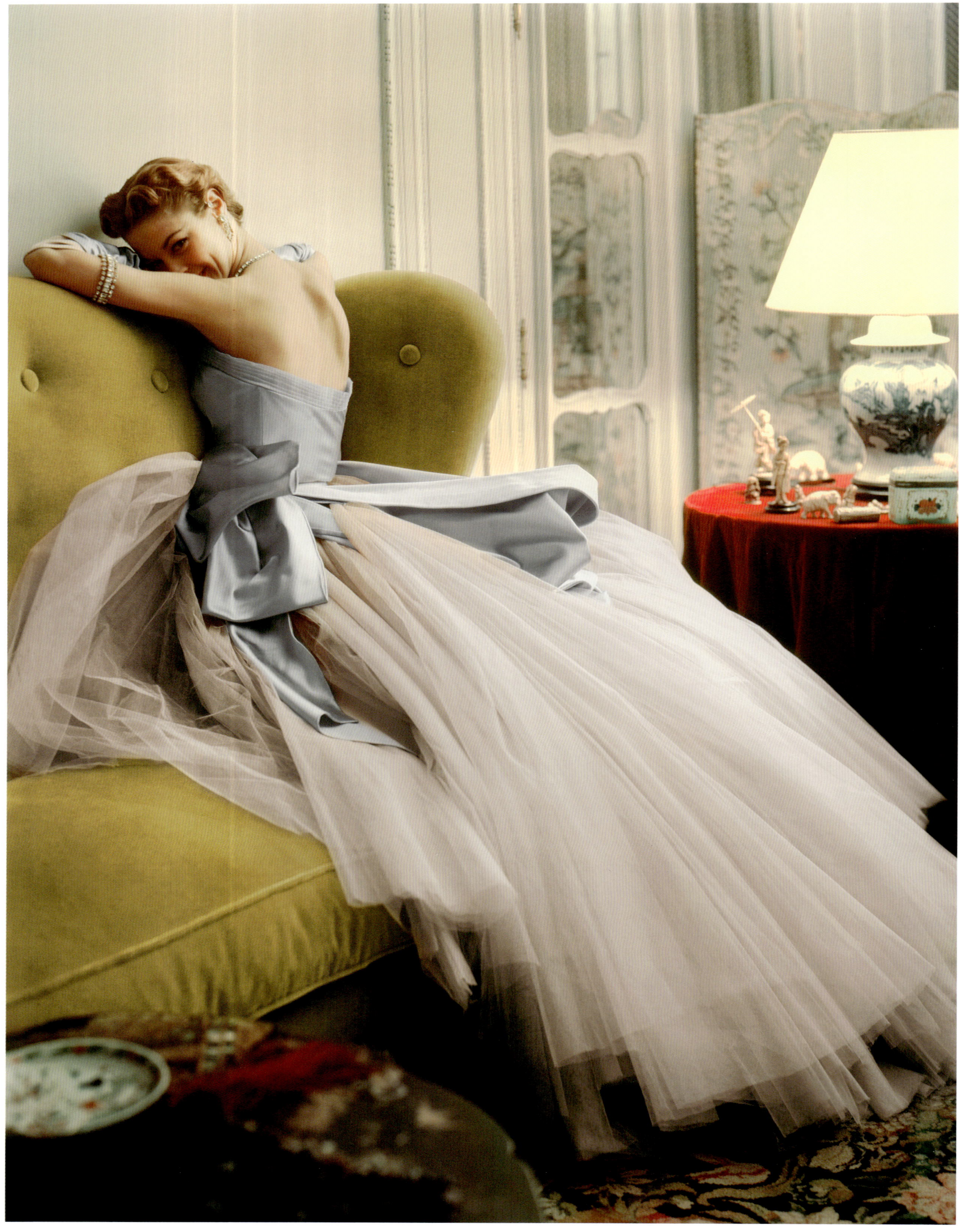

PARIS TO PRESTON, PRESTON TO PARIS

SATURDAY—12:00 MIDNIGHT, PARIS

Hello you dear people!

I am sure I will not finish this for I am waiting for a late date—it's done all the time in Paris—I think it's terribly gai, never having done it in the States.

I'm fine & dandy and having a glorious time you're never to worry about me!!

In February 1950, Jean Patchett came to Paris for the first time, to model the spring designer collections for *Vogue* sittings editor Bettina Ballard and photographer Norman Parkinson.

Less than two years before, Jean had dropped out of college, borrowed money from her father, a rural plumbing contractor, and left home for New York with dreams of becoming a high-fashion model.

RUE DE BOURGOGNE, PARIS

Today we worked—Ernie, Vogue's artist who does sketches drew me today. First we went to Balmain's to do two suits then to Dessès,' Schiaparelli's, and later around 6:00 we went to Dior!! His collection was the most fabulous—from each of the designers Ernie drew about two suits on me.

Jean was born in 1926. She came to New York from Preston, Maryland—"a tiny hiccup of a town," said Jean's daughter Amy Auer Hensley—down the Delmarva Peninsula on the state's Eastern Shore. Around Preston, broad fields of wheat and feed corn spread out to the highway, divided by dark stands of tall trees. Hawks hang in the stillness and yellow tractors amble slowly down narrow roads.

There wasn't much money around when Jean and her three siblings were kids. Growing up around Preston in those Depression years, Jean mowed lawns, swept the grocery, shined shoes, babysat, and waited tables at her father's little weekend tavern. At night, when it stormed, Jean loved the sound the rain made against the tin roof above her head as she slipped off to sleep.

SATURDAY — 12:00 MIDNIGHT, PARIS

This fellow I've been seeing is truly, awfully nice—quite rich, is editor of a French newspaper, have heard tell he has an 18-room apartment, and is taking a trip soon which will last 8 months through Africa, South America, Mexico, and on up to NY. . .

After high school came secretarial school in Baltimore, then a year and a half of soul-deadening boredom toiling for a firm that made stationery for banks.

Jean quit her job and studied history for a year and a half at Baltimore's Goucher College while singing at the nearby Peabody Institute for fun.

"I was all at loose ends," she later told the *Baltimore Sun*. "I didn't know what I wanted to do."

RUE DE BOURGOGNE, PARIS

We start photographing tomorrow with Mr. Parkinson. We'll be doing Dior dresses and it will be color and I have the possibility of having another cover!! Can you believe it? I have the March 1st and Mrs. (Jessica) Daves heard from Alex Liberman the art director in the States, that the picture that Penn took of me on Monday was divine so that's an April 1st cover and if this one turns out to be one it will be the May 1st.

Isn't that exciting. Must get in bed early tonight . . .

"Goucher was kind of tough," Jean told writer Dick Kucner, "because I didn't have a good high school background. A friend, Nan Perry, knew that I was struggling and suggested that I try modeling. At first, I laughed at the suggestion. But I thought it over and decided I liked the idea."

Page 2:
Made for You
Vogue
October 1, 1948
Dress by Henri Bendel
Photograph by
Horst P. Horst

Page 5:
April shopping list of a *Vogue* reader
Vogue
April 1, 1954
Photograph by
Irving Penn

Opposite:
Paris Spectaculars
(variant)
Vogue
1950
Evening gown by
Jean Dessès
Photograph by
Norman Parkinson

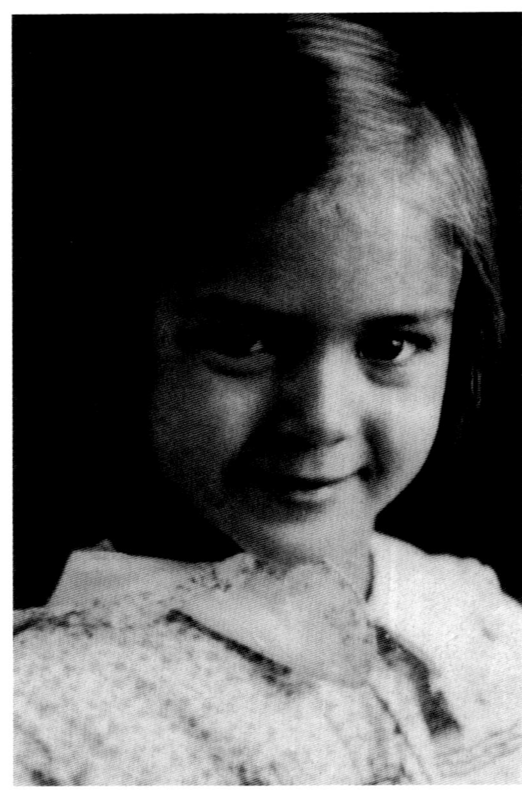

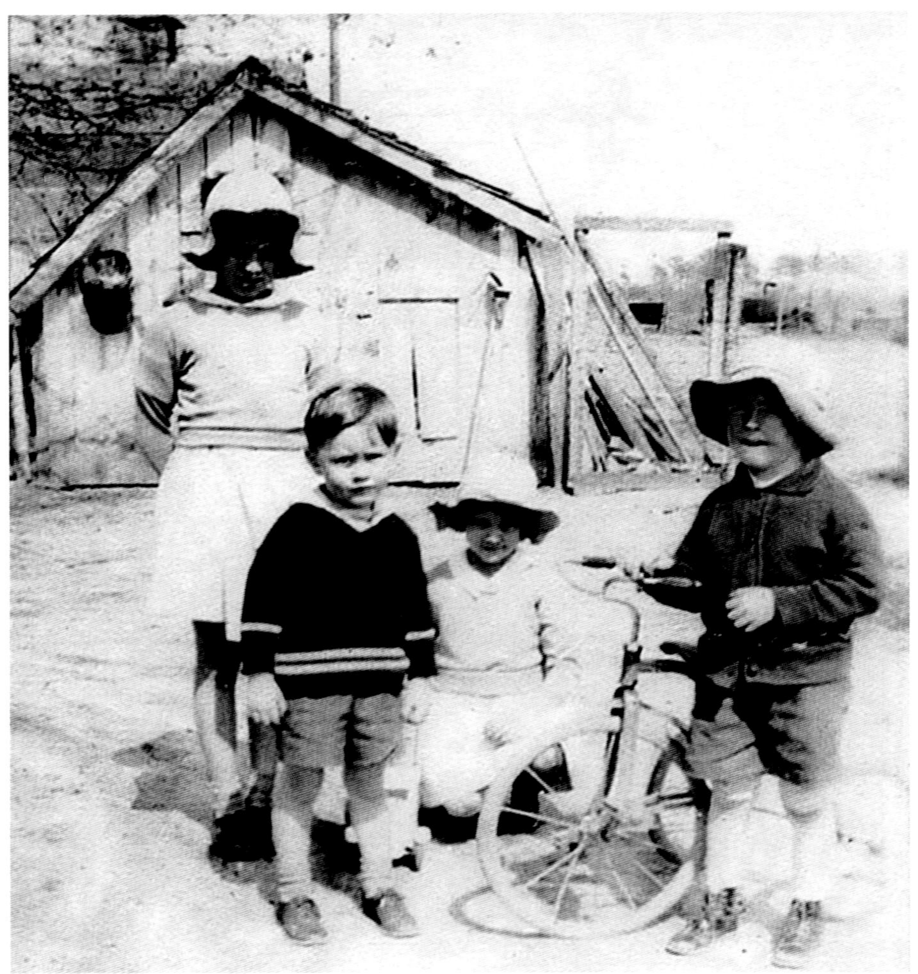

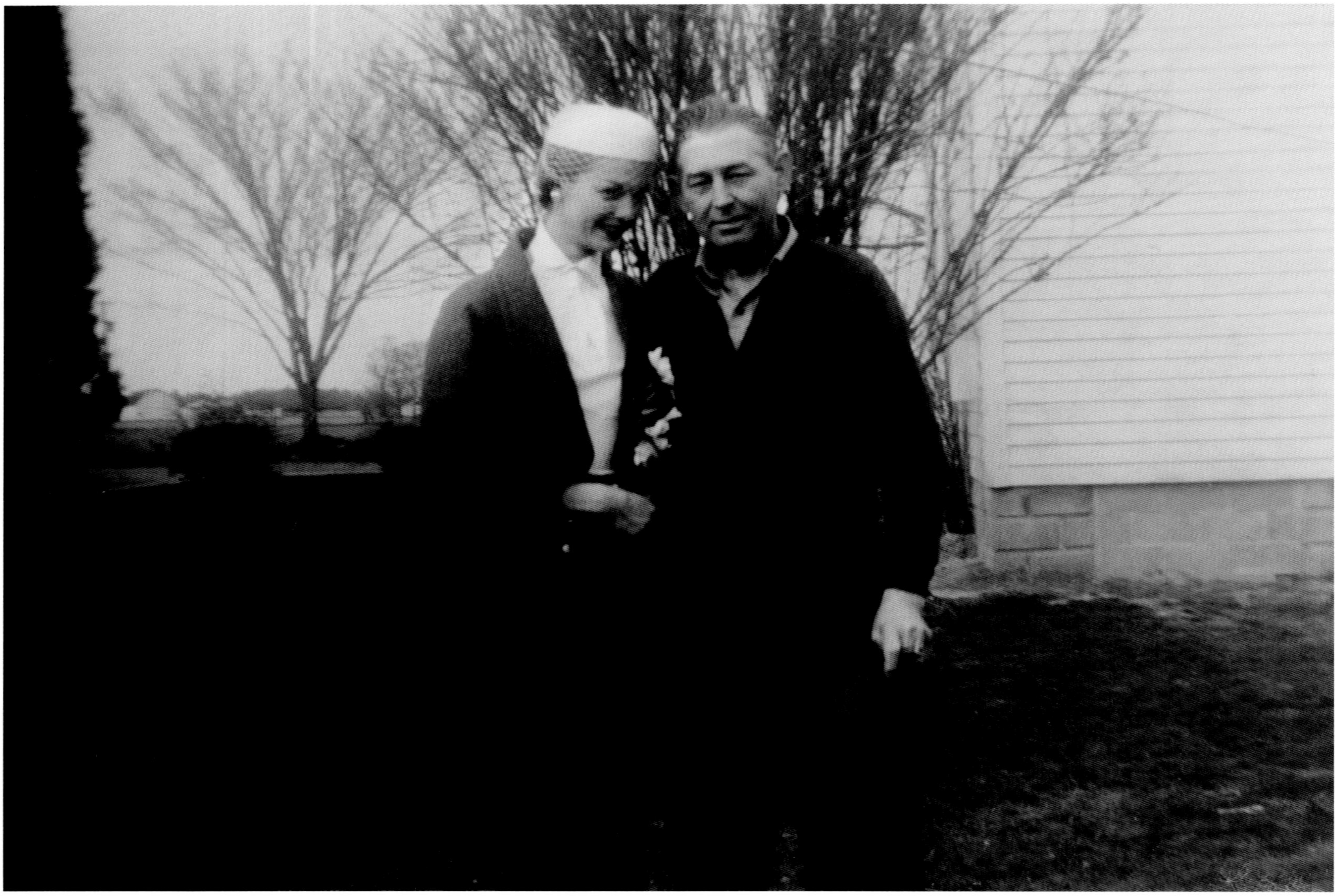

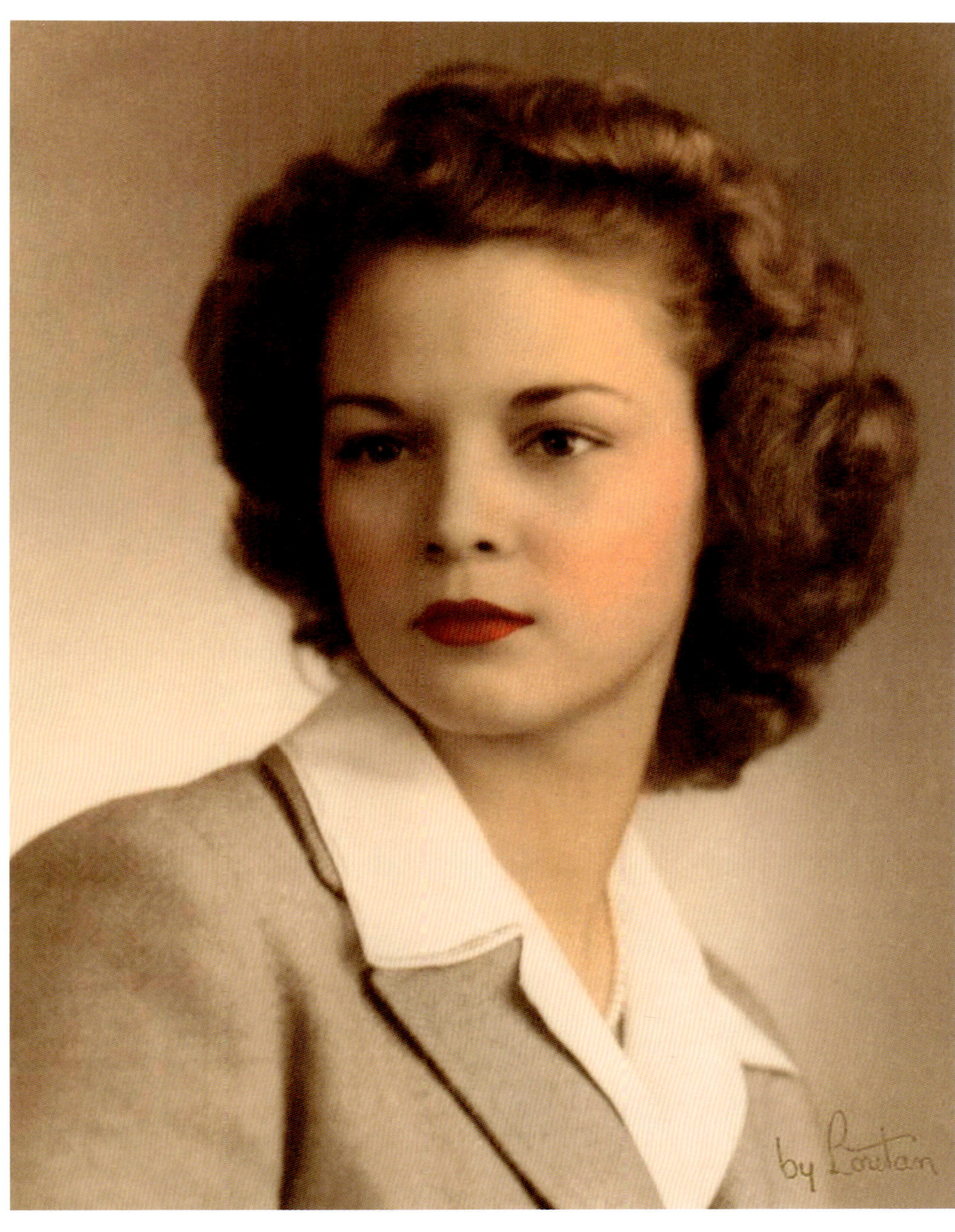

Opposite, clockwise from top left:
Jean Patchett age 6
1932

Jean Patchett age 7 with sister Betty and cousins Roger and J. Addison Patchett
April 1933

Jean Patchett with father James Frank Patchett
Jean wearing Jacques Fath suit from letter sketch on p.13
1950

Above right:
Jean Patchett
High School Graduation
1942

Jean's parents weren't happy with her choice. But they backed her, nonetheless.

On her 22nd birthday, Jean's father leant her six hundred dollars that would have gone to her college tuition, to underwrite the launch of her career.

HÔTEL DE CRILLON, PARIS

I can't remember what I told you all in my last letter, so I'll just start with Tuesday. That afternoon I went to the Jacques Fath collection which was quite wonderful and decided on a suit that I got. It's quite wonderful, gray flannel with a little white dotted Swiss man's sort of blouse underneath. I got it at cost—$200. If anyone else bought it would be $500, because they're all custom-made.

Once in New York, an aunt in Brooklyn helped Jean find a furnished room in Manhattan at a Methodist home for girls. She quickly signed with the Harry Conover agency, an industry leader notorious for failing to support its models, and started looking for work.

"I took a modeling course," said Jean in 1950 to the *New York Sunday Mirror*, "which didn't help at all—and had pictures made and went out to 'make the rounds' of photographers. Most times I never got past the secretary or the receptionist. In the first three months I made only fifty dollars. Total."

The modeling course cost one hundred seventy five dollars. The pictures cost thirty dollars. By May, Jean was running out of money.

But that month she met model Natalie Nickerson, then a silent partner in the modeling agency Nickerson's one-time secretary, Eileen Ford, had started with her husband Jerry.

Between pictures at a *Ladies' Home Journal* shoot, one of Jean's few jobs, Natalie suggested Jean leave Conover, and take her chances with the Ford Modeling Agency.

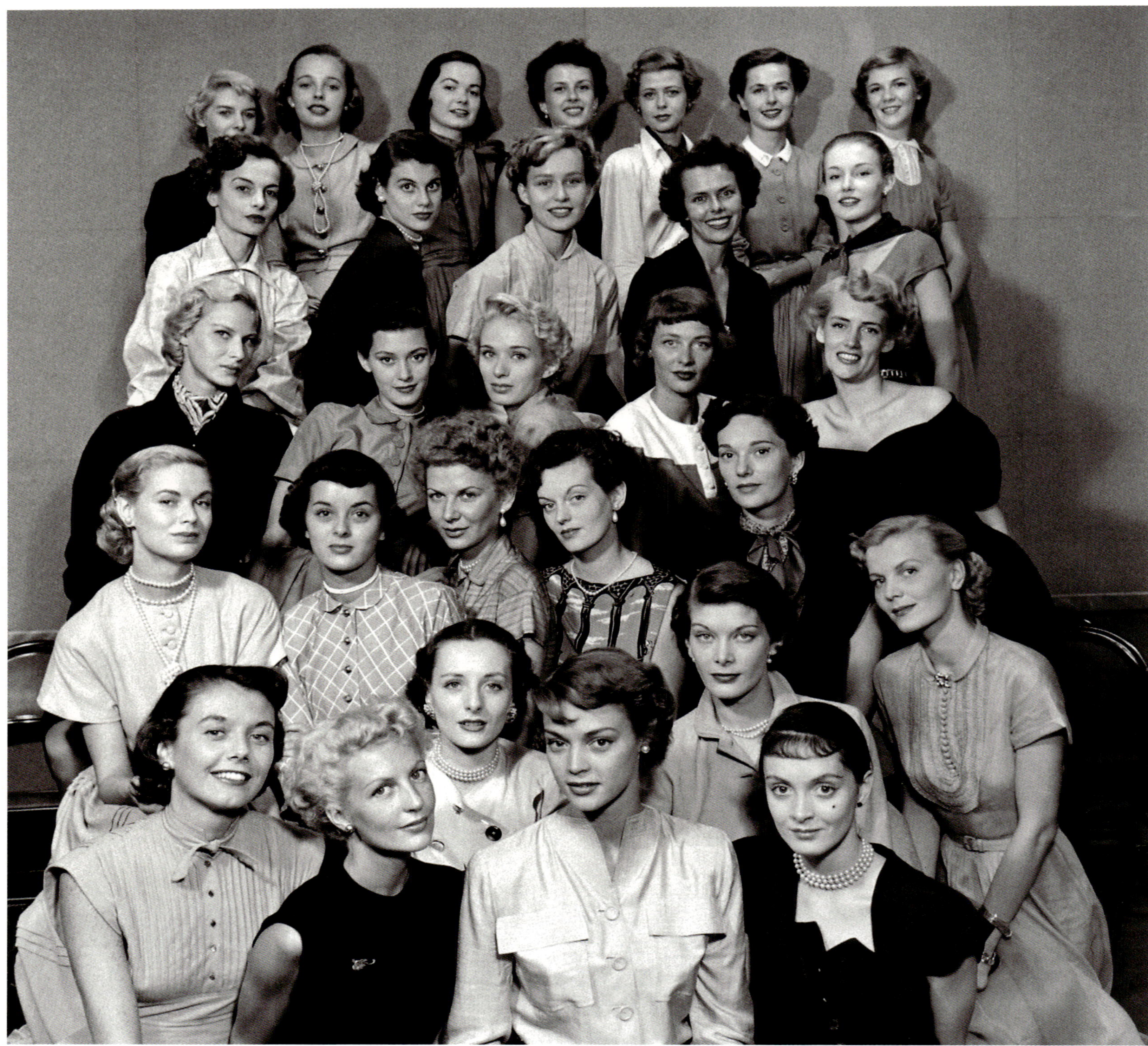

HÔTEL DE CRILLON, PARIS

Since Monday night I have been a real good girl haven't been out at all at night. But tonight that young man who took me out on Sunday night has asked me out again for dinner but shall try to be in early.

Now I want to buy some gloves for myself and some perfume for Eileen.

On April 10, Jean arrived at the red-doored brownstone where the nascent Ford Agency had its office.

"You just had to take a deep breath, even then," is how Eileen Ford described her first glimpse of Patchett to the *Los Angeles Times*. "She had on a black coat with black velvet at the shoulders and a black velvet beret—all made by her mother—and garnet earrings, bracelet, and necklace. She really was a country girl."

The country girl in the clothes her mother made for her took note of the two telephones Eileen Ford had draped over her shoulders—while talking into a third—and announced, "I'm Jean Patchett."

"First thing Eileen Ford told me," said Patchett to the *Sunday Mirror*, 'You're as big as a horse, you've got to lose weight.' I weighed 135 then." Jean was also quoted as saying Eileen had claimed she was "big as a house." Horse or house—either way, Jean cried.

RUE DE COURTY, PARIS

I'm waiting for Parkinson and his wife to pick me up to go to dinner. We have been working quite hard but it hasn't bothered me at all, you know me as strong as a horse—don't have the remotest idea when we'll be finished and really don't mind at all for just love Paris dearly . . . Parkie and I have been getting some divine pictures, so he tells me.

With Eileen Ford making her bookings, the days of Jean's competing with other young hopefuls, climbing dusty stairs to lounge in cramped waiting rooms as they struggled to get their portfolios seen, were over.

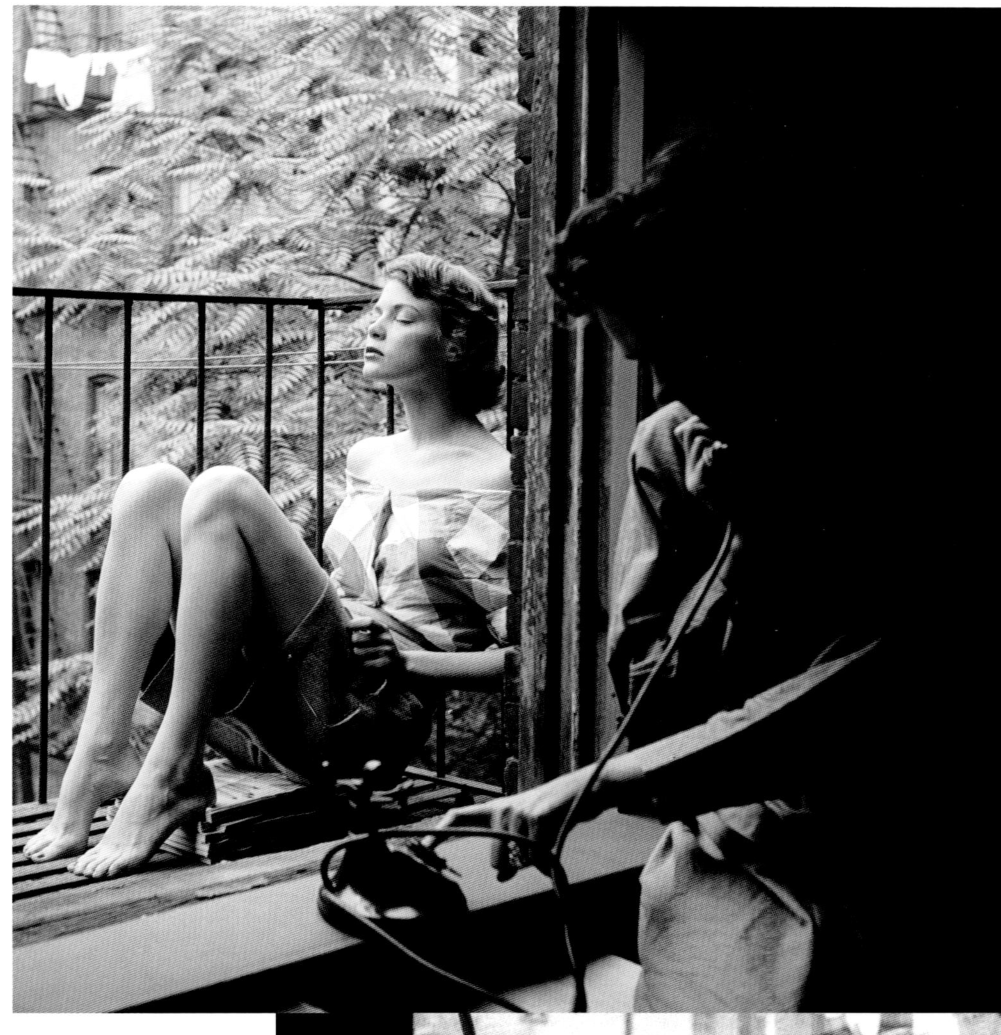

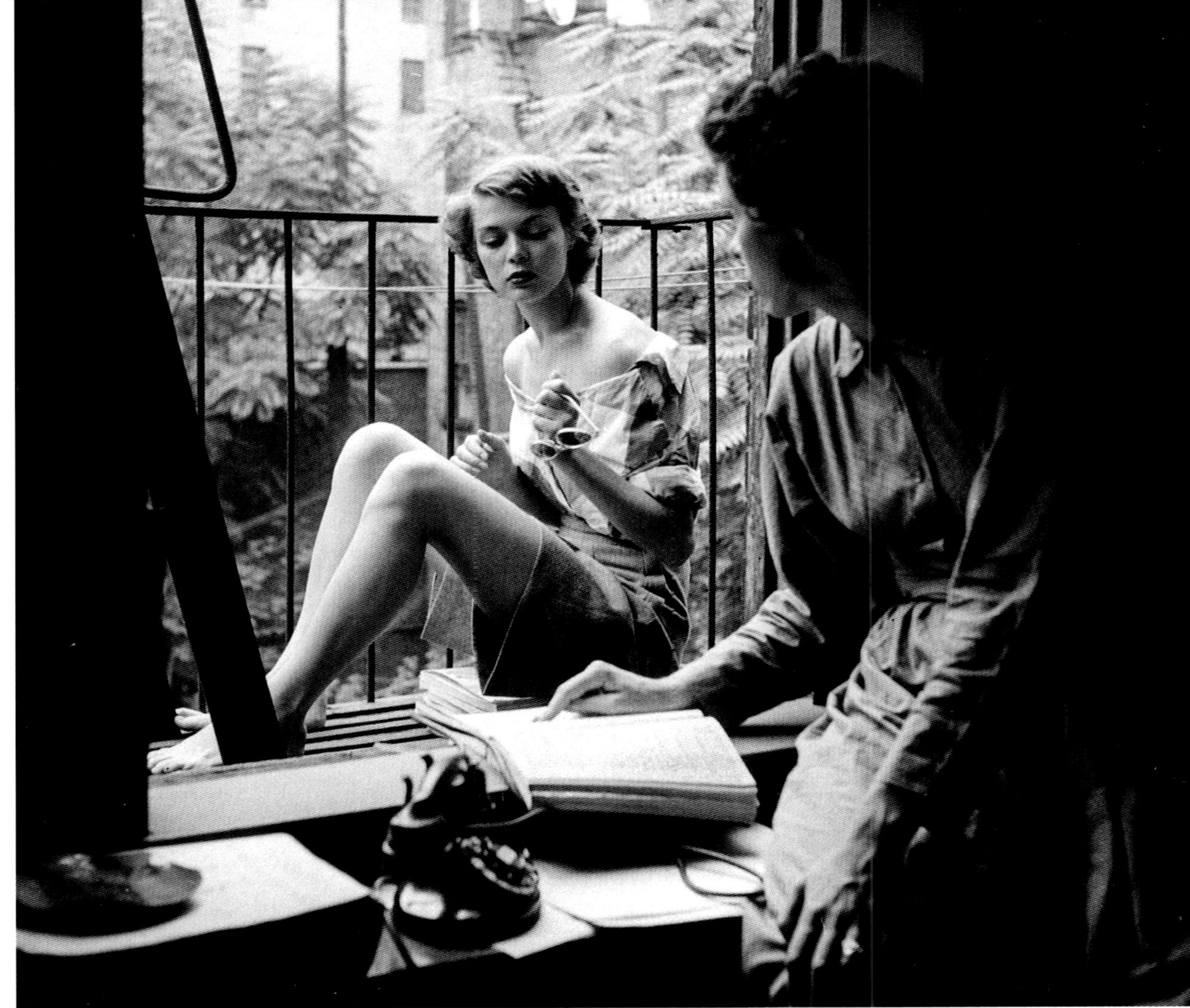

This page:
Eileen Ford and Jean Patchett
October 8, 1948
Photograph
by Nina Leen

Opposite:
Eileen Ford with Ford Agency models
1948
Front row: Jean Patchett second from right;
Fourth row, Eileen Ford second from right
Photograph by
Nina Leen

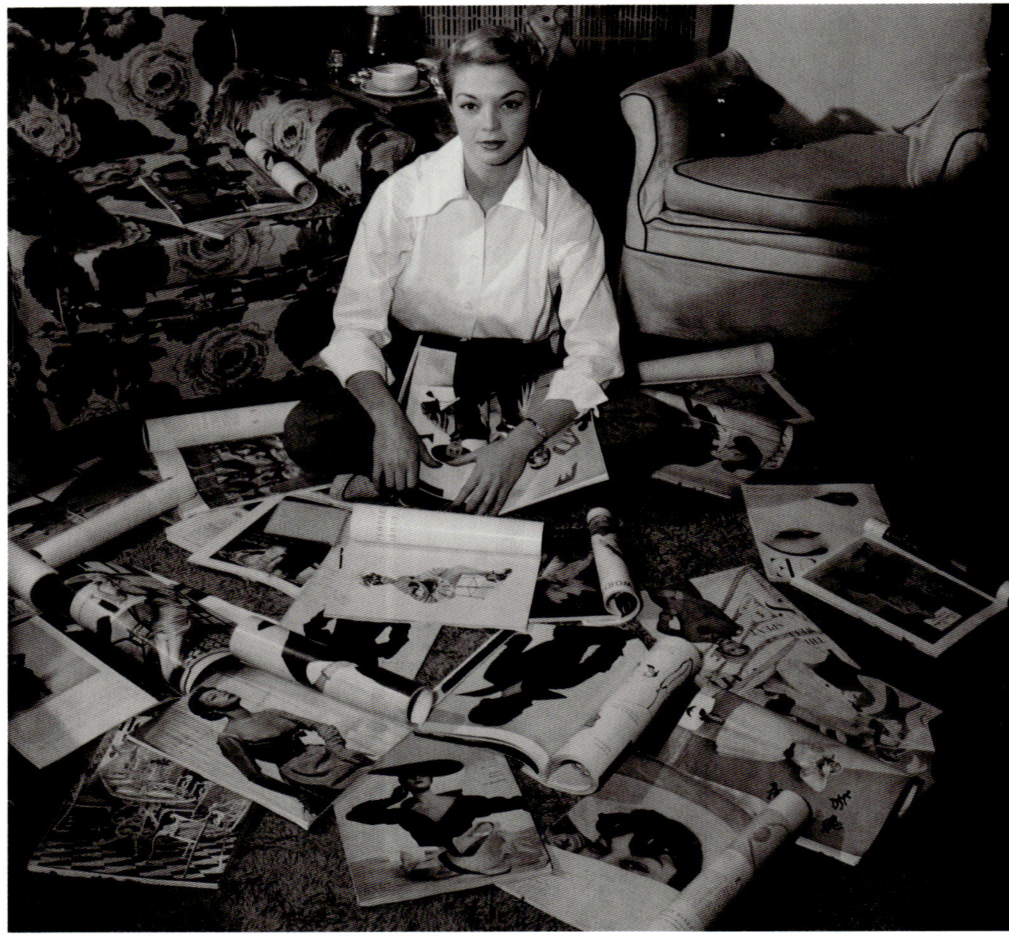

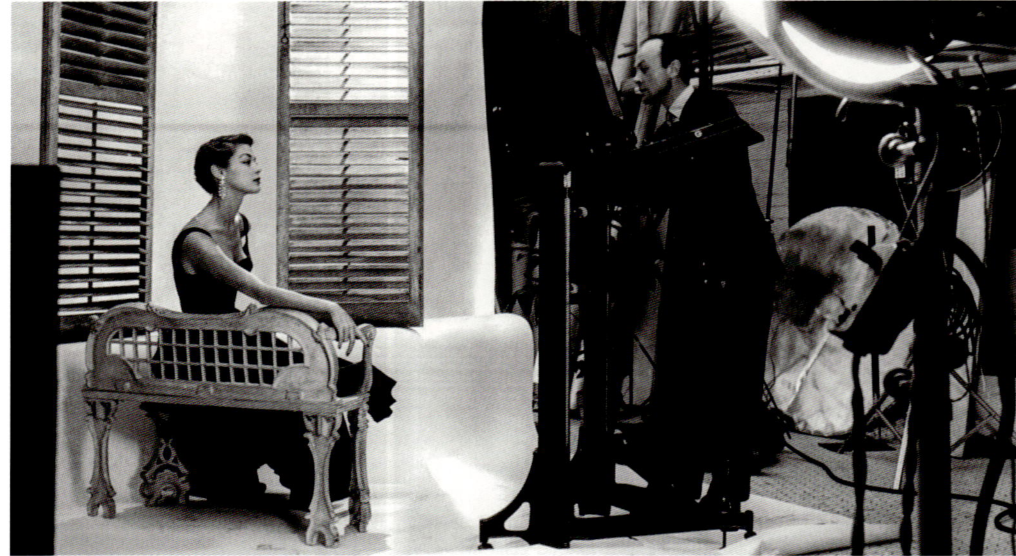

This page, from top:
Jean Patchett in her New York apartment
Baltimore Sun Sunday Magazine
February 1950
Photograph by A. Aubrey Bodine

Jean Patchett being photographed by John Rawlings
Baltimore Sun Sunday Magazine
February 1950
Photograph by A. Aubrey Bodine

Opposite:
Jean Patchett, letter to family from Paris 1950

Her weight came off and the jobs came in. "They put me to work the first week," Jean told writer Mary Frazer, in 1950. "By the end of May I had repaid my father."

On August 1, Jean's first editorial pictures were published in *Vogue*. The photographer, the veteran John Rawlings, was entranced by the charming new recruit. Looking back after a year, he told *Coronet* magazine, "I have seldom encountered a girl who excites me as much as Jean Patchett . . . Working with her provides emotional elation, with the result that pictures of her are almost invariably exciting and arresting in their moods."

September saw Patchett's first *Vogue* cover, photographed by Serge Balkin, with the prophetic headline "Fashion Stars Coming In, Fashion Stars Staying In" alongside her image. The following year would see Jean appear on four more covers for *Vogue*, in images by Cecil Beaton, Horst P. Horst, and Irving Penn, along with covers for *Glamour*, *House & Garden*, and *Life*, and in well over a hundred editorial photos and full-page ads.

Patchett had arrived.

RUE DE BOURGOGNE, PARIS

Well, your little twenty-four year ol' daughter is packing her clothes and coming home—sad, happy, more broad-minded and a little less sure that she knows everything!! Oh, this has been a wonderful trip . . . However, I think maybe someday I may come back to see you all . . .

That she did.

In June, Jean went home to Preston for a family reunion. The Patchetts gathered at a pavilion near an old tomato field, not far from the Choptank River. "A remote area," according to Jean's cousin Walt, just two years old at the time, but along with her cousin Dan, a keeper of the Patchett family lore.

In pictures from the event, Jean is a slim smiling figure in slacks. "Pretty progressive," laughed Walt. "Most of the other folks there,

HÔTEL DE CRILLON

R.C. SEINE 27.162

Paris, le .... 19.........

PLACE DE LA CONCORDE

Ad. Télég: "CRILONOTEL"

white ~~pattie~~ dotted-swiss man's sort of blouse underneath —
I got it at cost — $200. If anyone else bought it, it would
be $500 because they're all custom-made.

The dear little man from England who went
to dinner with us on Monday night who is
the artist from there drew this for me. Wasn't
that cute of him? He's quite a ~~proff~~
professional and does fashion drawing
in England for English Vogue.

Since Monday night I have been a
real good girl. haven't been out at all
at night. But tonight that young man
who took me out on Sunday night has
asked me out again for dinner but shall
try to be in early. I wrote Betts and
Ribby a letter yesterday and Jackie Stiteler.
Today I shall try to write Dottie.

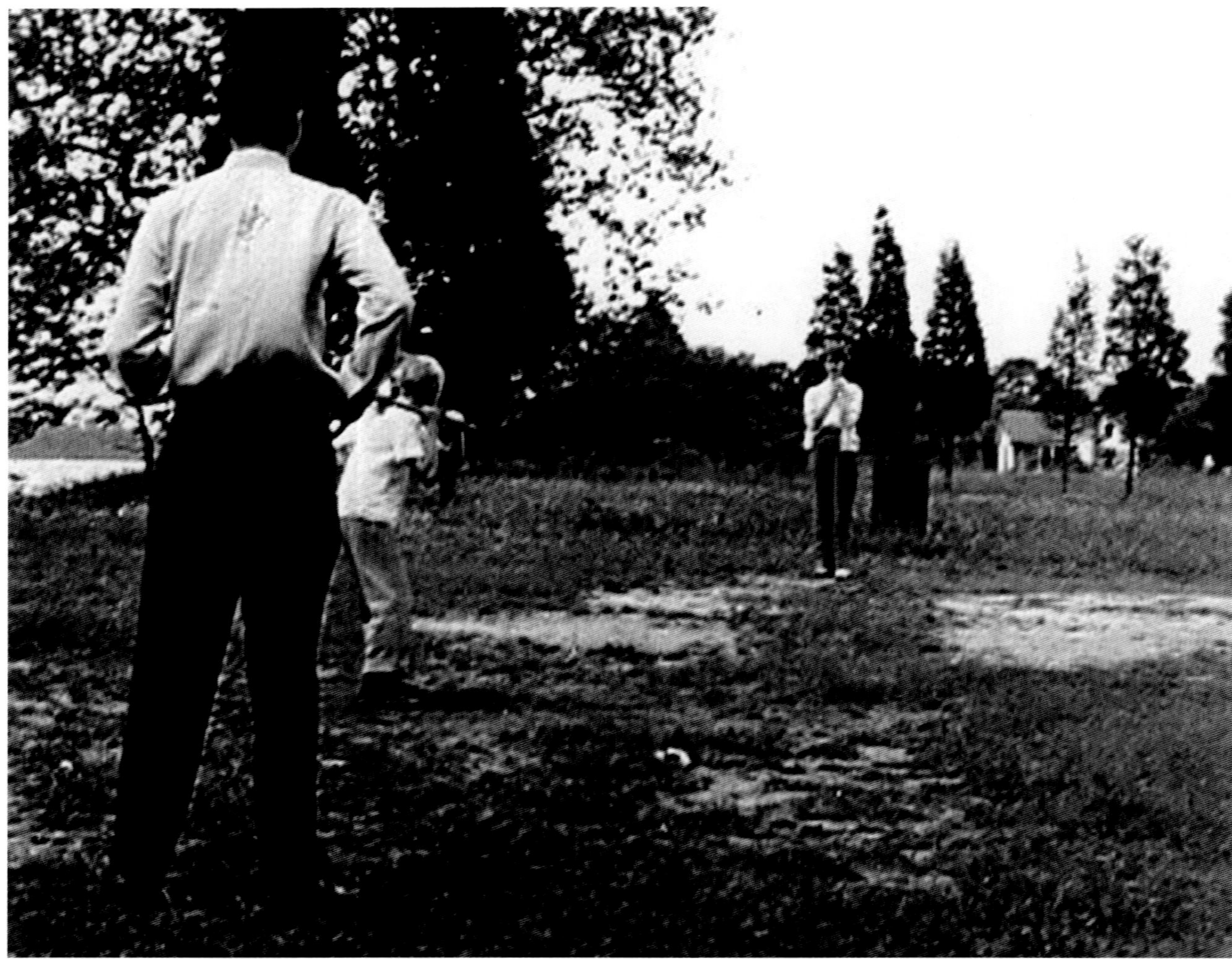

they had dresses and skirts on and so forth. They were—you know—a farming community."

A baseball game started up. Jean took the mound to pitch and promptly took an errant toss from her young cousin Roger—right off her famous face.

"Everybody took a collective gasp," said Walt, "because, you know, 1950, she was right in the prime of her modeling career."

Happily, Jean was unhurt. The following month she was back on the cover of *Vogue* ("Skin Milk Diet X") in another photo by Irving Penn. So far as we know, Jean's pitching days were over. She would later take up golf. But baseball does provide a useful analogy for measuring her career.

"Jean Patchett was to Ford what Babe Ruth was to the Yankees," said Jerry Ford to the *New York Post* on Jean's death.

Ruth made headlines when he made more money than the President. "Jean made more money than any model in history," said Eileen Ford in 1982, "until Brooke Shields and Cheryl Tiegs came along."

Ruth's impact can be quantified in his statistics, starting with his 714 home runs. As can Jean's—at least 58 magazine covers, including 18 for *Vogue* and thousands of editorial and advertising pages, shot by the greatest fashion photographers of the day.

Ruth was a pitcher and a slugger. Jean an artist and a muse. Ruth was a versatile star whose career stretched for decades, unusually long for an athlete. Patchett was a versatile star whose career lasted 14 years, unusually long for a model.

Ruth was a stocky symbol of the Roaring Twenties and Depression Thirties. Patchett was the face of mid-century design.

And Jean never forgot who she was or where she came from. The elegant model attending openings at the opera with her banker husband on her arm was also the down-home girl from Preston, Maryland. "You don't darn it, you patch it," was her standard line for art directors and photographers who struggled with her name.

Over the years, Jean Patchett had both the public success she earned and the private life she craved; a long happy marriage and children.

How did she do it? ➽

Above:
Patchett Family Reunion
Light's Beach, Maryland
Summer 1950

Opposite:
Vogue
September 1, 1948
Photograph by
Serge Balkin

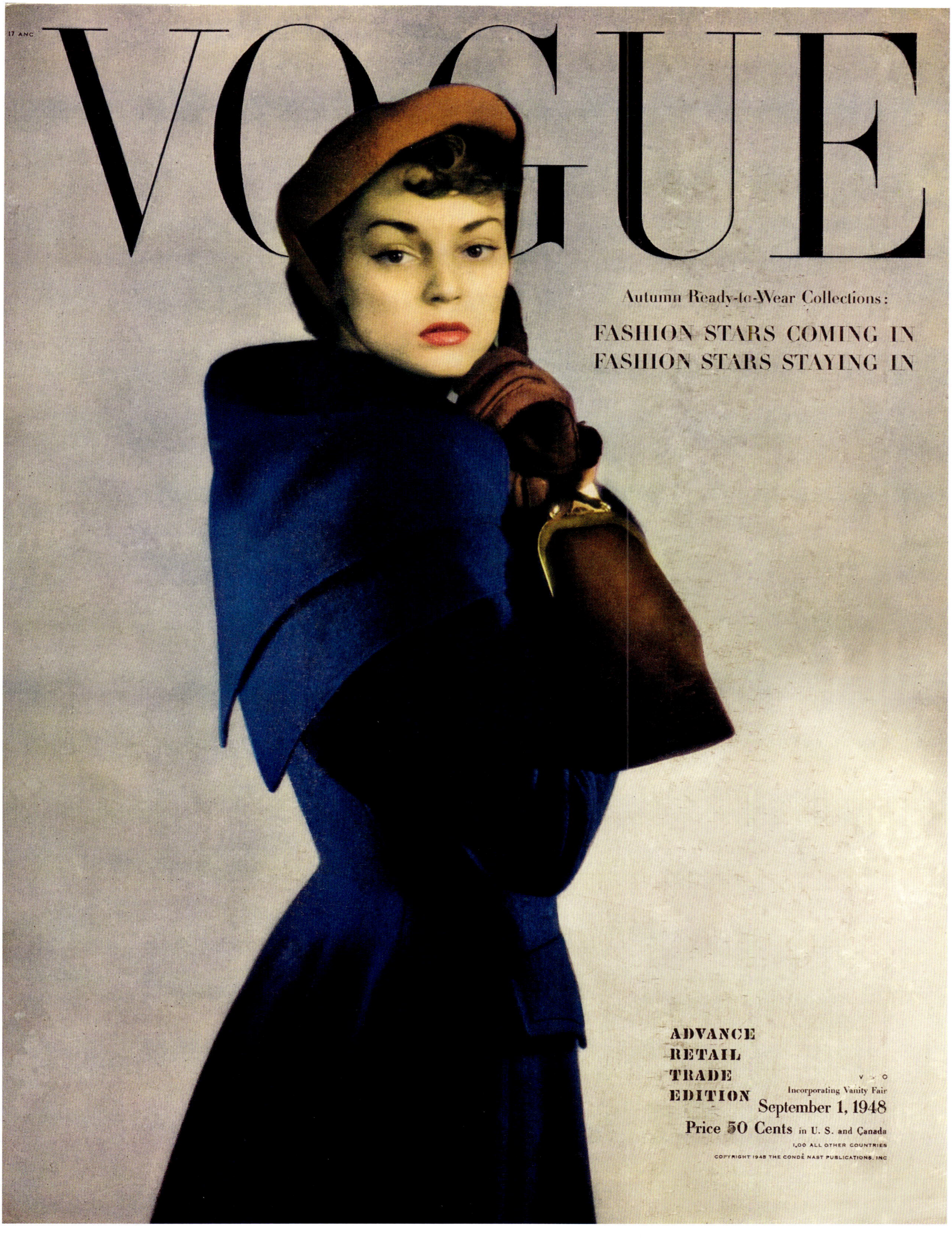

17 ANC

VOGUE

Autumn Ready-to-Wear Collections:

FASHION STARS COMING IN
FASHION STARS STAYING IN

ADVANCE RETAIL TRADE EDITION

V O

Incorporating Vanity Fair

September 1, 1948

Price 50 Cents in U. S. and Canada

1.00 ALL OTHER COUNTRIES

COPYRIGHT 1948 THE CONDÉ NAST PUBLICATIONS, INC

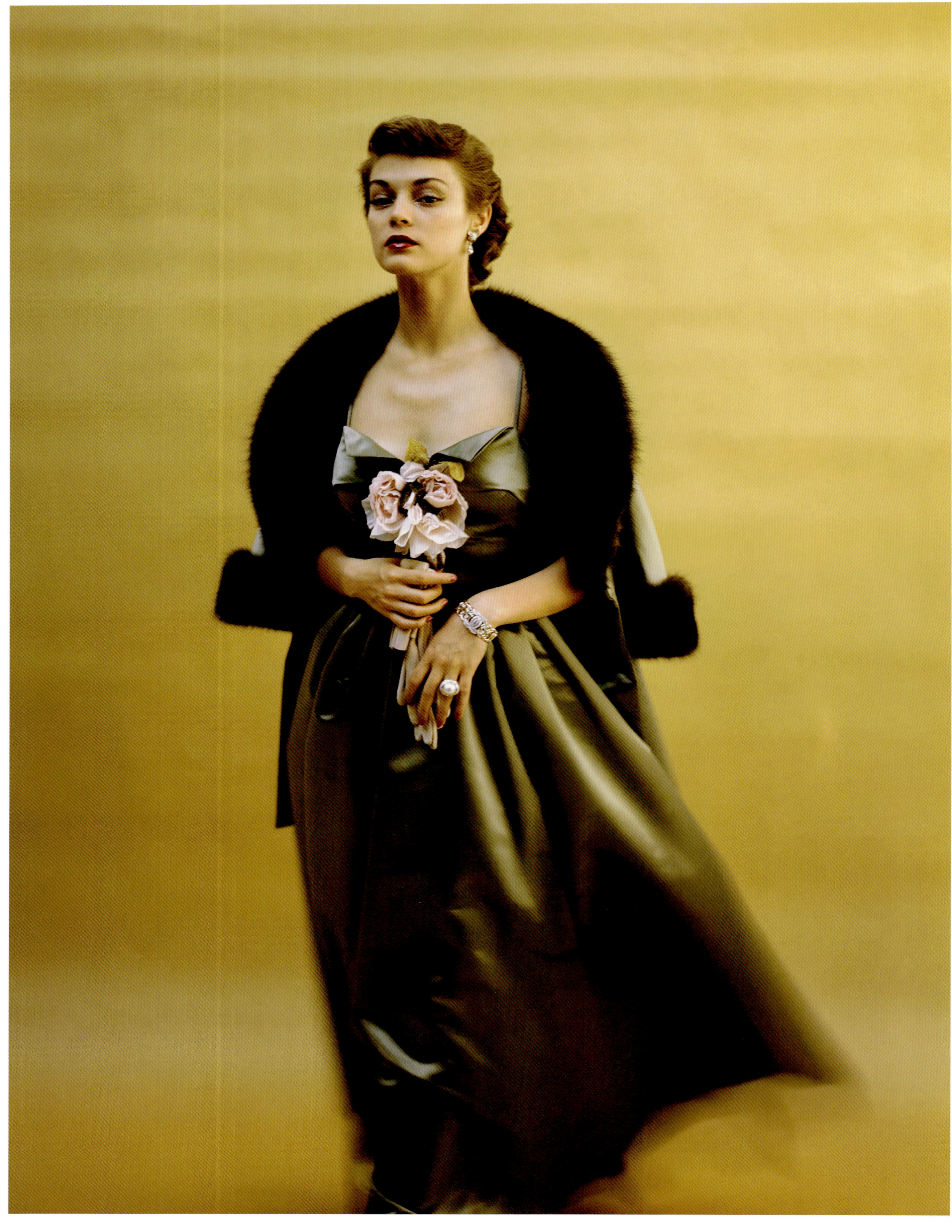

THE FANTASY OF TRANSFORMATION

It was like a dream come true, a fantasy of success. The small-town girl from rural Maryland came to New York and after a brief term of struggle and disappointment, met the agent/fairy godmother who was about to dominate the industry, and with her help, transformed herself into a glamorous era's top model.

It's a great story, and in its primal form a very old story, but one that only touches the surface of Jean's accomplishment in launching and then sustaining her career. It shares a core fantasy that gives the fashion industry some of its restless drive, one described by *Vogue* editor Laird Borelli-Persson as, "a dream of becoming. You can't be born a princess, but you can, through hard work, earn enough money to go to Dior and be dressed by Dior. Or you can have the dream that that could happen. And that's the fantasy of fashion; of transformation."

The fantasy holds its power to distract and command; it's acted out again and again, all over the world, every single day. But the reality of high-fashion modeling is different from the dream of transformation. For top performers like Jean Patchett, modeling was, and is, a high-stakes profession requiring discipline, stamina, physical agility, and strength, focus, intelligence and the ability to project a persona while acting a role in a collective fantasy. The critical qualities Jean Patchett brought to her career weren't owed to the transformative power of fashion, the magazine image makers, or the fierce support provided by the Fords. They came from Jean.

Just ask the professionals:

"Models are born, not made—like thoroughbreds for Hialeah,' said Eileen Ford to *Park East* magazine.

"I don't really think that you can teach how to model. It needs to come from within," said Cindy Crawford, a Jean Patchett from a later era, in a 2018 interview with *Town & Country*.

However, while models are born, not made, that doesn't mean they're born fully formed. Some things take time.

"A model is a kind of actress," said Jean Patchett in a 1955 interview with the *St. Louis Post-Dispatch* where she discussed the advice she gave young women who stopped her on the street, hoping to become models themselves. "A photographer will say: 'Now be petulant,' or, 'Look surprised,' or, 'Someone just stepped on your toe.' The girl must be able to respond immediately. This takes long practice."

Behind that active collaboration between a model and photographer lie more subtle, personal qualities. To really succeed at modeling, said Patchett, a model has to "have a feel for clothes and be able to catch in your face the mood of a dress."

It's a beautiful phrase, one that captures the mystery of the high-fashion model's art. But if modeling can't be learned, how did Jean find success, so quickly and so completely, and then sustain it?

Well, it's high-fashion modeling. Looks come first.

Jean was beautiful. And she knew it. "Just look in the mirror!" was her friend's clinching line, when she advised Patchett to leave school for New York City.

One look was enough for Francesco Scavullo. Then an aspiring fashion photographer who'd assisted both Rawlings and *Vogue*'s Horst P. Horst, Scavullo later claimed to be both the first to discover Patchett, and the person who sent her to Eileen Ford. He told author Charles Castle, "She walked into my studio, and I thought, 'This face is incredible, and she has a good body too.' I told her she could be a great model. . . she was fabulous."

Word of a fabulous new model spread quickly. For Cecil Beaton, whose first pictures of Jean appeared in the March 1949 issue of *Vogue*, Patchett was something altogether new in the world of postwar fashion photography. "Then came Jean Patchett," he wrote in his *Photobiography*, "young, tall, and

Opposite:
Furred Evening Suits
Vogue
September 15, 1948
Suit by Traina-Norell
Photograph by
John Rawlings

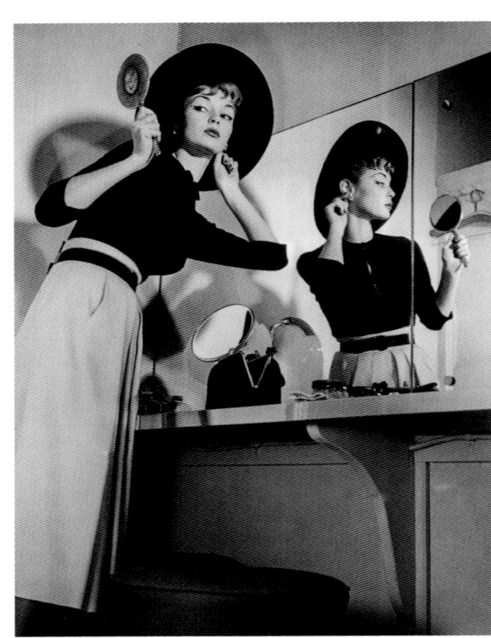

Above:
Jean Patchett prepares to be photographed by Cecil Beaton
Baltimore Sun Sunday Magazine
February 1950
Photograph by A. Aubrey Bodine

Opposite:
Valentina's White with Black
Vogue
April 1, 1950
Ensemble by Valentina, jewels by Verdura
Photograph by Cecil Beaton

healthy, like a pale wicked cherub with biscuit-colored hair and skin and an entirely new set of attitudes; diaphragm gathered in, the top part of the body thrown forwards, a trailing foot. . .keeping the necessary balance." Like other photographers who worked with Jean, Beaton seemed moved as much by her physicality and technical skills as her beauty.

A model must be able to project her personality to succeed, and to an enthusiast like Rawlings, no one did that better than Patchett. "Her ability to project herself is so striking that the very moment she walks into a room you feel her presence, even though your back may be turned," he told *Coronet*. "She has freshness without naivete, warmth without effusiveness, and an easy, unstudied elegance. Her gestures are completely natural and her ability to take direction is flawless."

"There are a lot prettier models," said *Harper's Bazaar* photographer Stephen Colhoun in 1951,"but none more sensitive. She is the quickest to understand what a photographer is trying to do with a certain picture and knows exactly what to do with her hands, head, and feet."

"Being pretty has almost nothing to do with it," an anonymous "top fashion photographer" told the *New York World-Telegram* in 1955. "She has a sense of fashion. She makes a plain white dress look elegant. On another pretty girl it could look like nothing."

And then there are variations on "pretty." William (Bill) Helburn, a wildly successful fashion and advertising photographer who used Patchett throughout her career, liked to say she was "commercially pretty." It was high praise for the top-earning model, coming as it did from a professional who preferred advertising work to editorial and whose personal goal was to out-earn the twin towers of 50s fashion photography, Richard Avedon and Irving Penn.

As for Penn, whose artistic relations with Patchett were the deepest and most meaningful of her career, and with whom she also shared an abiding affection, "pretty" was simply beside the point. "She is not conventionally pretty," said Penn of Jean to the *New York Sunday News* in 1951, "but has the real beauty of a person of deep intelligence and sympathy, and that all comes out."

Unconventional beauty is both a fair description of Jean Patchett and a key to her success, as it separated Patchett from her competition and helped her image spring off the page. "Jean's was a graphic face, like a poster," said *Vogue's* Henry Clarke to Castle. "As the clothes those days had graphic outlines and shapes, she was the perfect model for them." Jean's full pursed lips, high flat cheeks, and curving eyebrows and lashes, with a prominent mole peeking from the corner of her right eye, made other models look bland.

The mole would become Jean's trademark, but not without a fight—from Jean. "When I first began modeling," said Patchett, in 1955, "photographers used to retouch the pictures they made of me very carefully, to remove the mole." A search through the first 18 months of Jean's images in *Glamour*, *Vogue*, *Charm*, and *Bazaar*, shows that when her right profile was on display, her mole was invariably reduced to a shadow or wiped away.

Jean took that as a slight—and that brought out a quality in her that may not have been immediately evident in the polite young model, who endeared herself to veteran magazine editors with a soft, "Yes ma'am," or, "No, ma'am." "She was a tough girl," said Bill Helburn, "sure of herself. Patchett could walk off a set." The retouching "used to make me angry," said Jean, "so out of defiance, I began to darken it with eyebrow pencil. Then one photographer left it alone, and the advertising people started asking for me. That's how it all began."

The photographer who first highlighted Jean's "beauty mark" appears to have been Erwin Blumenfeld, with his cover shot of Patchett for *Vogue's* January 1950 edition. With an artistic background that included both German Dada and French Surrealism, Blumenfeld fractured and reduced Jean's

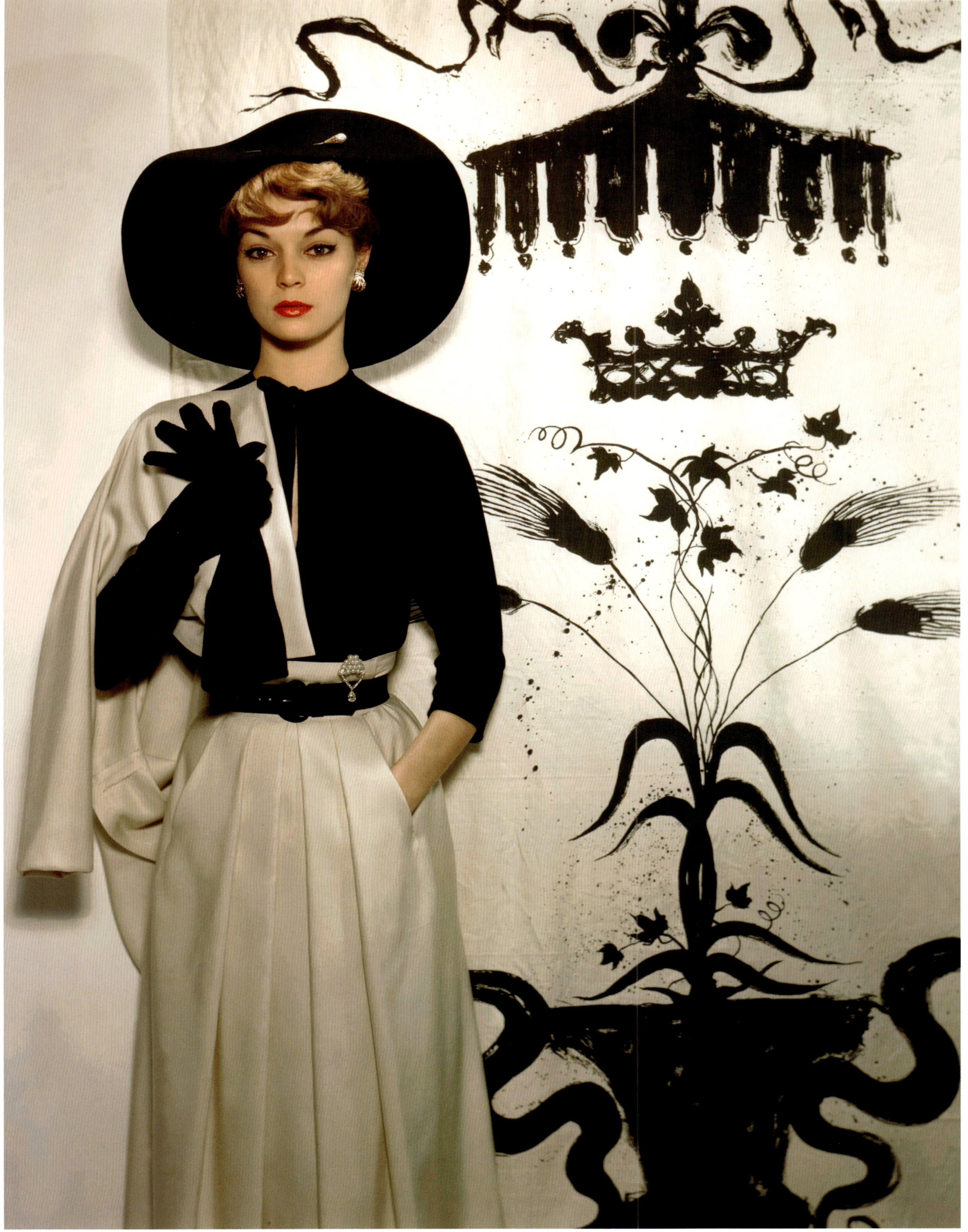

VOGUE

1950

MID-CENTURY
FASHIONS
FACES
IDEAS

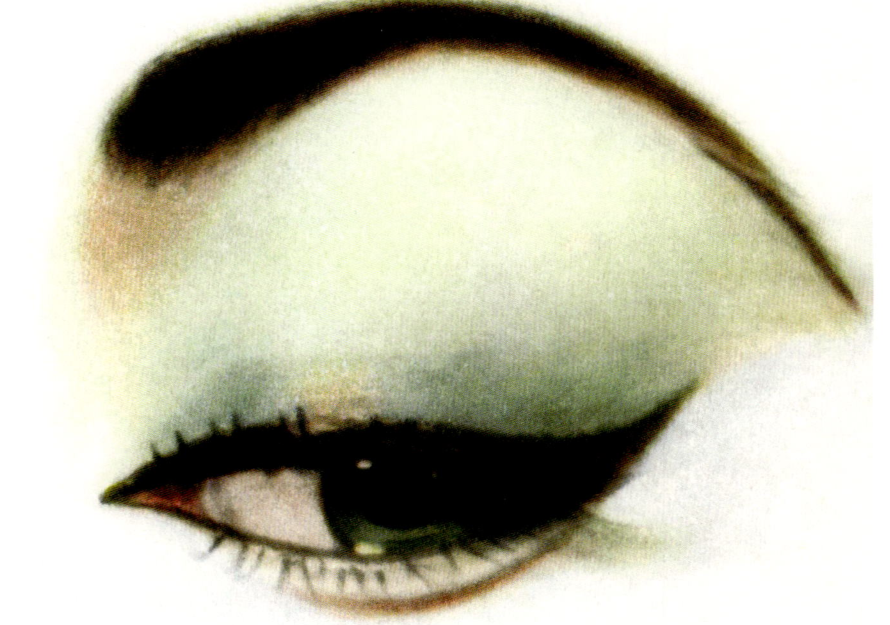

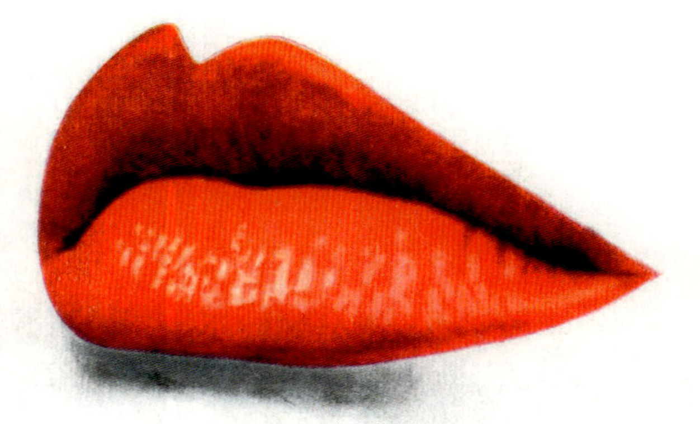

TRAVEL
HANDBOOK

Incorporating Vanity Fair
January 1950

Price 50 Cents in U. S. and Canada
$1.00 All Other Countries

COPYRIGHT 1949. THE CONDÉ NAST PUBLICATIONS INC.

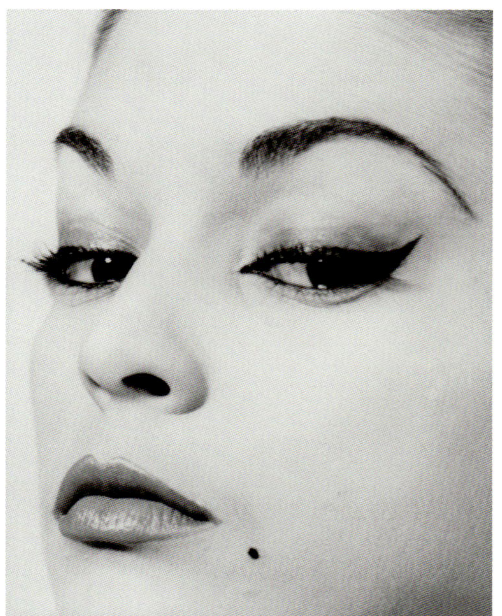

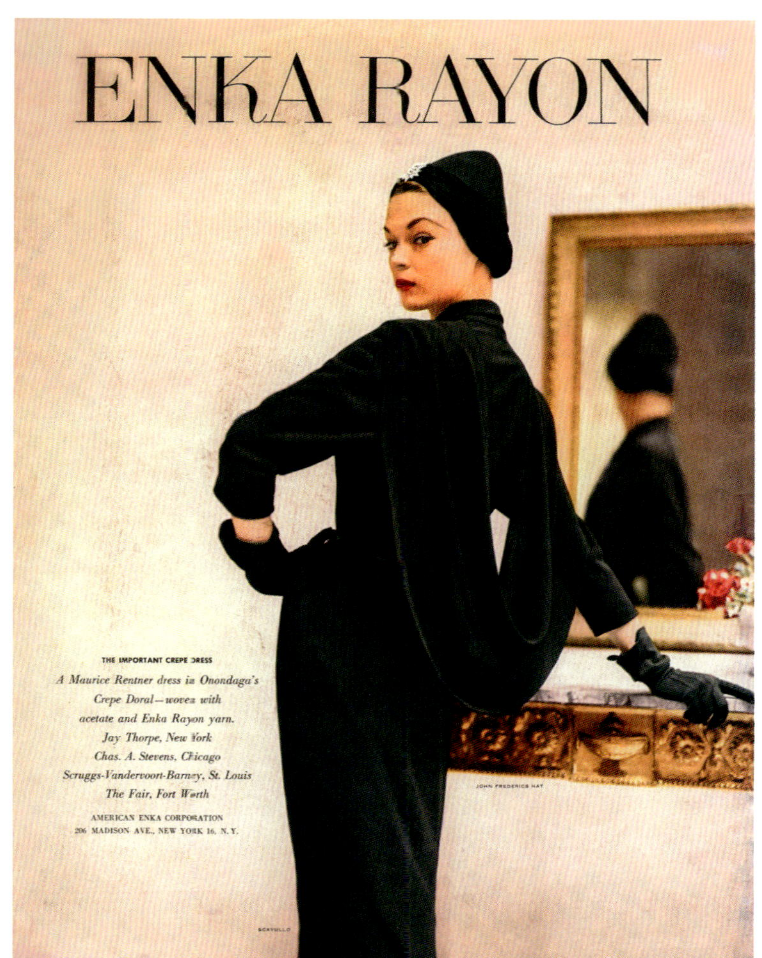

Opposite page:
Vogue
January 1950
Photograph by
Erwin Blumenfeld

This page, from left:
Mid-Century Beauty
Vogue
January 1950
Photograph by
Erwin Blumenfeld

Ad for Enka Rayon
1952
Photograph by
Francesco Scavullo

features, using an image he took for a hairstyle photo, with Patchett's mole drawn in below the left corner of her mouth. What remained was an unmistakable portrait of Patchett as a stylized mask of elegant hauteur, all red lips, black mole and green eye shadow, with her sullen "doe eye" staring out of a plain white background, daring the reader to turn the page.

It's one of the most famous fashion images ever made, and established Jean's mark as both, for a brief time, unique (imitators would soon appear) and to use a phrase that would not become current for another half-century, a special part of her personal brand. By spring, the mole's significance as Patchett's personal identifier and trademark was even more apparent, as it was ever more visible in her editorial features and ads.

Jean fought to display her mole but was shy to show her teeth when she posed, preferring to keep her mouth shut, particularly in the first years of her career. Unstained and perfectly even, they were small—so small Jean complained to the *World-Telegram*, "I have baby teeth. When I open my mouth, I look like a child." Her self-consciousness may have played into her choice of the basic roles she acted as a model. In a *Post-Dispatch* feature with the fine tabloid title, "Her Frozen Face Is Her Fortune" Jean explained that she had tried different expressions in her mirror and "the aloof look seemed to fit me best. Well then, I would be haughty, distant, frozen."

The "aloof look" also helped Jean close the gap between her youthful appearance, best suited for junior fashions, and the high-fashion clothing she was physically suited to wear. "I am so full and so long waisted I couldn't wear junior clothes," she explained to Edward R. Murrow, on his "Person to Person" program in 1955. "So, I decided to be a high-fashion model and didn't smile at all, which made me look a little older, I think."

In adopting the aloof look, Jean was also adapting to a convention for high-fashion models, then and now, one particularly appropriate for posing in couture designs. "Haute couture—it's high by definition," said Borelli-Persson. "It also means that the attention goes to the clothes. You don't want so much interaction with the person because you want to imagine you are the regal princess who's going to walk into the corporate party on your husband's arm. It was a way of keeping distance and keeping the attention on the clothes."

The haughty look was far from Jean's only pose, and she learned to work its variations as she shuttled from job to job. Patchett could be impassive, indifferent, sharp, surprised, cool, dismissive, and appraising—or warm, engaged, direct, fun, and sexy. Adopting a "frozen face" helped make her fortune—as it does for models today. But there was a lot going on with Jean, behind her taut mask and tight-lipped mouth. "The essence of Jean to me is that she was playing with it," said Borelli-Persson. "In her eyes you could often see a playfulness, and the beauty mark was just so flirty. So yes, she could be an ice queen but she always seemed kind of wholesome." Establishing her roles, then giving them depth, was all part of Jean's growth as a professional model; a skill set that allowed her talent to develop as she turned her craft into art.

For other, less glamorous parts of the job, Jean drew on the discipline she'd learned from her Depression childhood. She laid out the basics in a 1952 feature for the *Pictorial Review* that, like most stories published during her primacy, seemed stunned by her earning power—running under the headline, "$35-an-Hour Poser Tells Glamor Rules."

Like all models of the period, Jean was expected to show up at the studio with her makeup on and to do her own hair. She had to be prepared to stand in one position for an hour or more as required and to switch outfits quickly and without help. She was never ("Never, never") late or temperamental and prided herself on never refusing to model a gown, even one that might cost less at a store than five minutes of her studio time (then 58 cents a minute).

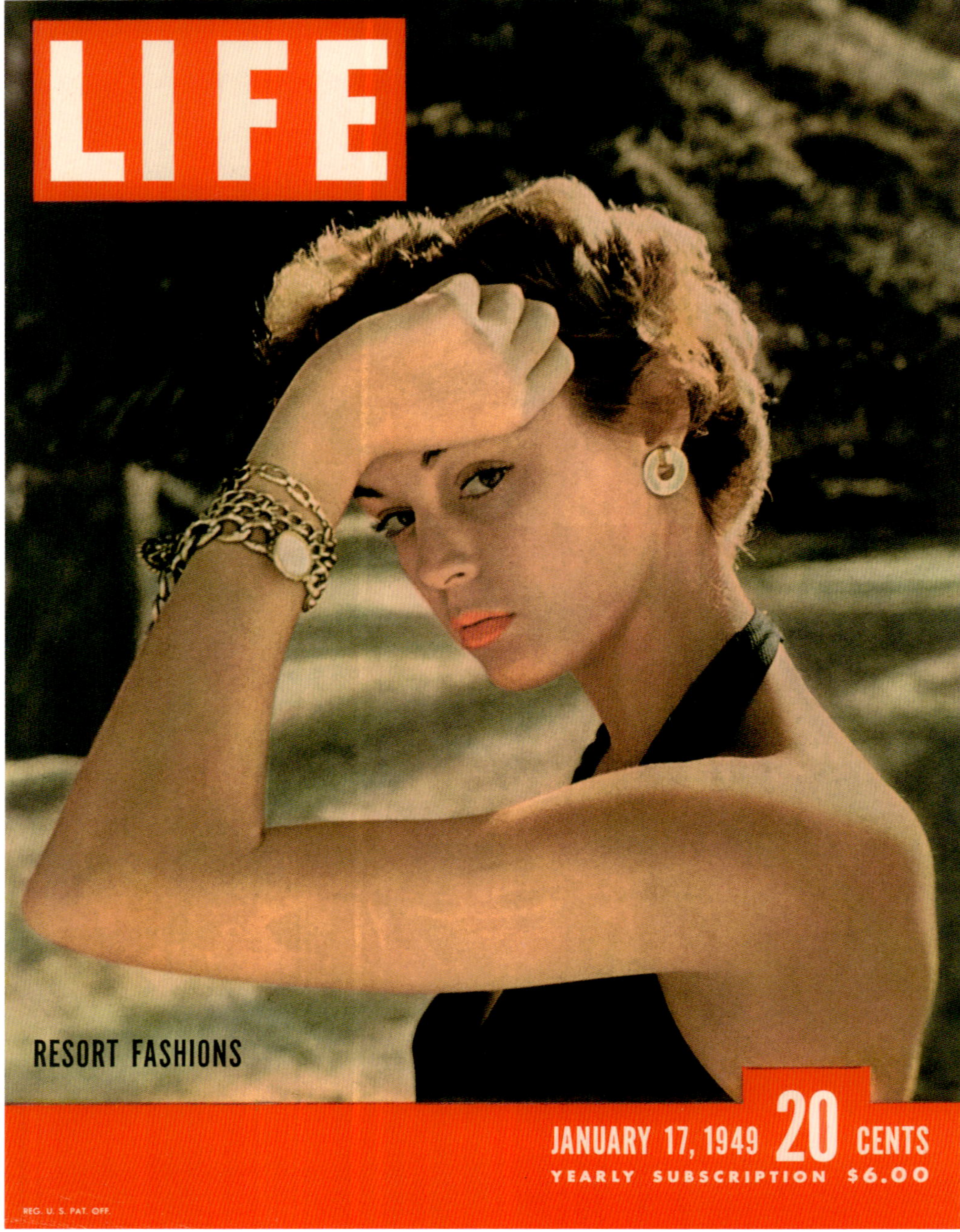

Good relations with her peers were also part of being a professional. Patchett may have played the ice queen on camera, but as *Glamour* told its readers in 1955, she was "'a model's model'. . . an ideal." According to Dolores Hawkins, a Ford model who was sometimes booked with Patchett, "When we did assignments together Jean was incredibly gracious and nice. . . always professional and wonderful with everybody."

Barbara Mullen, another Ford model, favorite of *Bazaar* photographer Lillian Bassman and a star in her own right, saw a different side of Patchett after Jean's first big success—one Jean was quick to discard. The two models met for whiskey sours—"Some cover had just come out on the stand," Jean told author Michael Gross in his book *Model*, "and I was just full of myself." Mullen, a tough Irish-American girl from Harlem, wasn't impressed. "She said, 'Look, just get off that high horse! Who in the hell do you think you are anyway?'" That was enough for Jean to reflect on how her covers, however beautiful or important to her career, would all end up in the trash with the rest of that week's magazines. "And," said Jean, "I just never let it go to my head again."

By the last months of 1948 Patchett was close to the top of her profession, thanks to eight months of bookings by Eileen Ford and Jean's own hard work and determination. In November she went to Cuba for a *Life* magazine cover story on "Resorts Fashions" that exposed her to a wider audience than could be found reading any fashion magazine. Jean then returned to New York, before flying down to Lima, Peru for a photo shoot she would later describe as "my first great trip and my first great picture," and the "real start" to her career. It was the trip that brought her together with the photographer for whom she would be an early muse and collaborator—Irving Penn. ➸

Above:
Life
January 17, 1949
Photograph by
Leonard McCombe

Opposite:
Mainbocher this winter
Vogue
December 1951
Photograph by
Horst P. Horst

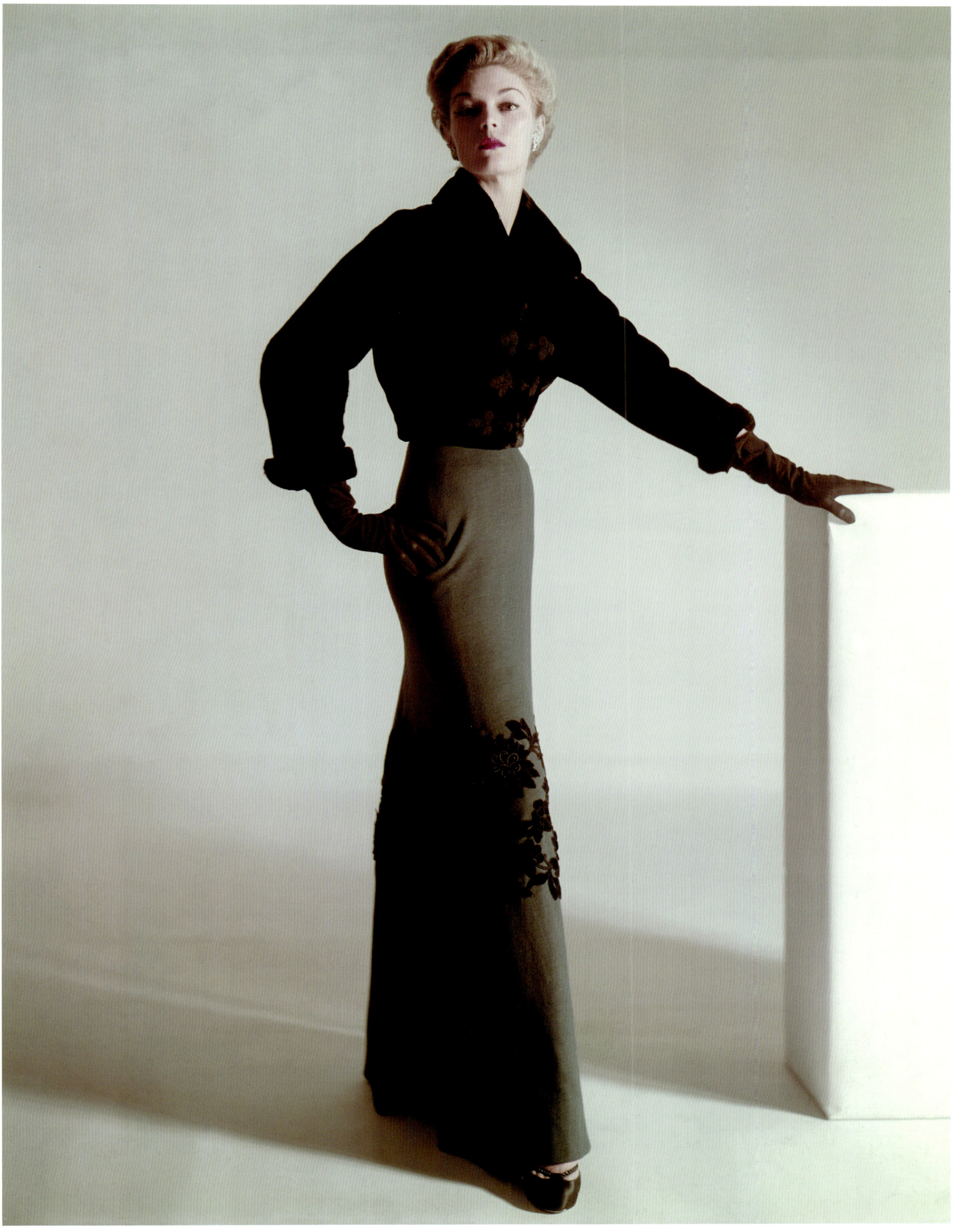

BEAUTIFUL PIGEON

On November 27, 1948 Jean Patchett boarded a Peruvian International Airlines flight for Lima. With her was the rest of the *Vogue* team assigned to produce a mock travelogue for *Vogue Patterns*, entitled "Flying Down to Lima": sittings editor Babs Simpson and photographer Irving Penn.

It wasn't a very happy team, at first. "I'd done only one sitting with Penn in New York," Patchett told Michael Gross. "I didn't even know who he was." As for Penn, Jean wrote her family that, "When he heard in New York that I was coming, he put up a protest."

Thirty-six hundred miles—and five days—later the photographer had changed his mind about the young model he was assigned.

LETTER FROM LIMA

Dear Mother, Daddy, James & children,

The trip down was uneventful and very, very tiring.

We went to bed yesterday morning around 6:30 and I slept until 1:00. . . Then Mrs. Simpson called and said that she and Mr. Penn were going for a walk and asked me to go along but I decided I would rather knit.

Do not worry about me for I am fine and dandy but just write if you find the time.

If an exhausted Patchett seemed anxious at the start of the trip, apparently so was Irving Penn. According to Maria Morris Hambourg, founding photography curator at New York's Metropolitan Museum of Art and a personal friend of Penn's who curated major exhibitions of his work, "This is something he did not want to do. It was clearly not for him. It's the one and only time that he took on this kind of site-specific fashion shoot and it was because of its difficulties that he ultimately realized 'I need to work in the studio. There are too many kinds of things—in the real world outside of the studio—to try to control.'"

Vogue's research staff didn't make it easier for the team by leaving the assignment's details to be fleshed out once they'd arrived, travel-weary, in a city Penn and Patchett at least, had never seen. Penn described the magazine's advice to Hambourg as, "'Here are the outfits . . . go to this place and this place and this place and this place. And here's Babs—you all go and figure it out.'"

"And for a man who wanted the outcome to be precisely the way he envisioned it," added Hambourg, "that was a contradiction in terms."

LETTER FROM LIMA

We've been working very, very hard, but I don't feel as if accomplishing a thing but maybe we are . . . I'm lying on the bed writing this . . . came back from the morning's sitting and are going out again this afternoon at 4:00. . .

I guess I best powder my nose and put on my best smile and meet my friends.

"We get to Lima," said Jean in *Model*, "and we don't take a picture . . . I was getting kind of nervous because I thought my face was turning green or something. I thought he didn't like me. We'd get up at 5:30 in the morning for the mist, and he'd look in his little Rolleiflex, and nothing would happen. He just couldn't take a picture."

Couldn't—or wouldn't. Penn couldn't stand the potential locations suggested by *Vogue*. "He said 'they were all horrible,'" laughed Hambourg. "I said, 'Why?' And he said, 'Well, because they were all Baroque.' It was not his style at all."

After several days (memories conflict on how many) of, in Penn's words, "using up a lot of shoe leather" and with tensions building as they searched for backdrops that might work, the photographer who hated the Baroque, "finally found this little café that looked like Third Avenue did in those days," according to Babs Simpson (in *On the Edge: Images from 100 Years of Vogue*.) They stopped in for refreshments and the breakthrough they had hoped for—just happened.

"There was a young man sitting across from me," Patchett told author Kennedy Fraser,

Opposite:
"Flying Down to Lima"
The Suit Dress
Vogue
February 15, 1949
Photograph by Irving Penn

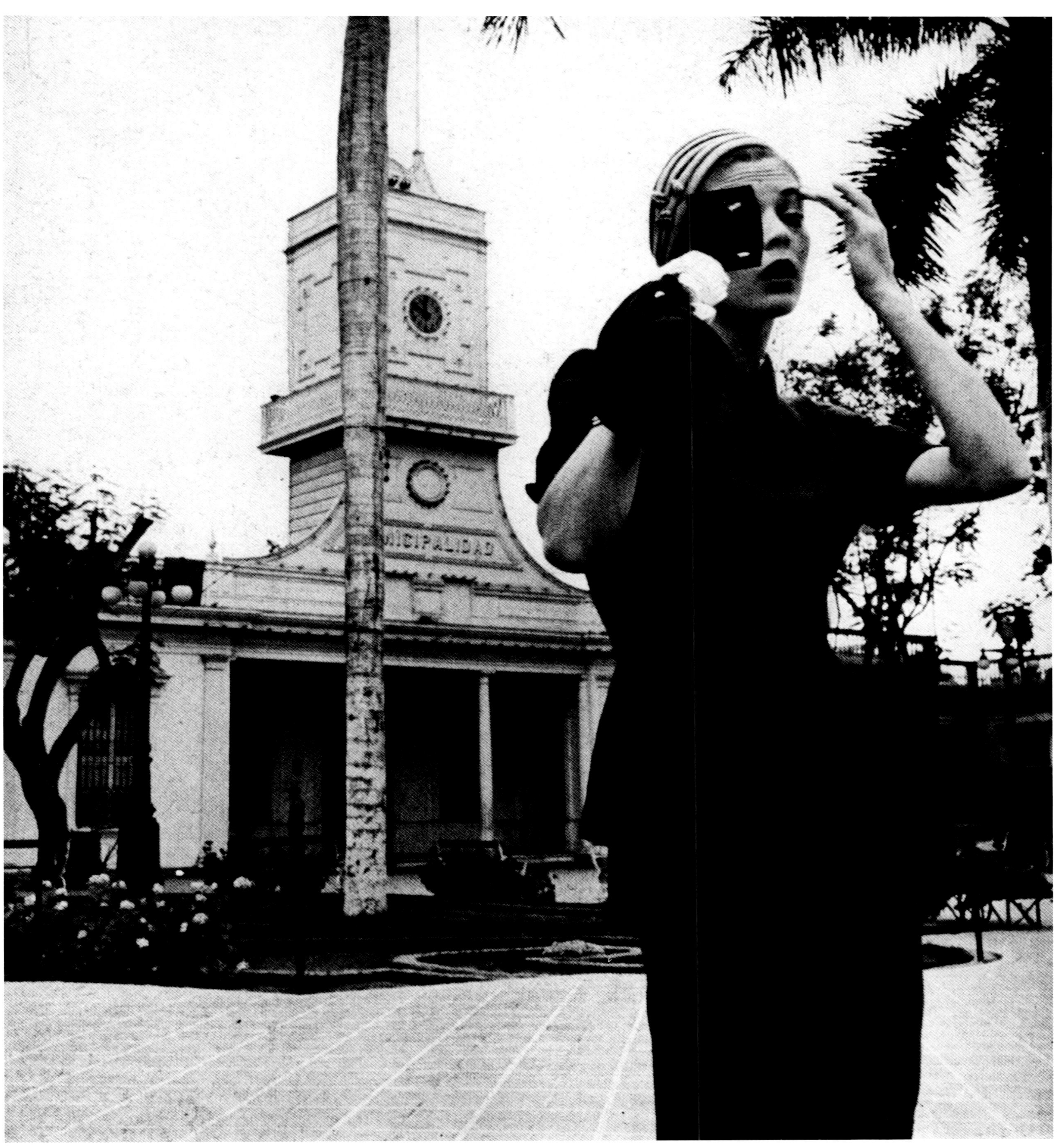

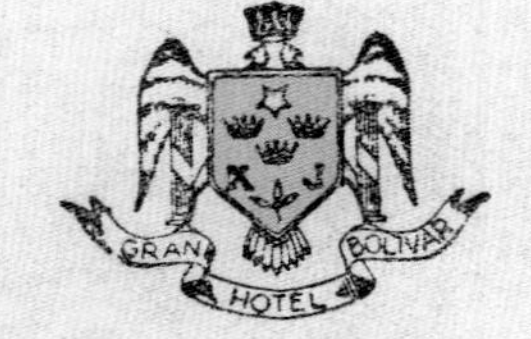

Friday - 11:30 A.M.

Dear Mother, Daddy, James & children,

Gee, It doesn't seem possible that a whole week has passed!! I am at the moment waiting for Penn to come back so that we can go to the airport and take some pictures. That sounds as if we could have used any airport in the states but we couldn't because this is a brand new one and quite lovely and we have to do it for P.I.A. since we flew down with them.

Everything I have seen since I've been here has been terribly interesting. But what I want to know is why haven't you written to me. Or maybe you have and I'll get it today ~~to~~ or tomorrow. I do hope you haven't been worrying about me because everything is just dandy and I'm just as safe here as I would be in my own back yard.

However, some news. I know that I shall be leaving here on the 19th which means that I shall get in Washington on the 20th or early morning of 21st. Then will have to go to Baltimore and will try to be home on the 22nd because if you don't mind I think I should try to get some Xmas shopping done - If you would rather for me to

Jean Patchett, letter
to family from Lima
1948

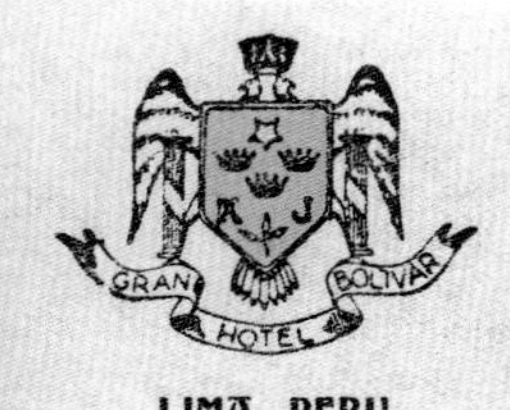

LIMA . PERU

come right straight home on the 21st I shall, just voice your oppinions. I truly didn't think I'd have to be here that long but it looks that way now and it is definite that I shall take the 19th of December plane out. It looks as if I shall have to leave half my clothes in N.Y. for the holidays.

This whole place is terribly fascinating and will almost hate to leave. But it will be terribly good to be back in the states and home again.

We worked very hard yesterday and shall again today. Sunday we are going to a bull fight which I am simply thrilled about. I've learned so much since I've been here.

Mrs. Simpson and Penn are both wonderful people and have been terribly nice to me. If it weren't for them I know I would be terribly depressed. They know of some of the funniest experiences and we practically laugh all the time.

I know I'm going to get some wonderful pictures

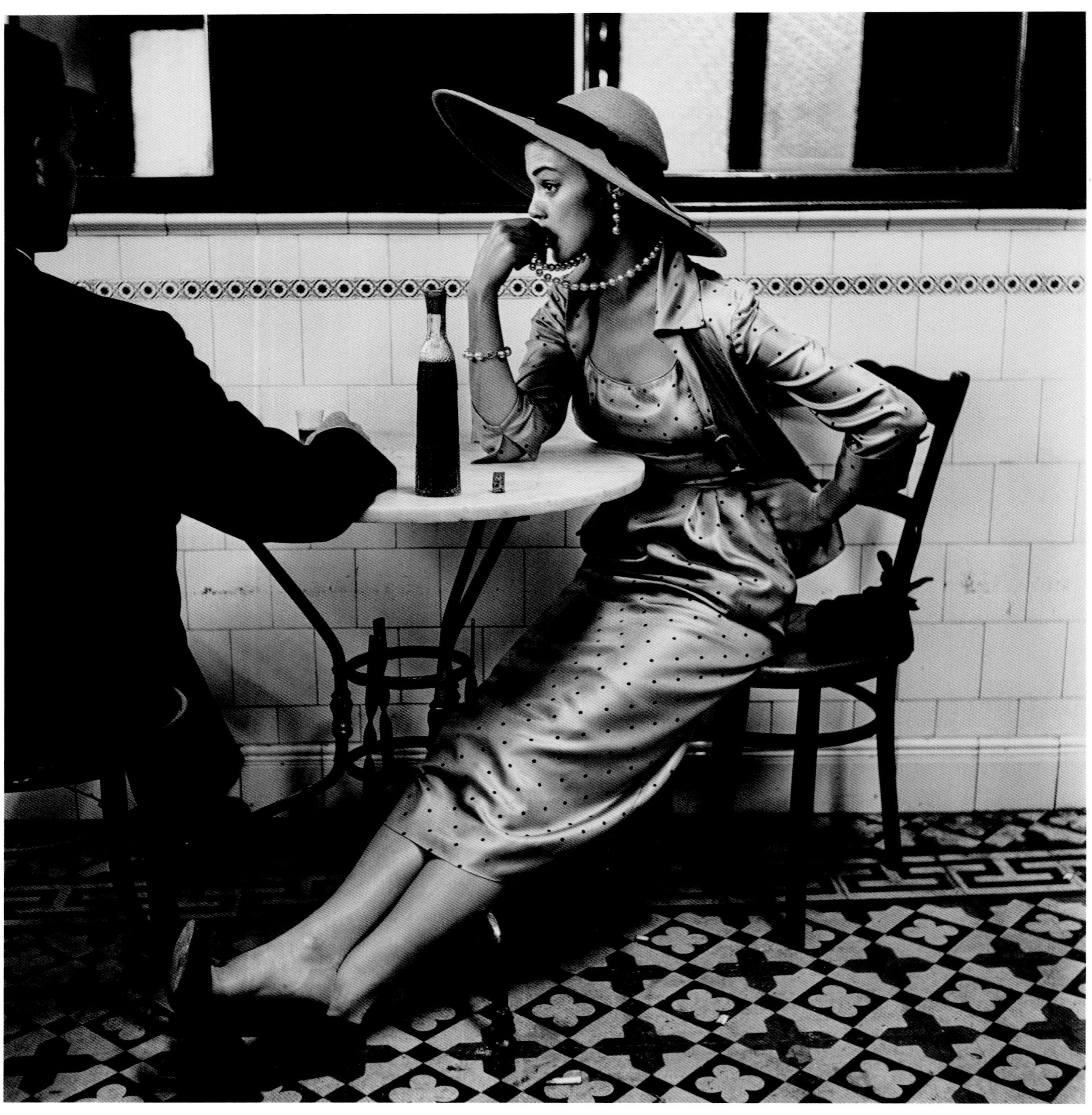

"Flying Down to Lima"
Café in Lima
Vogue
February 15, 1949
Photograph by Irving Penn

"and I was getting frustrated. So, I just sort of said to myself to heck with this and I picked up my pearls and I kicked off my shoes. My feet were hurting. And he said, 'Stop!'"

The image of a frustrated Patchett nibbling her pearls in that Lima café, was what both Penn and his mentor, *Vogue* art director Alex Liberman had been looking for. Weary of the stylized pictures of couture-draped models in striking balletic poses that regularly filled his magazine, images that reflected the mores and values of the bygone, prewar world, Liberman yearned for pictures that revealed the, "Interest and beauty in the everyday, in Patchett sitting in a chair," as he told biographers Dodie Kazanjian and Calvin Tomkins. "Instead of the artificial pose, here was a woman caught in an everyday moment. It's the imperfection of actual life."

The café image, now on view at museums around the world, also implied an embedded narrative beyond the limits of the frame. Who's the young man sitting with Patchett? Why are they there together and what's going to happen next? The *Vogue* team's anxious days of prowling the streets had made the picture possible. "By then she was used to being with him," said Maria Hambourg. "She'd been worn down from her anxiety; more like normal life. So, it made sense that it took a while. Penn was good at waiting things out."

LETTER FROM LIMA

We've worked so hard—much, much harder than N.Y. but I don't mind that so much.

We are now waiting for some lunch to be sent to Bab's room and then we're going out and photograph again this afternoon.

We are really going to get some beautiful pictures of me out of this trip, I hope. I can hardly wait to see them.

Vogue would publish 14 images from the shoot in its February 15th edition. Some feel as spontaneous and natural as Jean's café photo, others are more formal and posed. Spontaneous or formal, all of the images are superb examples of Penn's art and of Jean's range as a model as she enacts a series of roles, scripted by the clothes, by Simpson, the photographer, and herself.

It was hard work but rewarding. "Every bit of the time we were working," Jean told the *Baltimore Sun*. "To get one picture that's just right, Penn often takes 200 or 300. For that trip . . . he took 3,000 of me. People who think a model's life is mostly glamor and parties couldn't be more wrong."

As for the photographer, Patchett's patience, professionalism, and personality all seem to have won him over. "Her mind is always on the job," said Penn to writer Jess Stern. "She isn't thinking about what she did last night or what she is doing tonight. She has great physical energy and throws it all into the job."

They also appear to have had some fun.

LETTER FROM LIMA

Mrs. Simpson and Penn are both wonderful people and have been terribly nice to me. If it weren't for them I know I would be terribly depressed. They know of some of the funniest experiences and we practically laugh all the time. . . We all three get along beautifully.

Contact sheets from the shoot, given by Penn to Patchett, show her flashing an occasional impish smile that seems directed at the man behind the camera. "We had a very good time together," she told Michael Gross in *Model*, and were "very fond of each other."

It's also been suggested, notably by model Dorian Leigh, then in the process of ending an affair with Penn, that Penn and Patchett too had become an item. Patchett evaded the question, when asked some 40 years later and Penn's comments, if any, were either not recorded or are yet to be released.

"I know he loved her," said Maria Hambourg. "I know he really appreciated her. But more than that, I don't know."

What is known is that Penn had met and been dazzled by his future wife, model Lisa Fonssagrives the year before "Flying Down to Lima"—and that when Patchett saw Penn reading a long letter at their Lima hotel, he insisted it came, not from his future bride, but his tailor.

Small deceptions or unknowable intentions aside, a real intimacy had grown up between Penn and Patchett that would help spark one of the photographer's major achievements.

LETTER FROM LIMA

Gee, it doesn't seem possible that a whole week has passed!! I am at the moment waiting for Penn to come back so that we can go to the airport and take some pictures.

Penn thinks I am a terrific model and didn't realize it before.

With Lima behind them, Babs and Jean returned to New York with Penn's images while Penn went to the one-time Inca capital city of Cusco "on a hunch," rented a local studio, and took portraits of local people for the first of his "ethnographic" studies. Back in Manhattan, Patchett went to work, posing for ads for Henri Bendel, Miron Woolens, and Lonsdale Cottons, and for *Vogue* in editorial images by Coffin, Beaton, and Horst. A month later Penn and Patchett were back in *Vogue* with a new feature—"Beauty Magnified."

That summer, Penn began work on what he later described as "the major artistic experience of my life," a series of nude portraits of women, most of them of large, fleshy artist's models, which continued on weekends and holidays through the summer—a quiet period when Penn could have *Vogue*'s studios to himself. It was an intense, sometimes feverish experience for the photographer, an assistant, and his models—one of whom, as the series started, was the decidedly svelte Jean Patchett, according to both a Penn assistant—and Irving Penn.

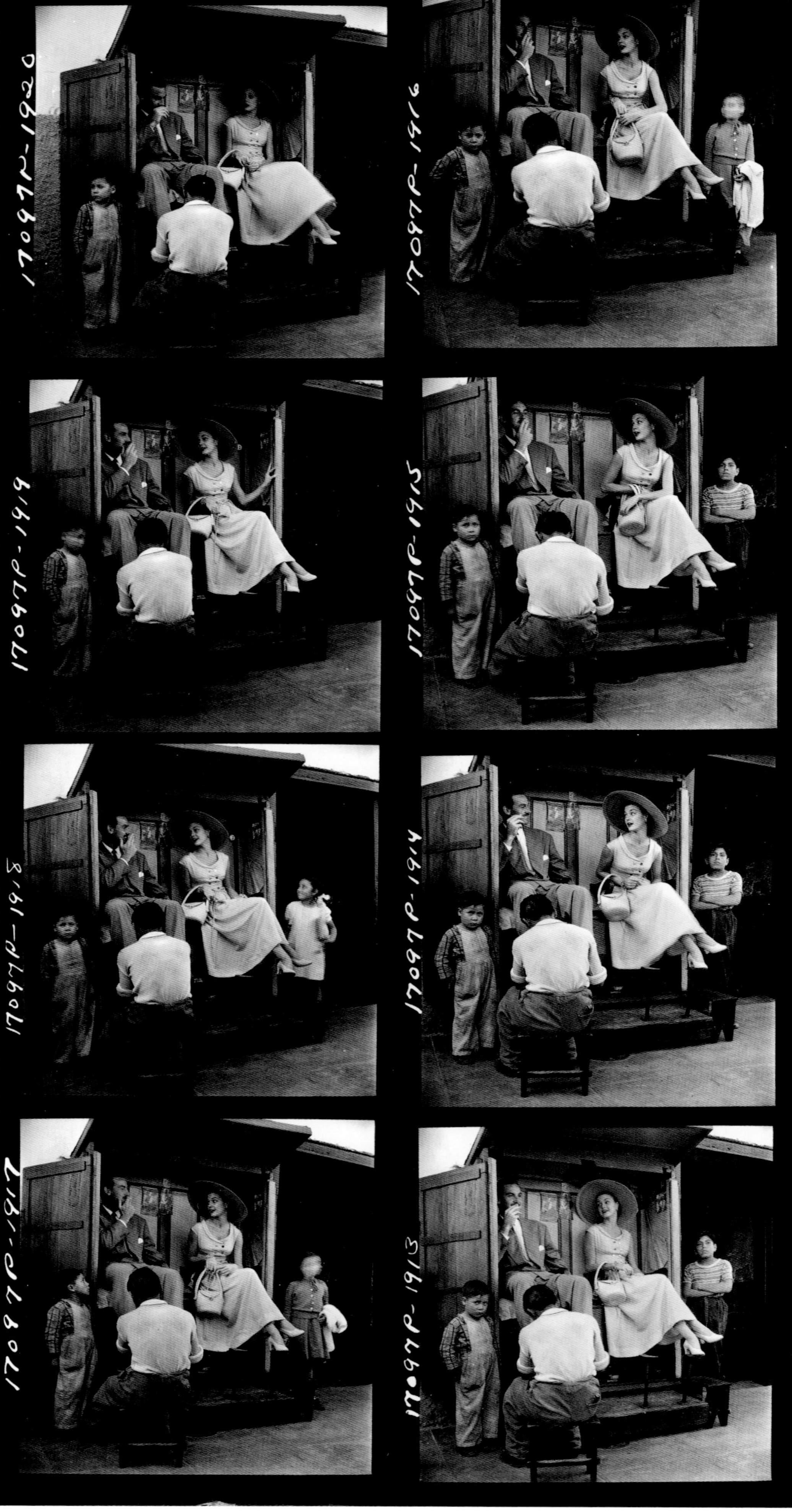

This spread, from left:
Shoeshine Stand
Contact sheet
Lima, 1948
Photographs by Irving Penn

Jean Patchett in Saya y Manto costume
Contact sheet
Lima, 1948
Photographs by Irving Penn

Following spread, from left:
Jean Patchett at the Beach
Contact sheet
Lima, 1948
Photographs by Irving Penn

Jean Patchett in Bullfighter's Hat
Contact sheet
Lima, 1948
Photographs by Irving Penn

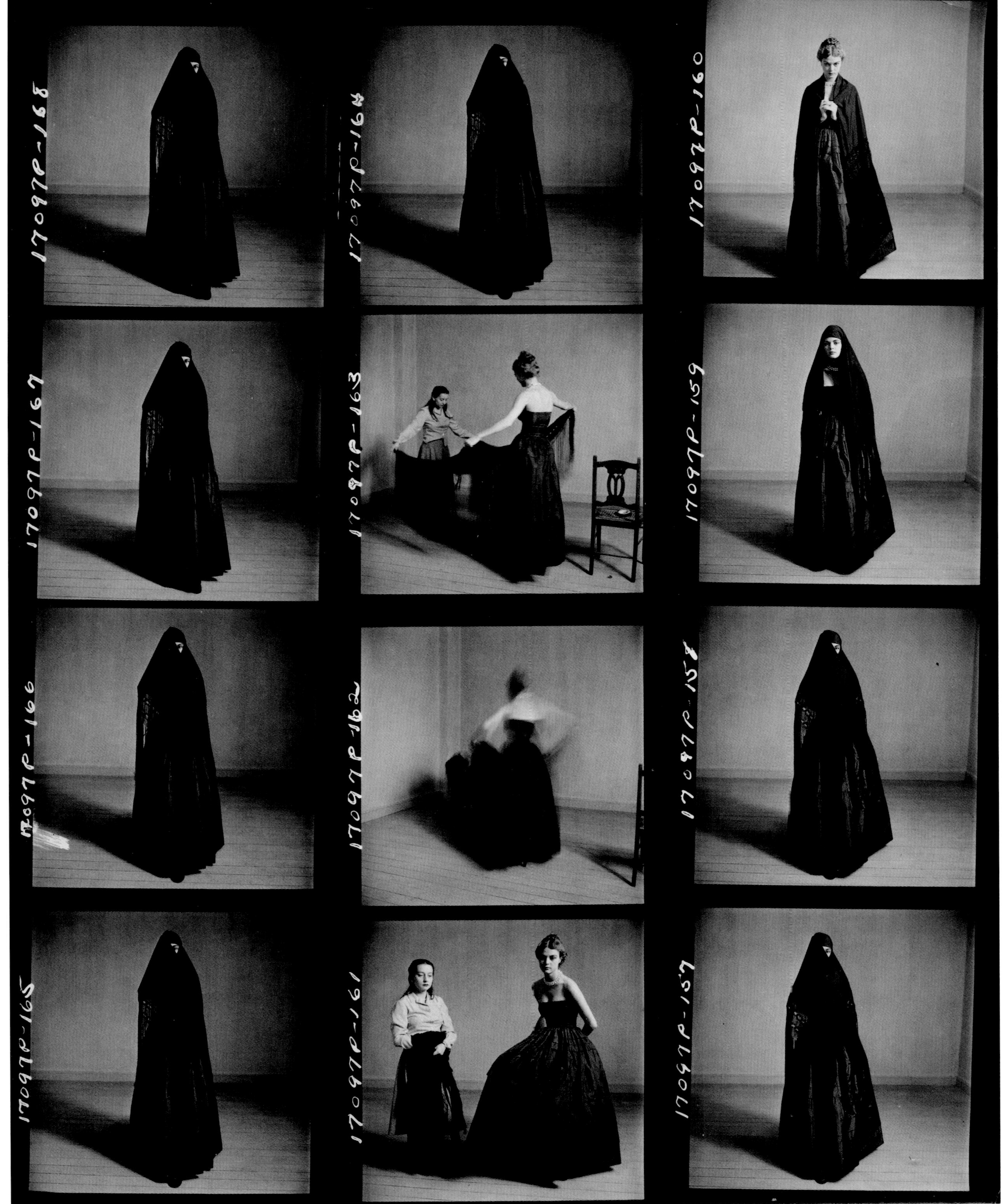

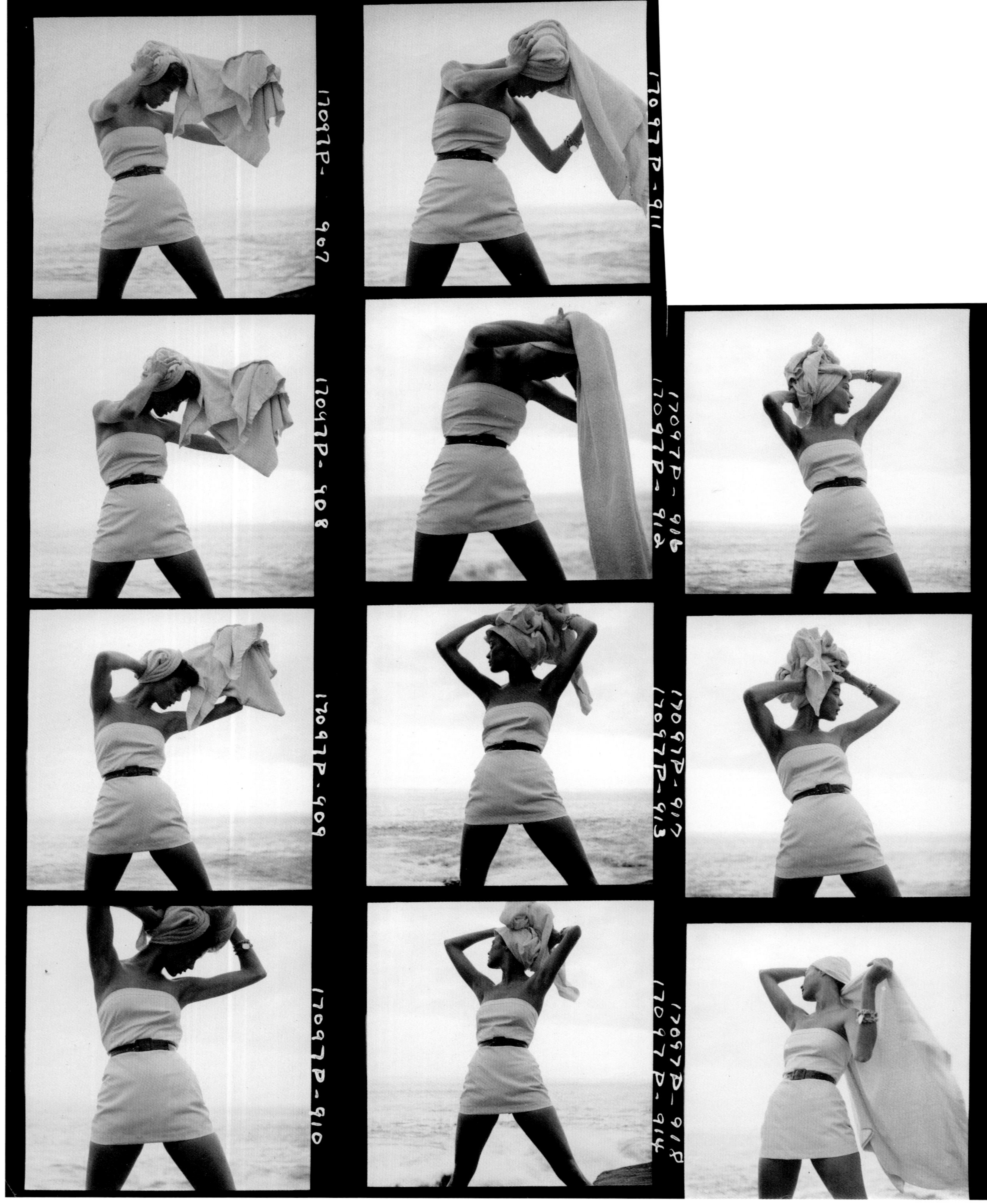

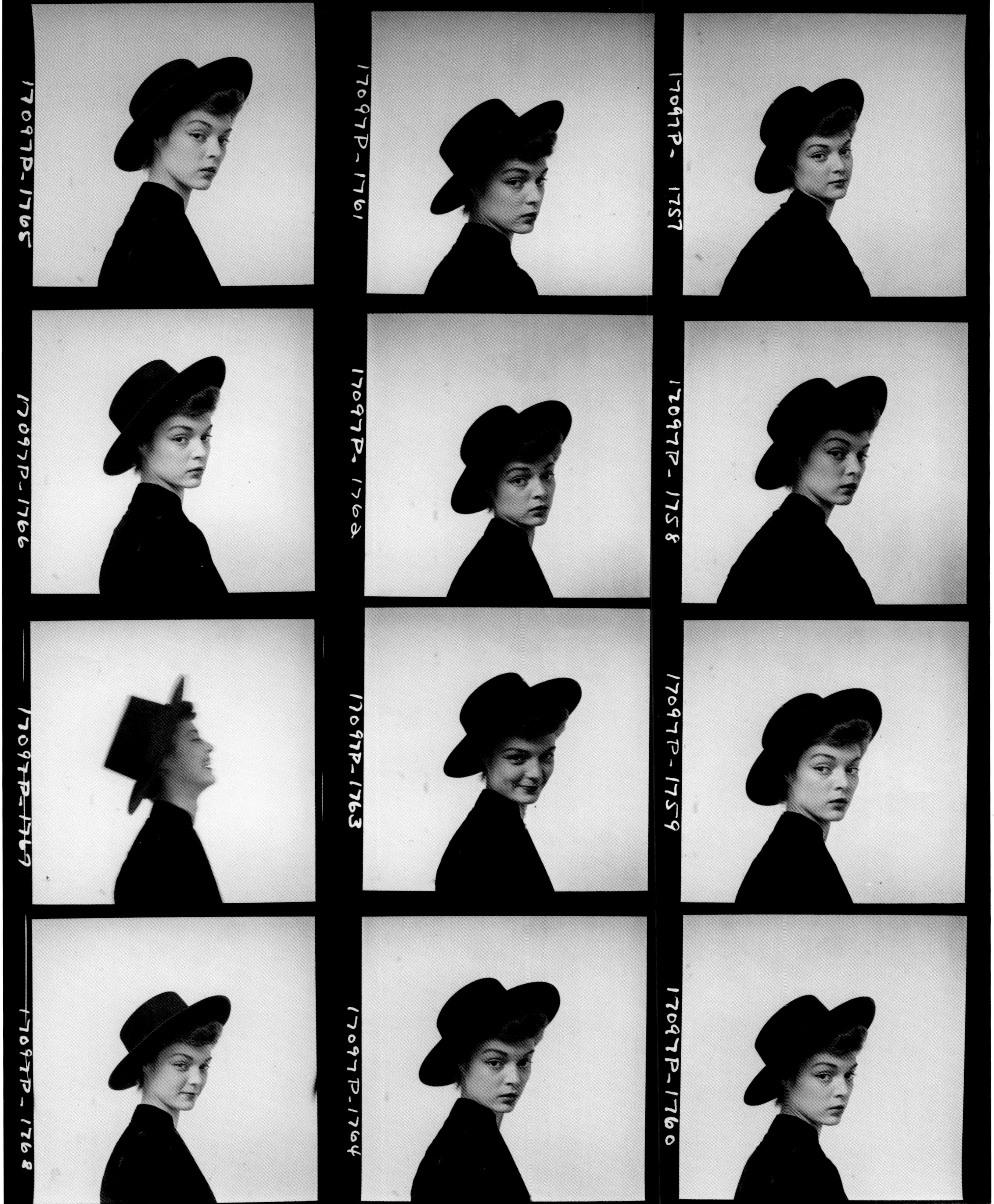

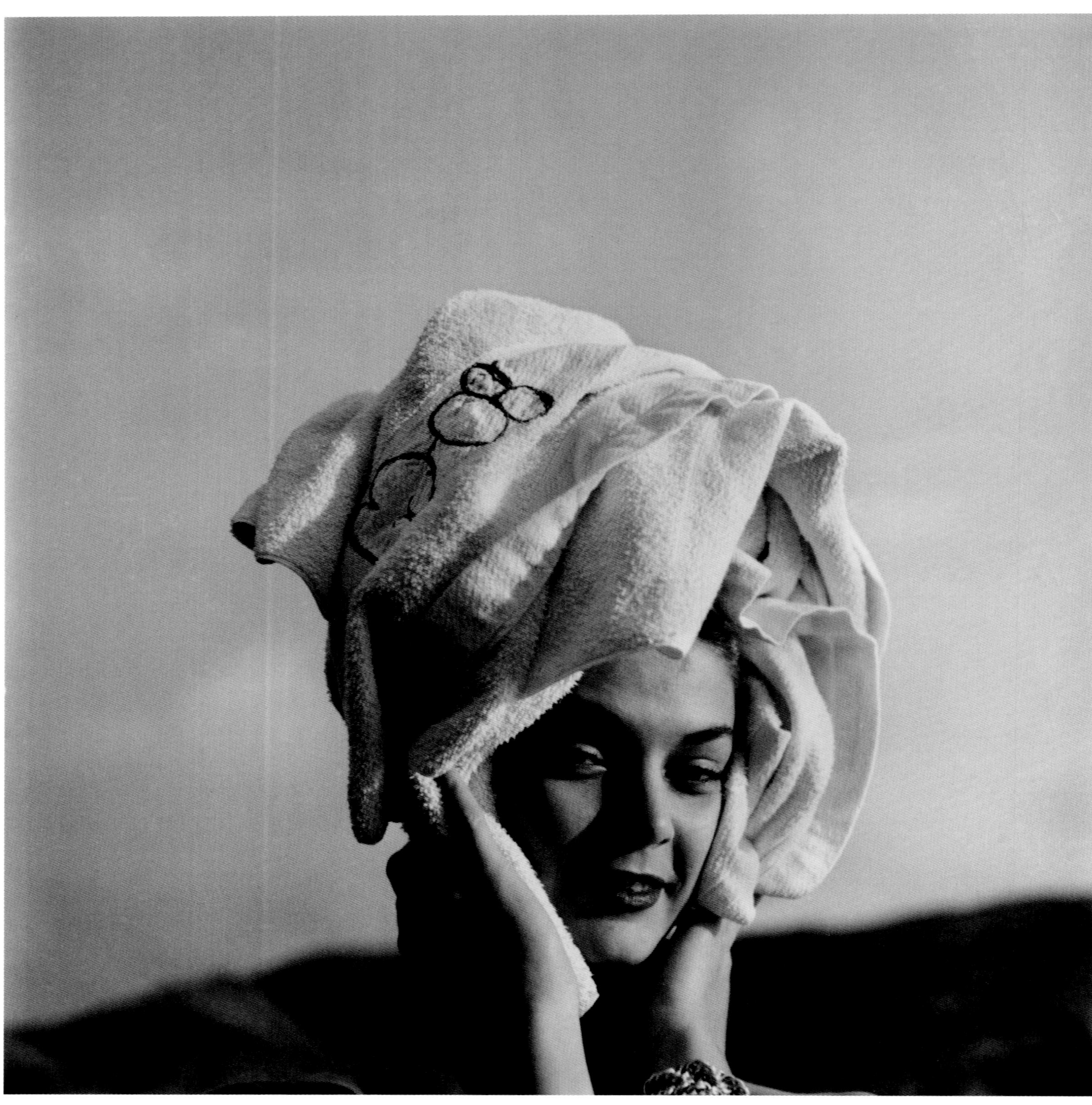

"For the longest time, he wouldn't acknowledge that she was it," said Maria Hambourg, "perhaps because she didn't want to be acknowledged as being one of the models." Patchett would be the only model Penn identified besides Pearl Bond, who sat for the image that helped initiate the series, and whose name was written on the back of the print. For her part, Patchett never discussed taking part in the sessions at all. As for why she took part, Jerry Schatzberg, who photographed Patchett for *Vogue* towards the end of her career, suggested that freedom from the constraints of a small-town childhood was motive enough, compounded by the photographer she would work with. "Those are the people that just dreamed of doing this," said Schatzberg. "And then you get to do it with somebody like Penn—a master." While identifications are difficult, there are some 18 images of slim, nude models (first shown in 1980 at New York's Marlborough Gallery) who may be Jean.

Penn's description of shooting the series to Hambourg, in her book *Earthly Bodies*, is remarkably sensual and passionate. With his assistant helping him switch cameras as he directed his models, Penn, "kept talking all the time. . . with coos, murmurs, and supportive breathing to convey that everything was wonderful, just right in this perfect situation. The smell in the studio was 'sweet, powdery, a little sweaty. . . There was no physical contact except an appreciative embrace at the end. All the women responded the same way.'"

Looking back at her work with Penn, in a 1990 interview in *Lear's* magazine, Patchett described their professional relationship as if it were a troika between the photographer, herself, and the camera he preferred. "I liked the Rolleiflex," said Jean. "I felt very close to the Rolleiflex and loved Penn for what he did with it. He made me feel pretty. We had a communal relationship through the camera.

Below:
Nude #3
Vogue
July 1950
Photograph by Irving Penn

Opposite:
Jean Patchett
Lima, 1948
Photograph by Irving Penn

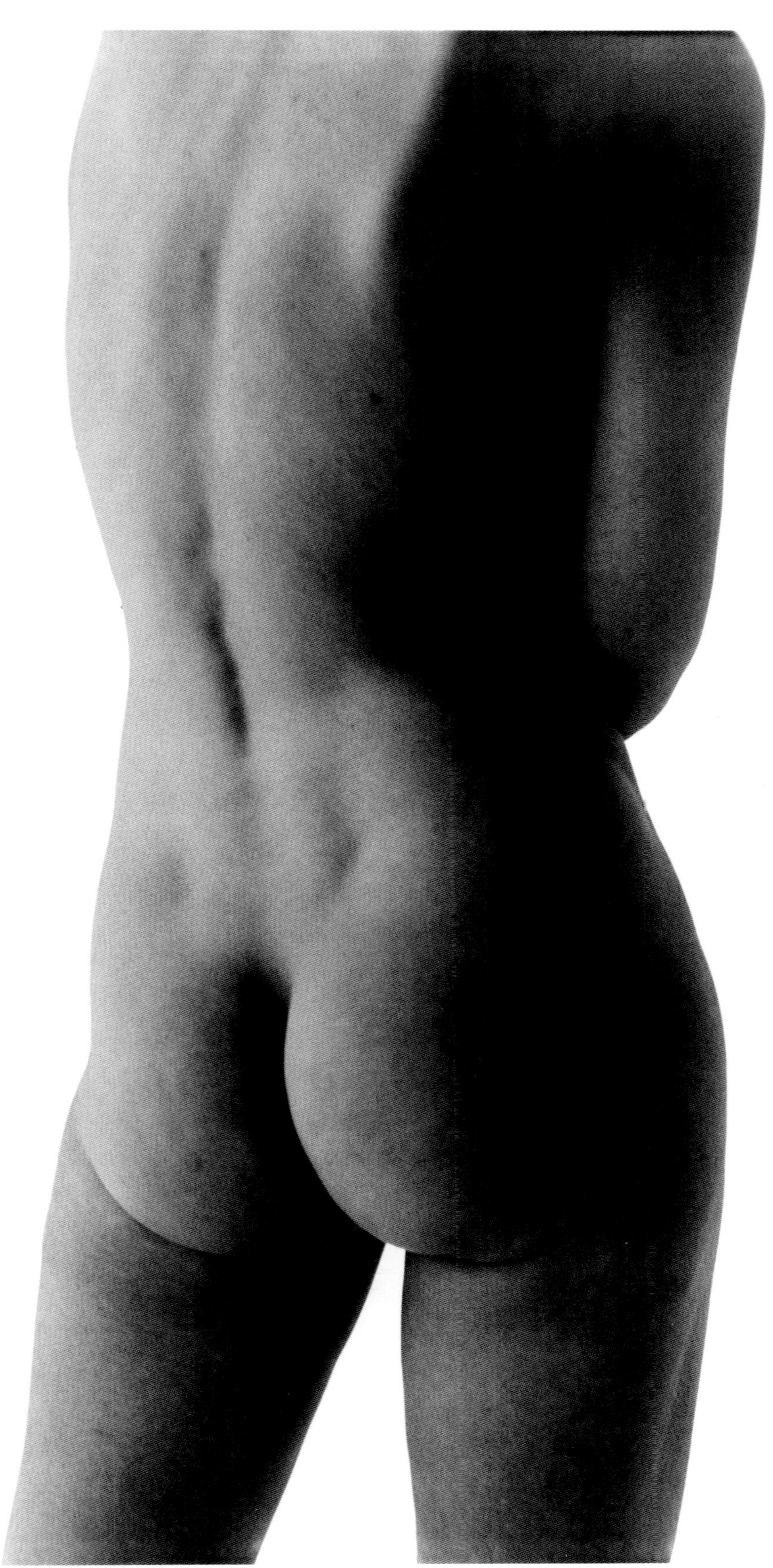

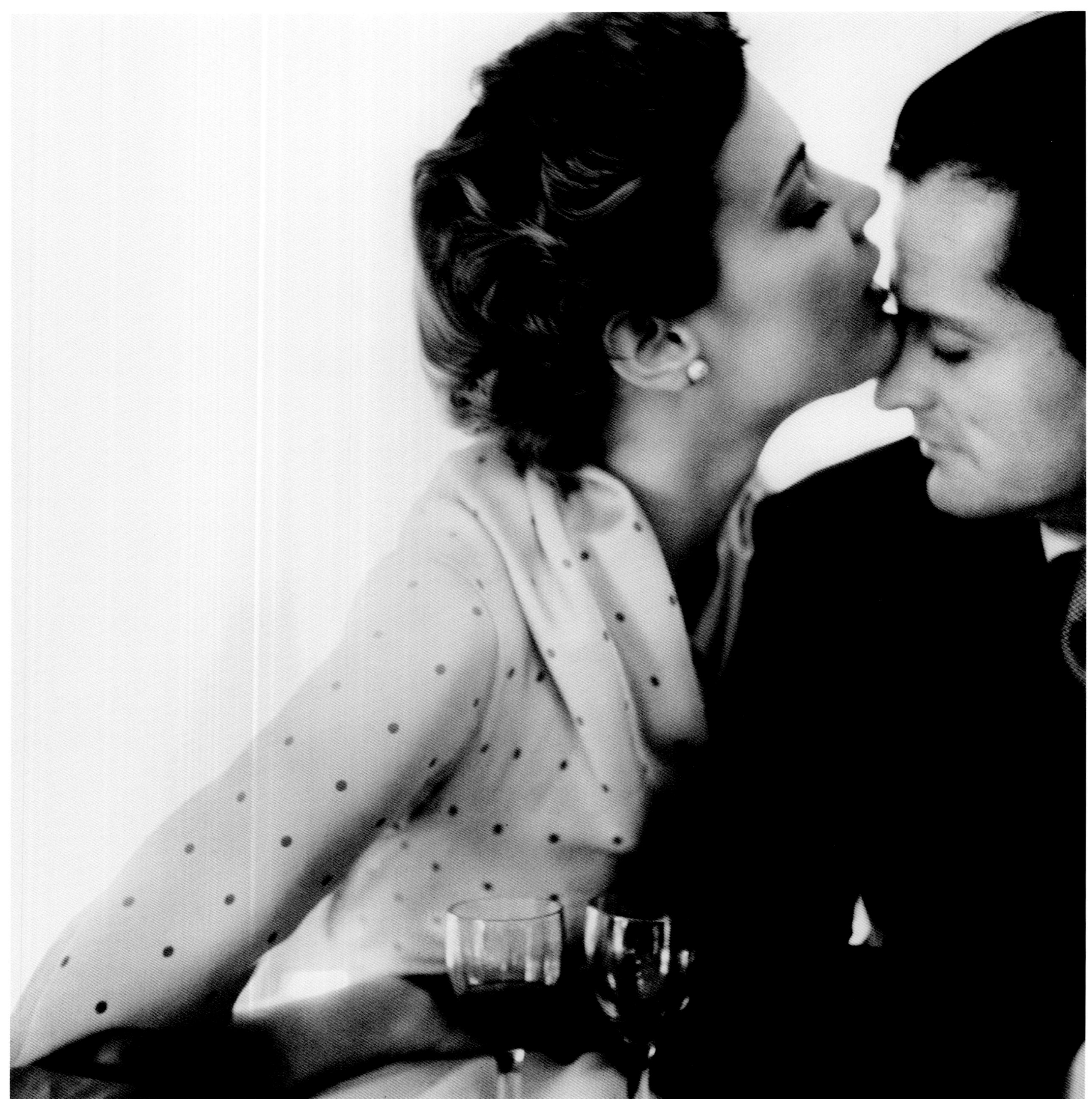

Above:
Fashion Photo
Vogue
New York, 1949
Photograph by Irving Penn

Opposite:
Self-Portrait Italy
circa 1944–45
Photograph by Irving Penn

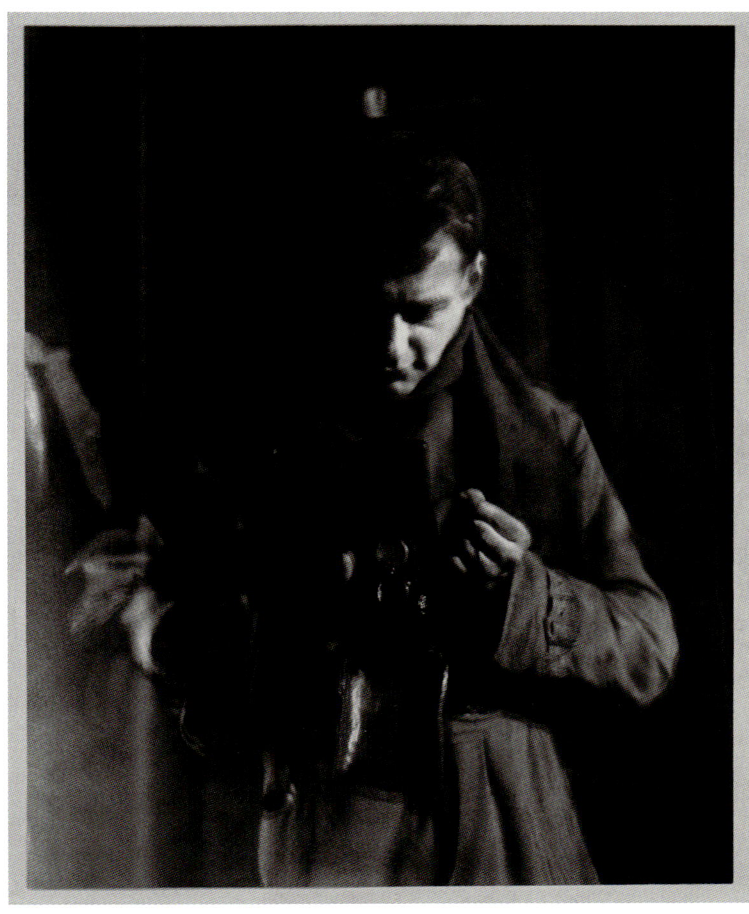

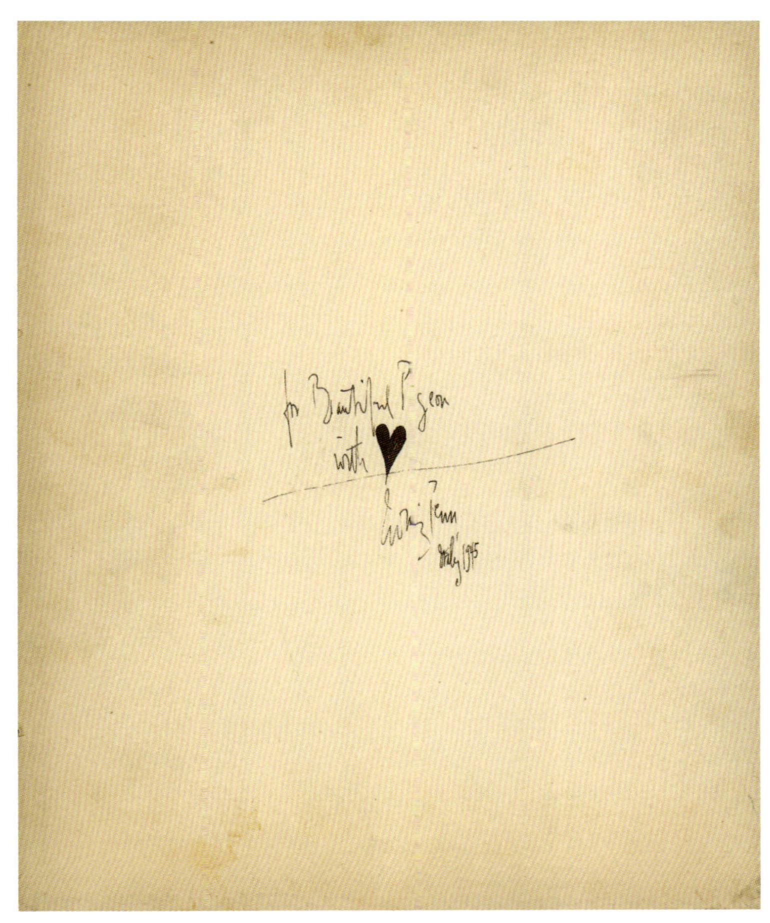

It was like making love to a camera, not to the photographer."

Along with that communal relationship with the camera came a series of close collaborations between model and photographer, with Penn directing Patchett like an auteur with a Method actor. "Penn and I had a great rapport," she told Charles Castle. "I'd get into an outfit and stand on the white paper in the studio and he would tell me a story . . . he would say, 'You're at the Caravelle having lunch with somebody, and you're wearing this lovely suit. Show me how you feel.' Or it's at the opera, and I'm looking for this lovely man I'm madly in love with. It's intermission, and I can't find him. Suddenly, I see him in the distance and I'm trying to catch his eye over everybody's heads. Another time I would have to pretend to be on the street looking for a taxi cab, or at Cartier's looking at a jewel." Penn also collaborated closely with Liberman, who often sketched for the photographer what he hoped to see on film, then personally picked the final published images from Penn's contact sheets. "At one sitting, we would easily take five hundred pictures for one outfit," said Patchett. "He called it chasing a bluebird."

Looking through Penn's photographs of Patchett, from 1949 to 1956, there's more of a collaborative, "model as actor" feel to their work through 1952, the year Liberman warned Penn that *Vogue's* editors had complained that his pictures "burned on the page." After April 1953, Jean's postures in Penn's photos seem more formal, her features more mask-like as Penn "began to make a commodity" rather than "a picture," to satisfy his critics at *Vogue*. "Liberman didn't believe in the Capital 'A' art of photography," said Hambourg. "He was really all about communication. Painting and sculpture, that was Art, but photography was in the service of a publication."

In 1964, eight years after Penn's last published image of Jean Patchett in the pages of *Vogue*, the photographer—admittedly tired of fashion photography—told a session of Alexey Brodovitch's Design Laboratory that he didn't think a model's personality "should ever intrude . . . The greatest ones are fairly anonymous people who look at the photographer and suddenly become somebody, but they are, in fact, mirrors under those circumstances."

While Patchett may have been a mirror for Penn's camera in the latter years of their collaboration, she brought all of her ability to project her personality and inhabit a role to the work they did before. "It's really not about the clothes," said Hambourg about Penn's approach to fashion. "It's about the image of a woman who's alluring. He wanted the heart, the soul, or some essence of the person, even in a fashion shot, to be present."

Heart and soul were there to be shared by Penn and Patchett. Jean's daughter Amy may have put it best: "He had a deep affection for my mom and she for him." If further proof is needed, among the contact sheets and other images which Penn presented Jean is a picture of himself in his uniform of the American Field Service, which he volunteered for and served in during the last years of the Second World War. On the back of the picture he wrote a dedication to Jean in black ink—"for Beautiful Pigeon with ♡ — Irving Penn, Italy 1945." ➻

A DANGEROUS PLACE

"The fashion world's a dangerous place," warned essayist Kennedy Fraser, in 1992. "The most vulnerable don't survive it." And fashion models living off that most transient source of personal capital, their looks, are among the most vulnerable of all. A finite source of self-esteem is soon depleted in adversity—and it's all too easy to lose faith in oneself if the people around you care only for the income they can glean from your looks. What follows often, when the cycle is complete, is a crash.

"So many tragic lives," said Richard Avedon to author Michael Gross, of more than a few of the models the photographer worked with in the late 40s and 50s. "They ended up destroyed," added designer Bill Blass, a "sketcher" in New York's garment center in the early 40s, where he saw the rag trade's seamy side up close.

The names of the damaged and destroyed include some of Patchett's peers at the very top of the modeling profession. Sunny Harnett, a stunning blonde whose advertising and editorial pages in the mid-50s rival Patchett's output at her most prolific, suffered a mastectomy, weight problems, and a nervous breakdown as her career declined. She was hospitalized and died at 63 after a fire in a geriatric ward. Dovima, a favorite of Avedon and Helburn and as big a star as Harnett or Patchett, gave her money to husbands who abused her, retired from fashion to work as a restaurant hostess in Florida and died alone, leaving just one hundred dollars behind in a safety deposit box.

Jean Patchett was different. Confident enough to borrow a large sum of money from her father then leave home to find her way in a strange city and highly competitive profession, Jean knew what she wanted in her private life and took nothing for granted in her career. "My impression was that becoming a star fell into her lap," said Amy Auer Hensley. "I didn't get any sense this was calculated. Obviously, she had the smarts and realized, 'I'm good at this. I photograph magnificently and I'm going to work my tailbone off, be professional and make the most of my time.' Everything that came was unexpected and gravy. She knew she was blessed."

Success was gravy, but there was plenty of cream as well. The young woman who'd waited tables at her father's country bar loved the Stork Club, a New York nightlife institution that started as a mobbed-up speakeasy before becoming the favored spot of columnists Walter Winchell and Dorothy Kilgallen, along with tourists, Broadway and Hollywood stars, poohbahs, politicians, and J. Edgar Hoover. Patchett was a regular at Friday "model lunches" staged by Stork owner Sherman Billingsley and enjoyed evening dates with the second-generation heirs to beer and fuse box fortunes she met there. But model lunches aside, Jean drew a careful line between business and pleasure, not too difficult given the lack of prospective husbands in her strata of the fashion world. "Girls who model for the Seventh Avenue dress houses meet big buyers and executives," Jean told writer Mary Day Winn in 1950, "but almost the only people I ever meet in the line of business are photographers and women fashion editors."

And Jean did not date photographers. Some of course were women, some gay men—in the closet and out—and some were straight guys on the make, who used the power of their position to get all the sex they could. Advertising and magazine art directors might suggest a model for a job, but top photographers often selected their models themselves, sometimes a single favorite they would go to again and again. As in every other field, having the power to give work or withhold it gave the less scrupulous room to exploit the needy, beautiful, often insecure women who would come to their studios and disrobe.

Their names were known to many in the industry and models would pass the word on who and what to avoid. But not always to Eileen Ford, a fierce mother hen

Opposite:
Model Jean Patchett in Crowd, Metropolitan Opera Gala Opening
November 8, 1954
Photograph by
Jerry Dantzic

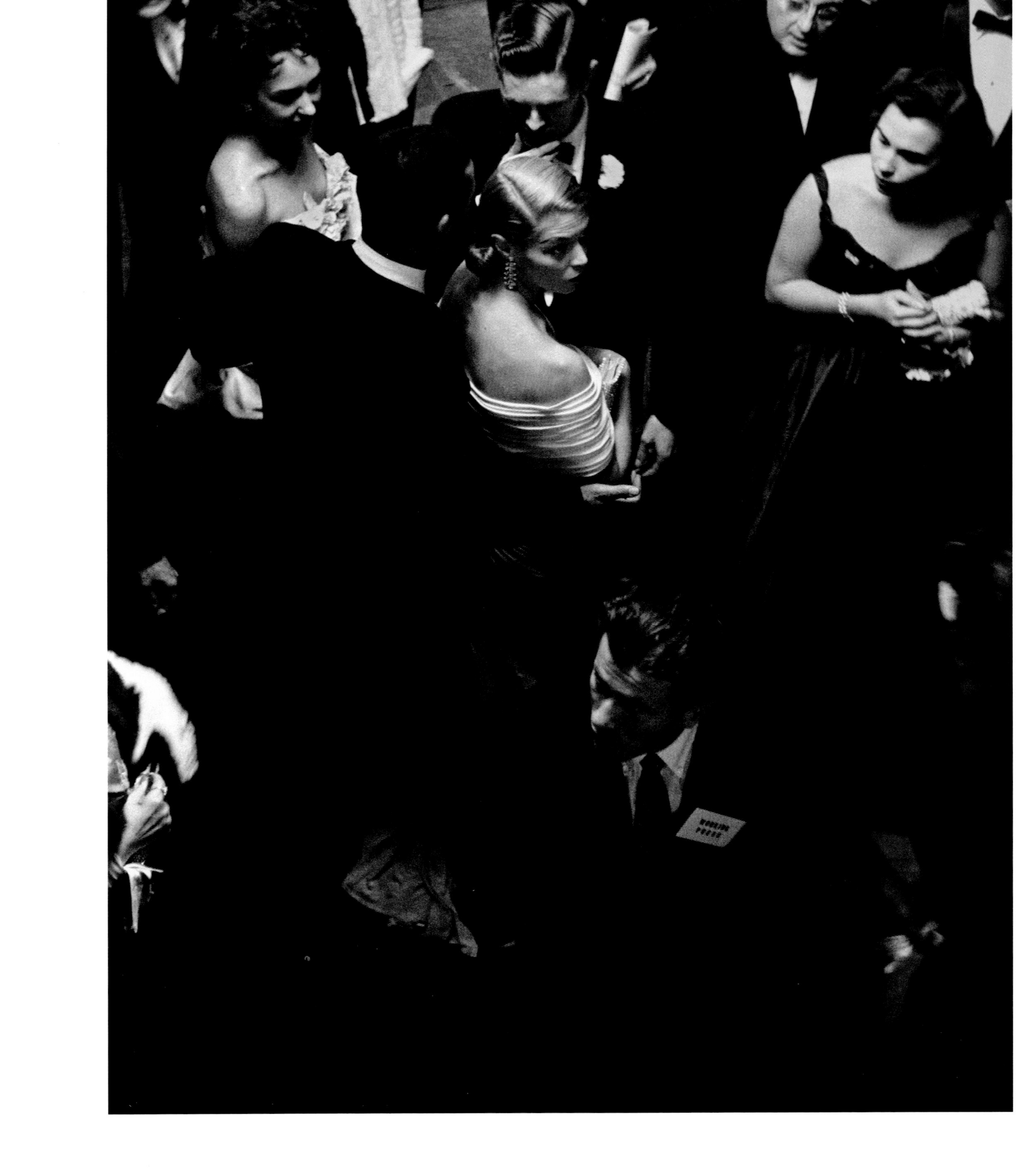

© 2019 JERRY DANTZIC ARCHIVES. All Rights Reserved.

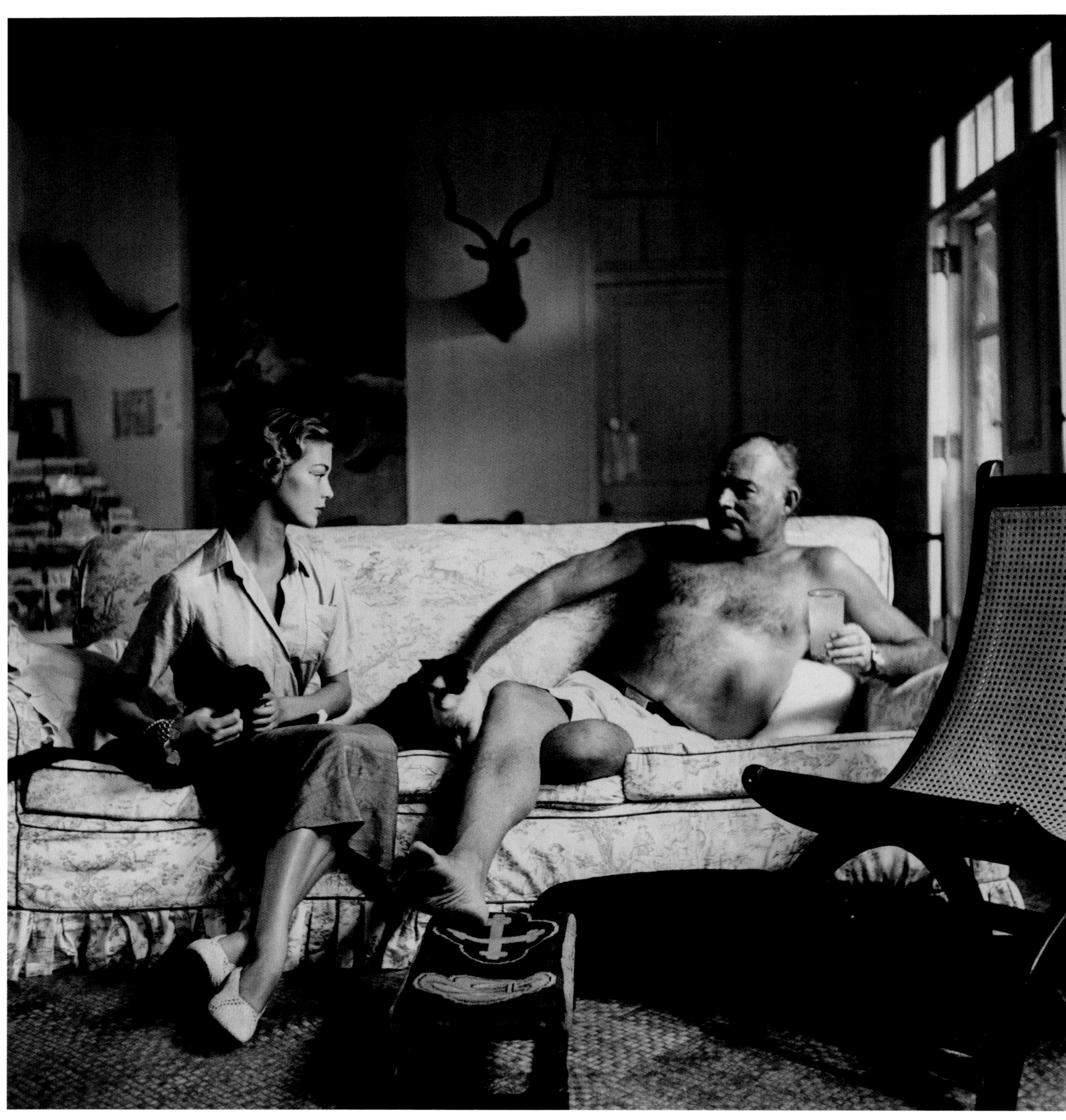

Jean Patchett and Ernest Hemingway, Finca Vigía, Havana
Vogue
November 15, 1950
Silk shirt and wrap skirt
by B. H. Wragge
Photograph by Clifford Coffin

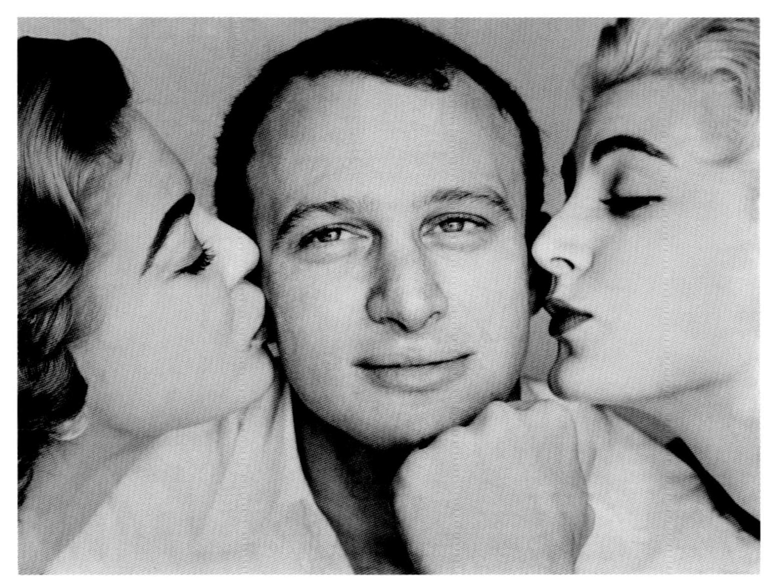

Jean Patchett and Carmen Dell'Orefice kissing William Helburn
circa 1952
Photograph by William Helburn

to generations of young Ford models who insisted she would never send one of her "girls" to a photographer who liked a little sex with the session. Bill Helburn, a friend to both Jean and Eileen, said having beautiful women going in and out of his studio made him feel like "Willy Wonka in the chocolate factory." And Bill loved chocolate.

"I was awful," he would later say of his casual affairs and wandering eye, not to mention his active hands. But Helburn, unlike some contemporaries, had charm to burn and understood there were limits. "Billy was a naughty boy," said Jean to Michael Gross. "But he adored me, and I adored him and I never had any trouble with him." "He had a reputation with the models," added Carmen Dell'Orefice, a star model from 1946 until today. "But a lady has a right to say 'no'— and I never heard that he was anything but a gentleman if they said no."

Patchett was less forgiving after an encounter with novelist Ernest Hemingway. On a trip to Havana with Babs Simpson and the irascible Clifford Coffin for a *Vogue* "Sun Fashions" feature, the trio went to Hemingway's Havana home, looking for the writer and a background for the shoot. When they arrived at half-past seven in the morning, the house was decorated with "half-filled champagne glasses" but Hemingway was nowhere to be found.

When the 51-year-old novelist sauntered in, according to Simpson's account to *Vogue*'s Dodie Kazanjian, he was accompanied by a young Basque priest who "got on very well" with Babs, while Hemingway "took a great shine to Jean, of course." It was anything but mutual. "She said he stank," said Amy Hensley, "and she's sitting on the couch, trying to get away from him and she's like— yecch." The image *Vogue* published in its November 15, 1950 edition, with the neutral title "On the Scene in Havana," shows a corpulent Hemingway in shorts, gripping a drink and staring at Patchett with a dazed, carnal expression while she recoils slightly and primly returns his look. The print is a composite of two negatives according to Coffin biographer Robin Muir, "one where Patchett looks at her least stunned and the other of Hemingway at his most attentive.'

"They wanted to spend their lives with us," said Simpson. "So we got the first plane we could out of there."

Back to New York, and for Jean, the daily struggle familiar to all fashion models of keeping down her weight. Some chose artificial means to suppress their appetites, easily done in that dawning age of "miracle drugs." Amphetamines were readily available, prescribed as diet pills or purchased over the counter in an inhaler. Other models were pushed into using speed by photographers— allegedly including Coffin, who, according to Muir, was described by a contemporary as prodding his models to take "thyroid pills and uppers to keep them slim." Amphetamines also worked as confidence-boosters for some struggling models, at least before the drug's more pernicious effects began destroying their health.

There's neither any evidence nor even a suggestion that Jean Patchett ever tried controlling her weight with drugs, nor would that have been consistent with the reliably disciplined manner in which she approached her job. Regular exercise was part of Patchett's routine, but to keep off the pounds, Jean relied on her diet. At 5'9" maintaining her 34–22–35 figure took constant effort— and sometimes a waist cincher to complete the effect. Breakfast for Jean was often "five cups of coffee and half a grapefruit; lunch a sandwich grabbed on the run, with most calories coming at dinner, a hearty (but not too-hearty) meal."

"I am afraid I have gained a few pounds gee—!! I hope not—it only means I'll have to go on another diet," Jean wrote her family from St. Croix and a *Vogue* shoot with Norman Parkinson in 1950. A few days later Jean obsessed again about her diet in a letter from Jamaica's Montego Bay, "The food is out of this world," she wrote, "and I must try not to eat too much for I simply can't afford to gain weight." Not even Irving Penn and Lima could distract her from worrying about her waistline. "The food here is very, very good and I'm sure I've gained 100 pounds, I feel tremendous," she wailed in a letter home, after a footsore day spent searching for locations.

If Jean objected to the prevailing standards of the time, she seems to have kept it to herself. And not just regarding her weight. Between 1950 and 1960 the median age for a woman's first marriage was around 20 years old. While at least a third of American women were either working or looking for a job at the decade's start, many expected to sacrifice their careers to marriage and children and Patchett told reporters, more than once, that she intended to do just that. Just four months before her wedding day, she assured one writer that when she married she planned to become a full-time housewife because "marriage is a career in itself."

What she did was a little more complicated. In 1948, a few months before her decisive encounter with Eileen Ford, friends introduced Jean to a Milwaukee-born Macy's trainee who would go on to a successful career as a banker. "A couple of models I knew who lived at the Barbizon [a residential hotel] said, 'We've got a girl for you,'" Louis Auer later told the *Los Angeles Times*. The couple would enjoy evenings together at the Stork Club, El Morocco, and 21, but their first date was at a Manhattan luncheonette. He would soon give her a nickname—"Poncho"—that friends would use for decades. "Patchett, Patcho, Pancho. . . that's how it evolved," said Louis.

The relationship built over time. Louis was a favorite date, but Jean realized he'd become

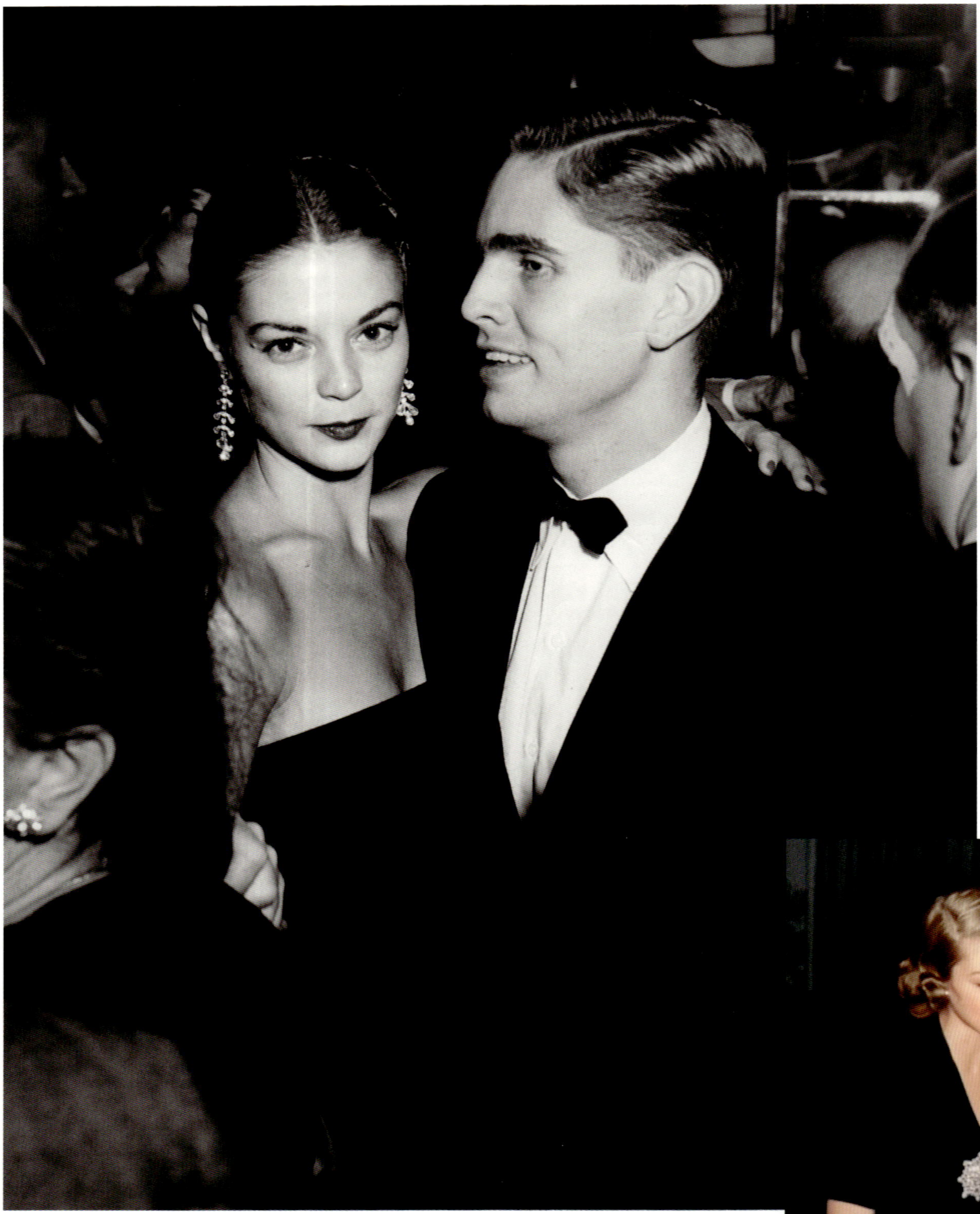

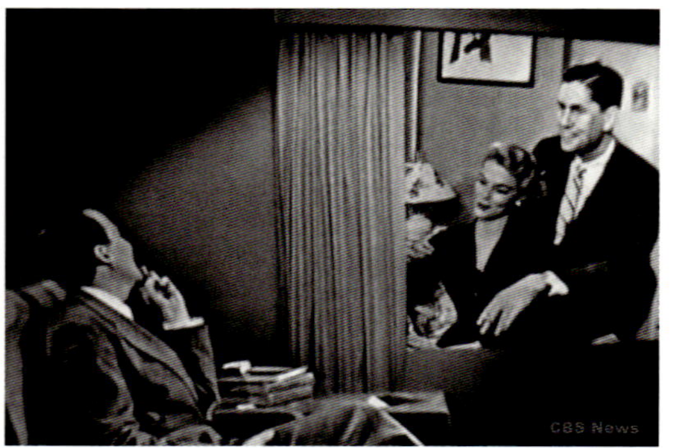

This page, clockwise from top left:
Jean Patchett
and Louis Auer
The Stork Club
circa 1950

Wedding Day, Jean
Patchett and Louis Auer
New York
March 30, 1951

Edward R. Murrow
Interviewing Jean Patchett
and Louis Auer on
"Person to Person"
June 28, 1955

Opposite:
Jean Patchett
The Stork Club
circa 1950

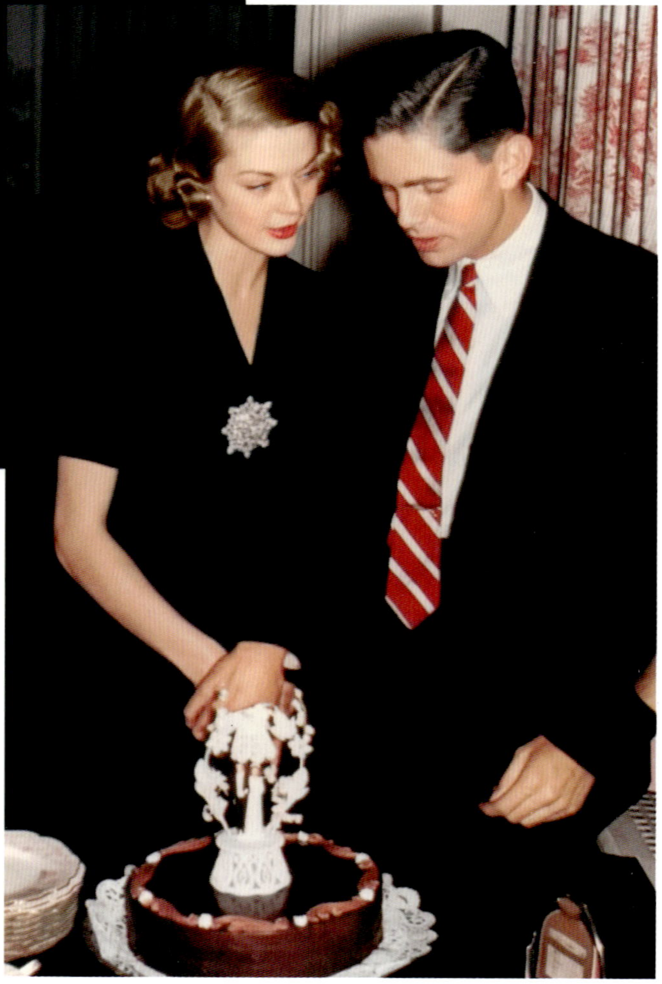

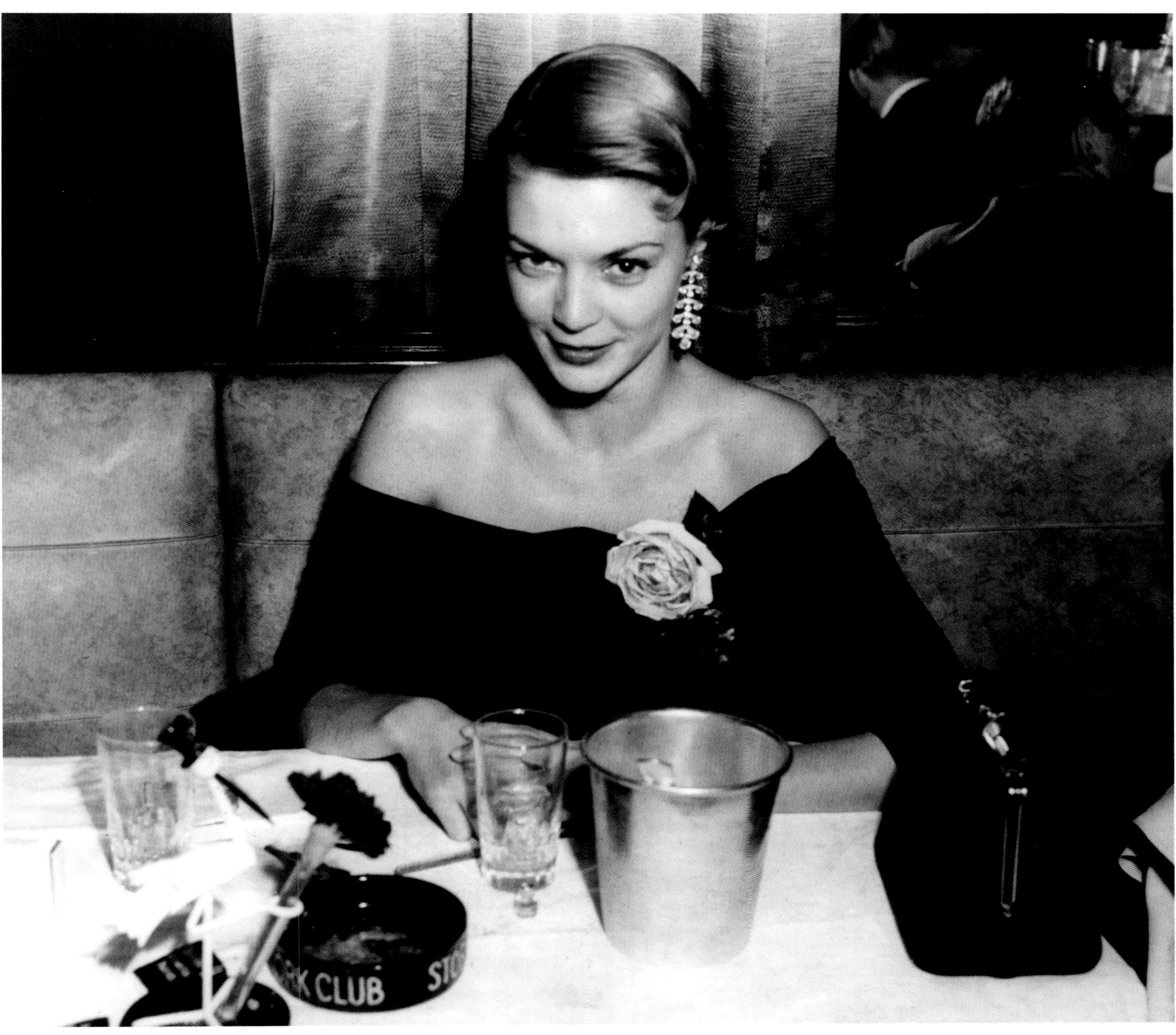

much more to her when she went to Paris with Norman Parkinson—and found herself thinking of Louis Auer. They were married on March 30, 1951—the end of a busy week for Jean, whose work diary shows appointments with Stephen Colhoun, Mark Shaw, and *McCall's* magazine, in the days before the ceremony.

After their honeymoon, Jean cut her hours and days, working three and a half days a week with no jobs after 4:30 or 5:00, to give her time to shop and make a hot dinner for them both. While Louis agreed to help with the dishes, when it came to money traditional rules applied—Jean gave her checks to her husband to manage, taking a weekly percentage back to pay their bills.

Children were supposed to follow marriage, and quickly, in those baby-boom years. And Patchett publicly yearned for kids. A month after her triumphant "Doe Eye" cover for *Vogue* was published, the haughty doyenne with the startling graphic face told the *Baltimore Sun* her ambition was "to work one more year and then get married and have children." One year later and already married to Louis, she told another reporter she expected to leave modeling once "the baby comes" in a year or two, because she didn't want to raise her children in New York. The children did come, but not until Jean's career was in its final years. The Auers adopted their son Bart in 1959 and daughter Amy in 1961.

Home and Louis both were a comfort to Jean. Evenings at the Stork Club were fun but infrequent and often ended early. "I'm no good at all after 'the night before,'" Jean told writer Sam Boal, four years after getting married. "So when I'm tempted to stay out late—I go home to bed." The Auers loved movies, Broadway shows, and occasionally went to the opera. But despite their affluence they didn't own a television when Edward R. Murrow and his production crew put them live on the air that year for a national audience.

"Tell me," the avuncular Murrow asked Louis, "how is she doing at this business of being both a model and a housewife?"

"Well I hate to say it in front of her Ed," said Louis, "it's a little bit of a commercial, but she's much better as a housewife than she really is as a model actually. She's top notch as a housewife."

In the 21st century that may sound like sexist slander that demanded a rebuff. But in 1955, when women were expected to put home first, it was more likely an act of gallantry—defending his wife's choice to have both a career and marriage—and a compliment ➸

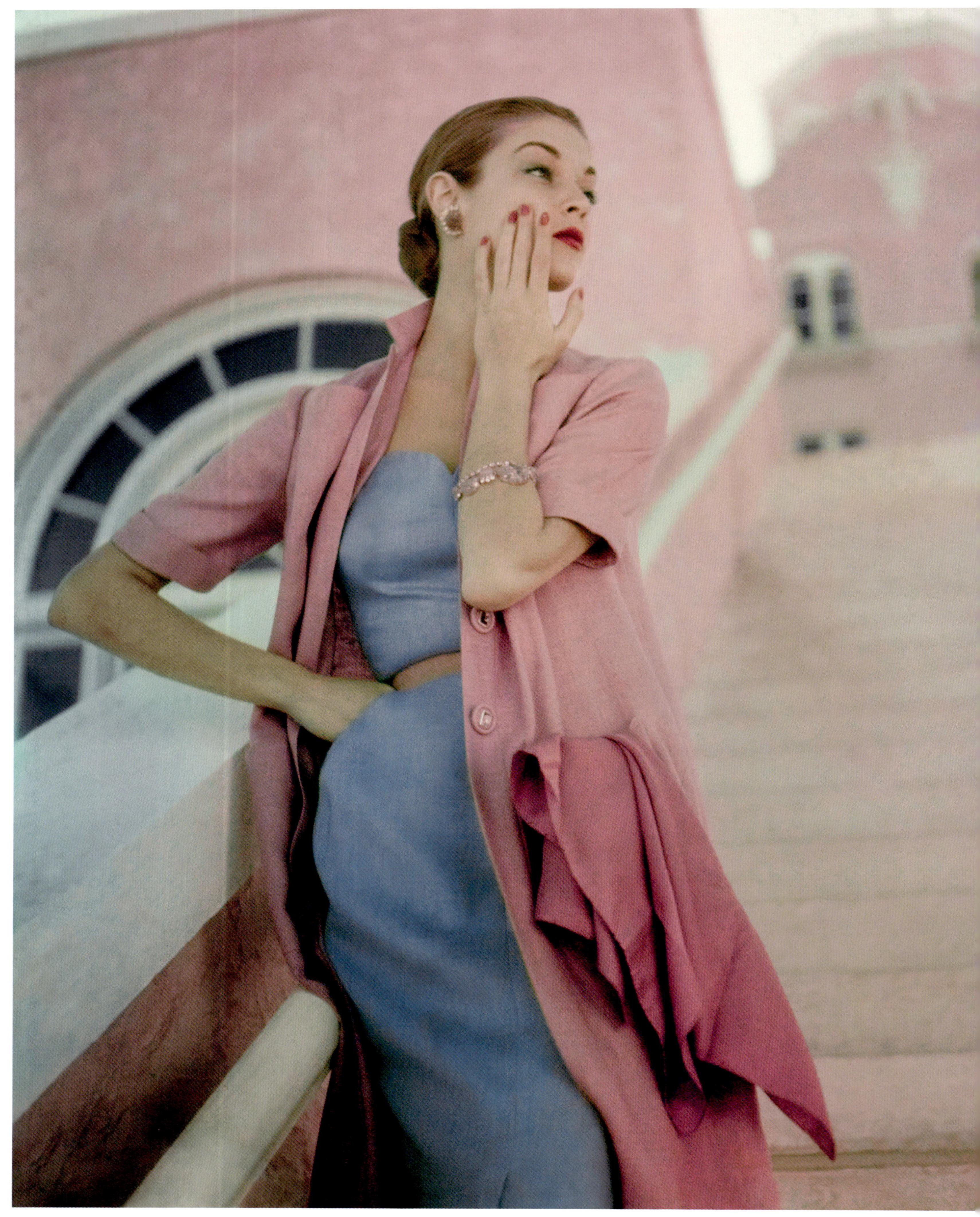

WORKING WOMAN

"In all her pictures there was a presence that was unique. Her class is in her face in the same way as Grace Kelly."

Photographer Melvin Sokolsky was starting his career at *Vogue* as Patchett's reign was ending. While he never framed Jean in a shot, he understood what she brought to the job.

"She was a thoroughbred. It's a talent when you learn how to harness it and you learn how to project it and you can do it in the moment. Then you're worth money."

How much money? Patchett earned between fifty and sixty thousand dollars a year for much of her career (an annual take of around half a million in 2019 dollars). Sixty dollars an hour towards the end of her career, when Jean was still the highest paid model in the business. Thirty-five dollars an hour in 1951, the year Jean and Louis got married and the sole year for which Jean preserved her daily work diary and appointment book

It's a fascinating document: heavily detailed, sometimes revealing and sometimes obscure. Social notes are few—there's the occasional "Stork Club" or "dinner with Eileen and Jerry," two trips to Preston to see her family and a big "My Wedding Day!" on March 30. A pair of shopping lists show Jean and Louis dining on standard American fare—hamburgers and steaks—but with more fresh vegetables than the average American might have thought necessary for survival in 1951. But for the most part it's all work and little play, with some shoots identified by photographer, others by the magazine or commercial client paying the bills. In page after page, Jean is booked four to five times a day, five days a week, nearly always within a few square miles of Midtown Manhattan, a necessity to make the quick turnarounds required to make it to the next job on time.

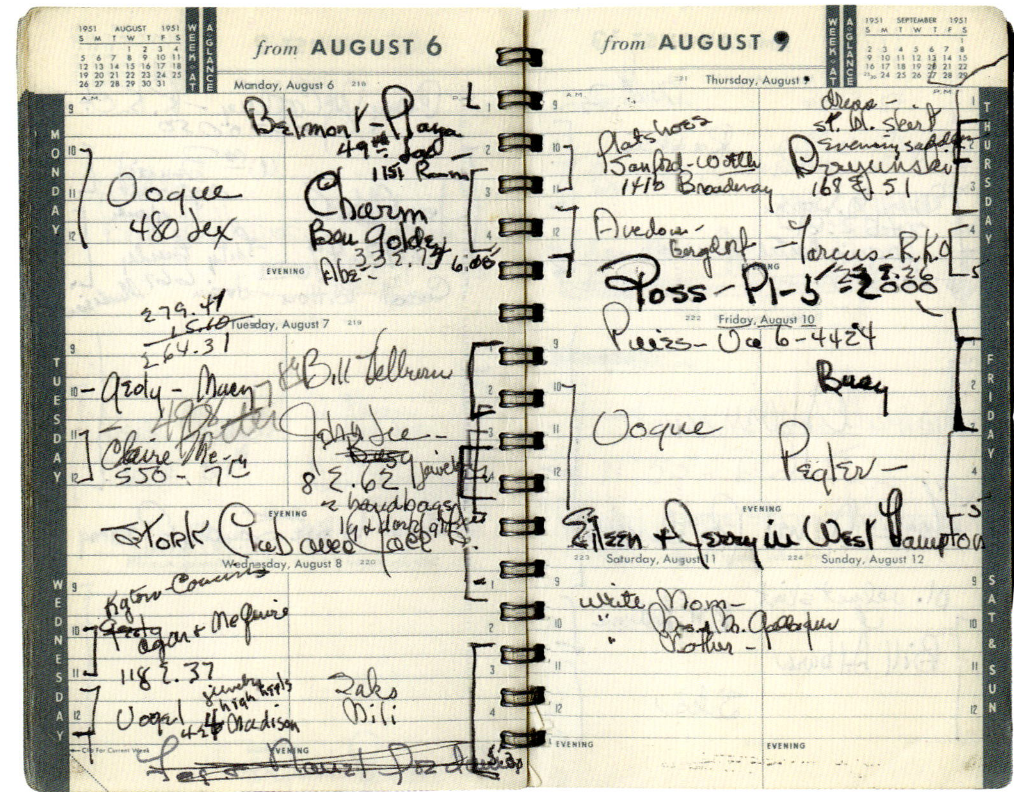

Left:
Frosted Summer Colors
Vogue
May 1, 1951
Photograph by
Clifford Coffin

Right:
Jean Patchett
Appointment Book
August 6–12, 1951

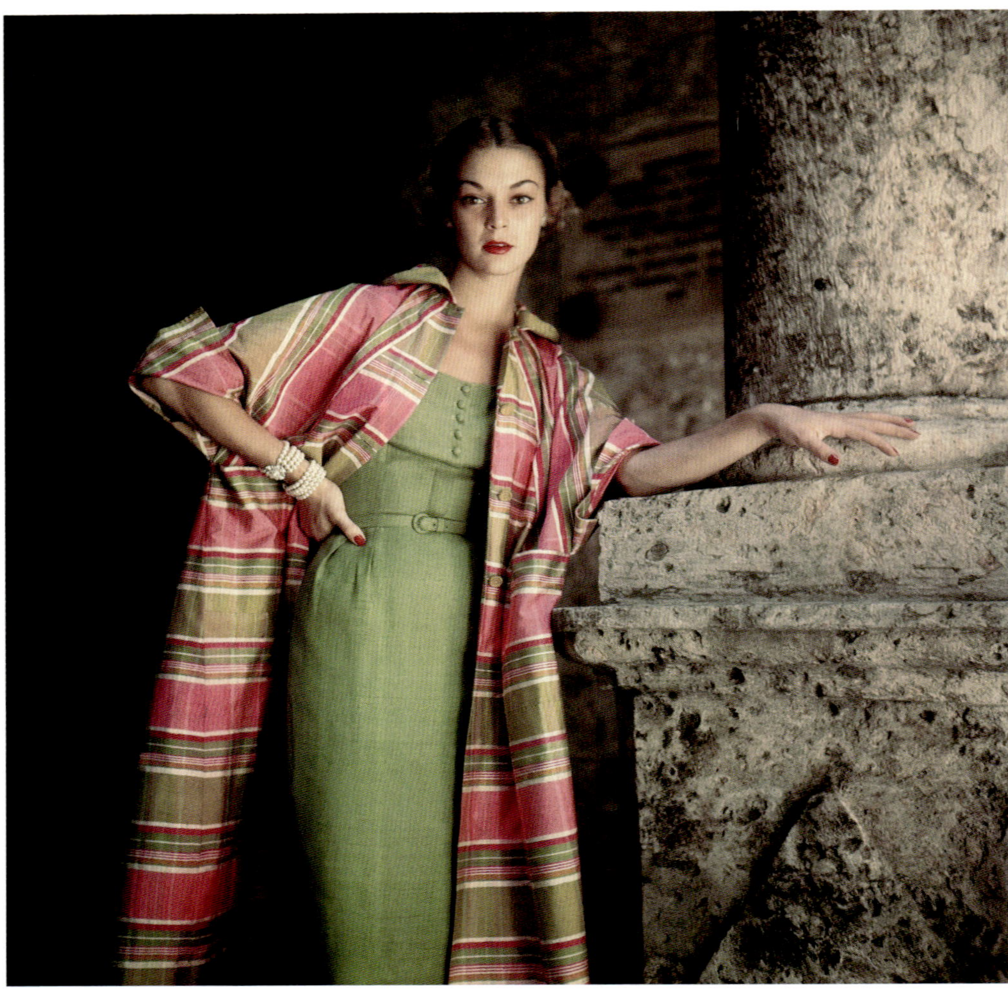

"A normal shoot was an hour and a half to two hours," said Bill Helburn. "A popular model—a Jean Patchett or Dorian Leigh—they were booked very close. They wouldn't start till 10:00 and then maybe, if you got friendly, you'd get them in there earlier." Or later, as Jean would sometimes stretch her workday into the evening hours, even if that meant working 12-hour days, as she sometimes did for days at a time.

Helburn had Patchett in his studio at least 29 times that year, more than any other photographer whose name she recorded. Some of those Helburn shoots were editorial assignments for *Charm* but many more were for ads, jobs which helped fill Jean's calendar but were not her favorite. "Modeling for fashion ads sounds fun but isn't," she told the *Detroit News,* that October. "I don't have to tell you that not every fashion advertiser makes clothes like Hattie Carnegie or Mainbocher, and no girl likes to pose in clothes which she knows are perfectly awful. Worst of all are fittings where you stand and stand for hours while people stick pins all 'round you and occasionally, in you."

Surprisingly, Irving Penn's name appears only twice in the diary; though as Jean appeared in seven of his *Vogue* layouts that year, it's likely some hours tagged "*Vogue*" might as easily have been marked "Penn." Similarly, Clifford Coffin's name appears just once, although they produced eight layouts for the magazine.

Of course, Jean may simply have preferred not to write his name down at all, as Coffin was famous for his brutal behavior with models. "He was very tough to work with—beastly to the girls," an unnamed fashion editor told Robin Muir. "Very unpleasant. He reduced models to floods of tears." It's hard to imagine Patchett putting up with that, and while Coffin took many striking pictures of Jean, including one of her best-known *Vogue* covers, wearing a striped cowl, she hinted at her displeasure in a letter home. "I do believe this is going to be a very pleasant trip," she wrote in 1952, on assignment for *Charm* in Mexico with Bill Helburn, "for we haven't anyone here who is temperamental—no one like Coffin . . . so it should be rather enjoyable."

1951 also saw Jean working regularly with two old friends, Francesco Scavullo and John Rawlings. Much of that work, again, appears to have been for advertisers, in particular Enka Rayon, a manufacturer which enjoyed booming sales before enduring a series of takeovers, finally closing its last U.S. plant in 2009. Throughout the 1950s, Enka was one of many fashion firms whose advertising teams hired the same models and photographers as the magazines, producing striking ads as worthy of admiration (and preservation)

Above left:
Dresses in Havana
Vogue
November 15, 1950
Plaid silk coat by
Tina Leser
Photograph by
Clifford Coffin

Opposite:
Vogue
Cover image
July 1951
Photograph by
Clifford Coffin

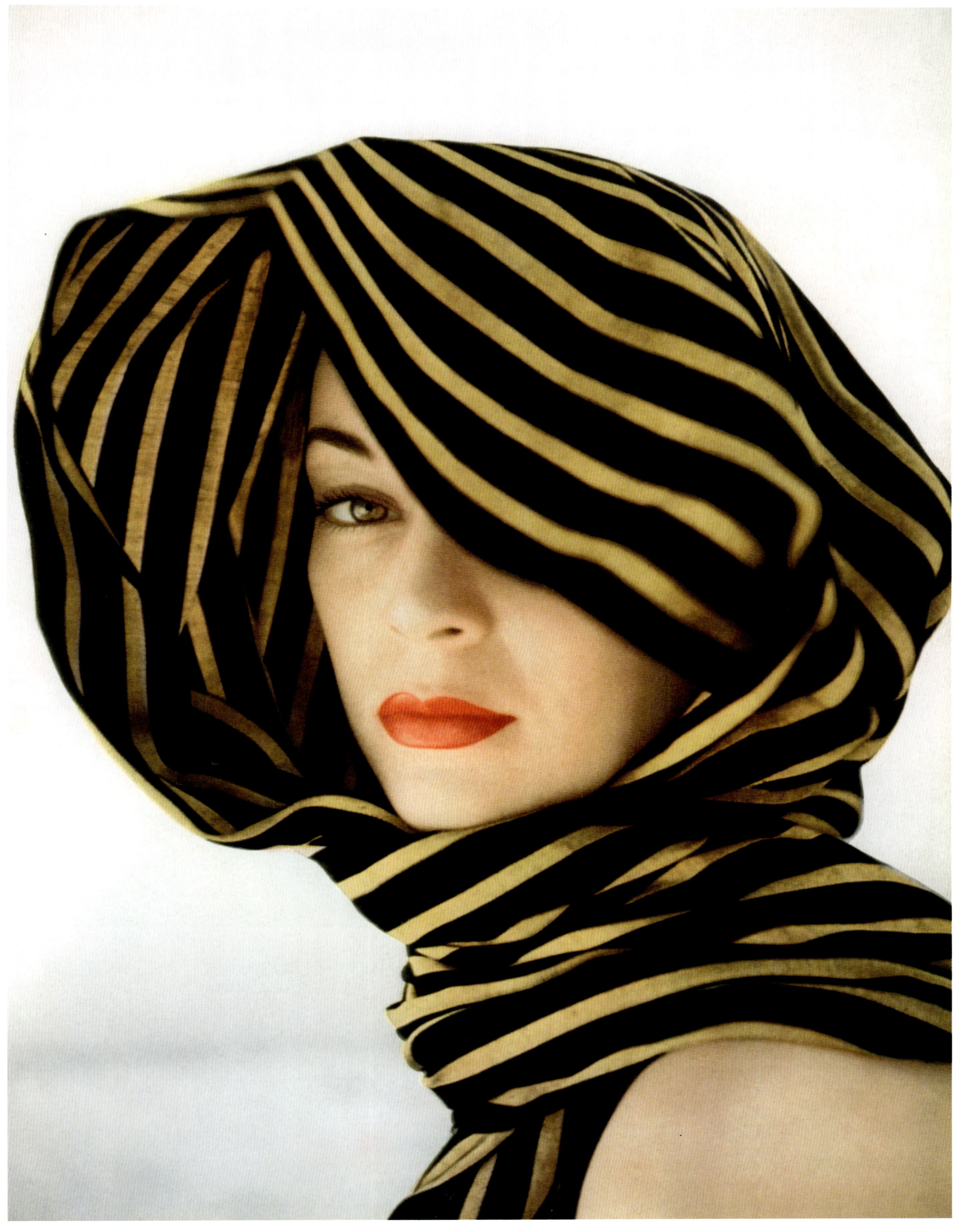

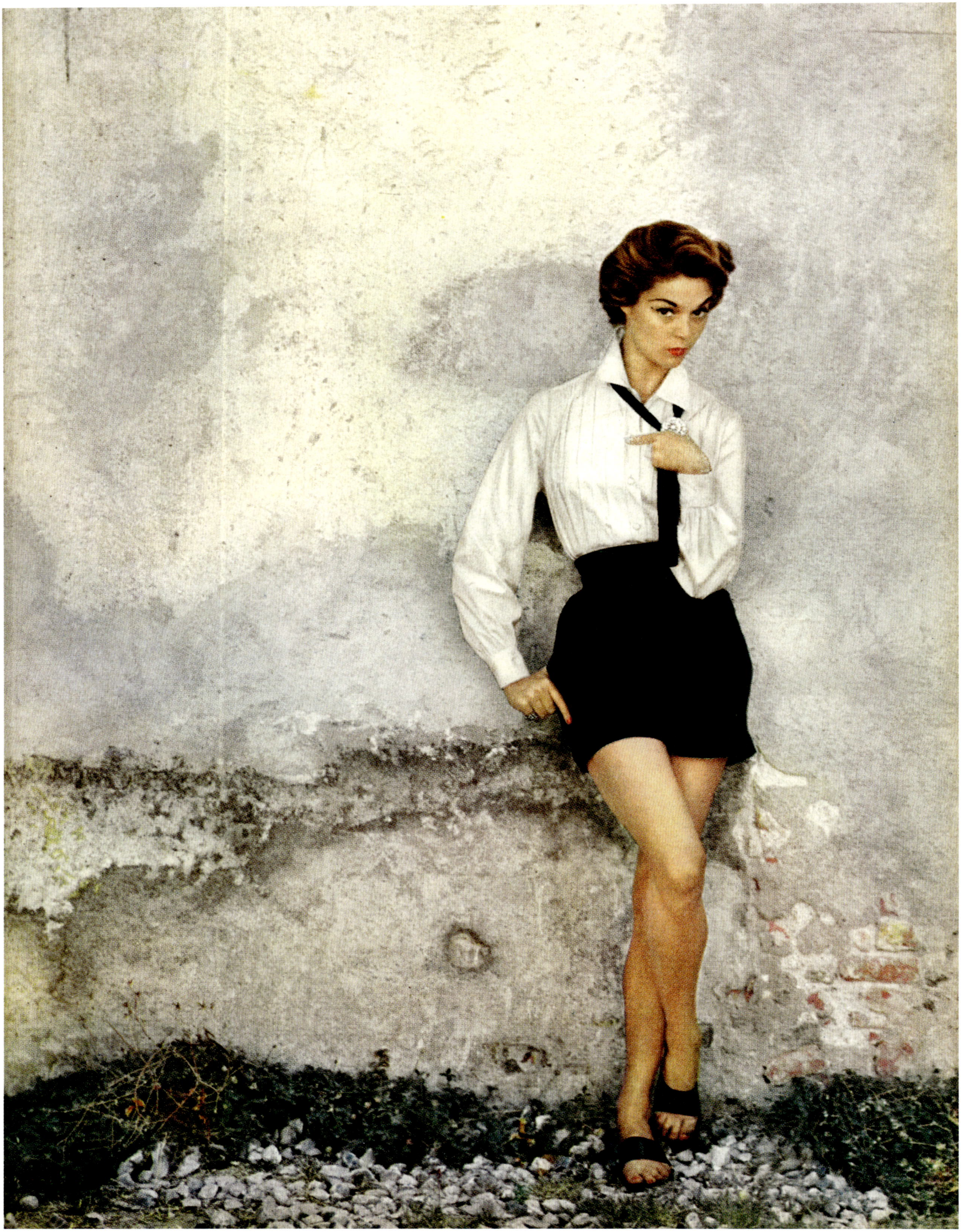

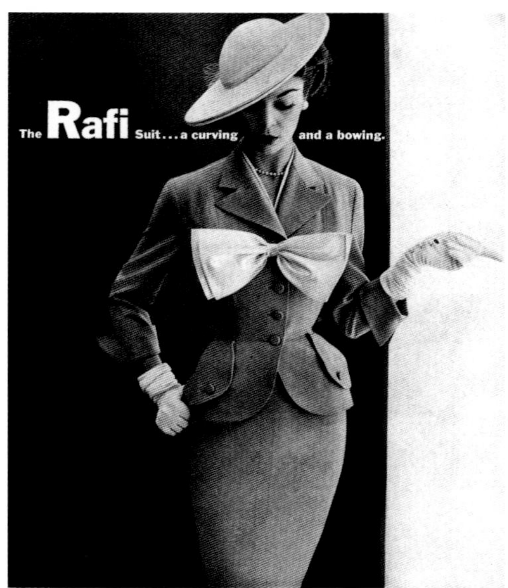

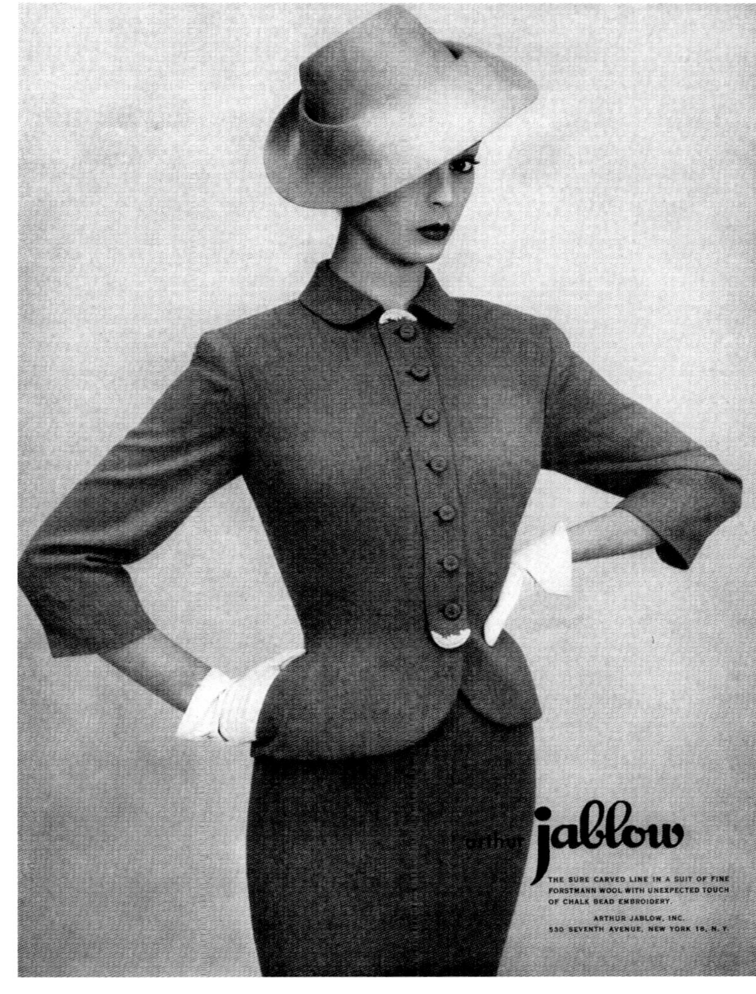

as many of the era's best-known editorial images. Other memorable ads featuring Jean were crafted for designers Mollie Parnis and Christian Dior, Supima cotton, coat and suit makers Rafi and Arthur Jablow, swimsuit manufacturer Cole of California, and cosmetics and perfume makers Helena Rubinstein, Max Factor, and Revlon.

For top photographers, "That's where they made their money," said Etheleen Staley, once a stylist with industry giant Grey Advertising, later co-owner of the Staley-Wise Gallery. "A lot of the editorials paid poorly but the photographers were happy to do it because it moved them on to advertising jobs."

Ads helped provide a very good living for all concerned. Irving Penn's commercial accounts included Jell-O Pudding and Pie Filling, Plymouth cars, cosmetics firm Clinique, and Helena Rubenstein's Noa Noa perfume. Ads also helped bring Patchett together with the man generally credited as the most influential photographer in the fashion world, Richard Avedon.

Patchett and Avedon would produce ads for clients like New York luxury department stores Bergdorf Goodman and B. Altman & Co., and, in a series of brilliant two-page layouts, Revlon cosmetics. They worked together steadily between 1950 and 1960, including at least 20 times in 1951, according to the diary. Still, Patchett was quoted several times as saying she never felt entirely comfortable working with Avedon, especially when compared to Irving Penn.

"I looked entirely different when I was photographed by him," she told Charles Castle, and certainly Avedon had unique ways of posing Jean, especially when it came to arranging her makeup and hair. She also found Avedon less collaborative—"we had to do what he wanted"—and claimed working with him left her feeling "inadequate." Whatever Jean's feelings, her professionalism

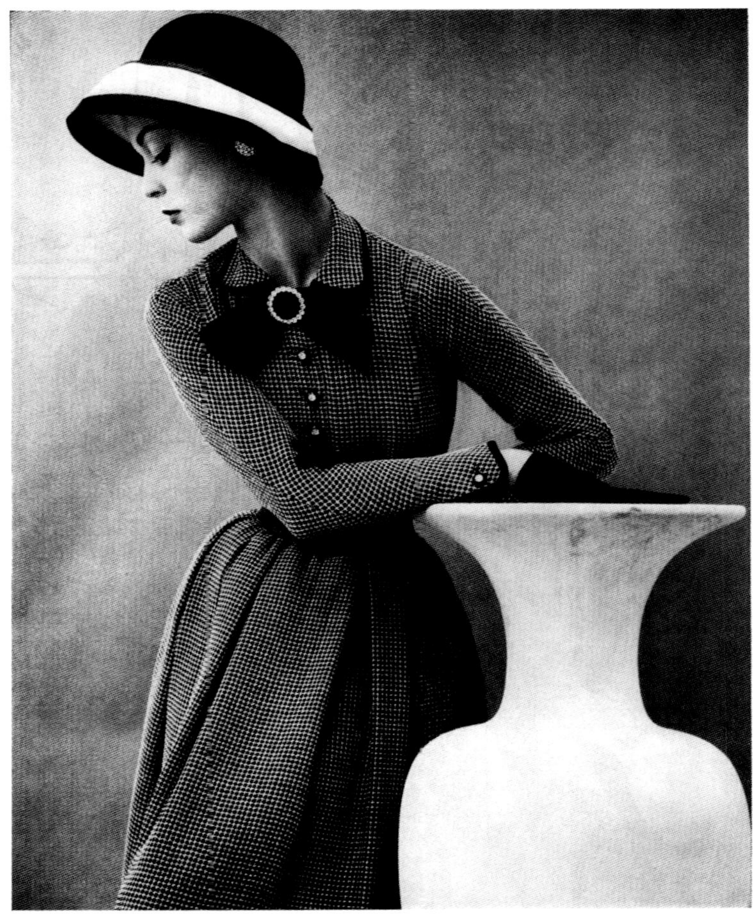

This page, clockwise from top left:
Ad for Rafi
1952

Ad for Jablow
1953

Ad for Mollie Parnis
1952

Opposite:
Vacation in Mexico — Formal Playcloths
Charm
June 1952
Photograph by William Helburn

Following Spread:
Ad for "Cherries a la Mode" by Revlon
Vogue
November 1, 1955
Gown by Galanos
Photograph by Richard Avedon

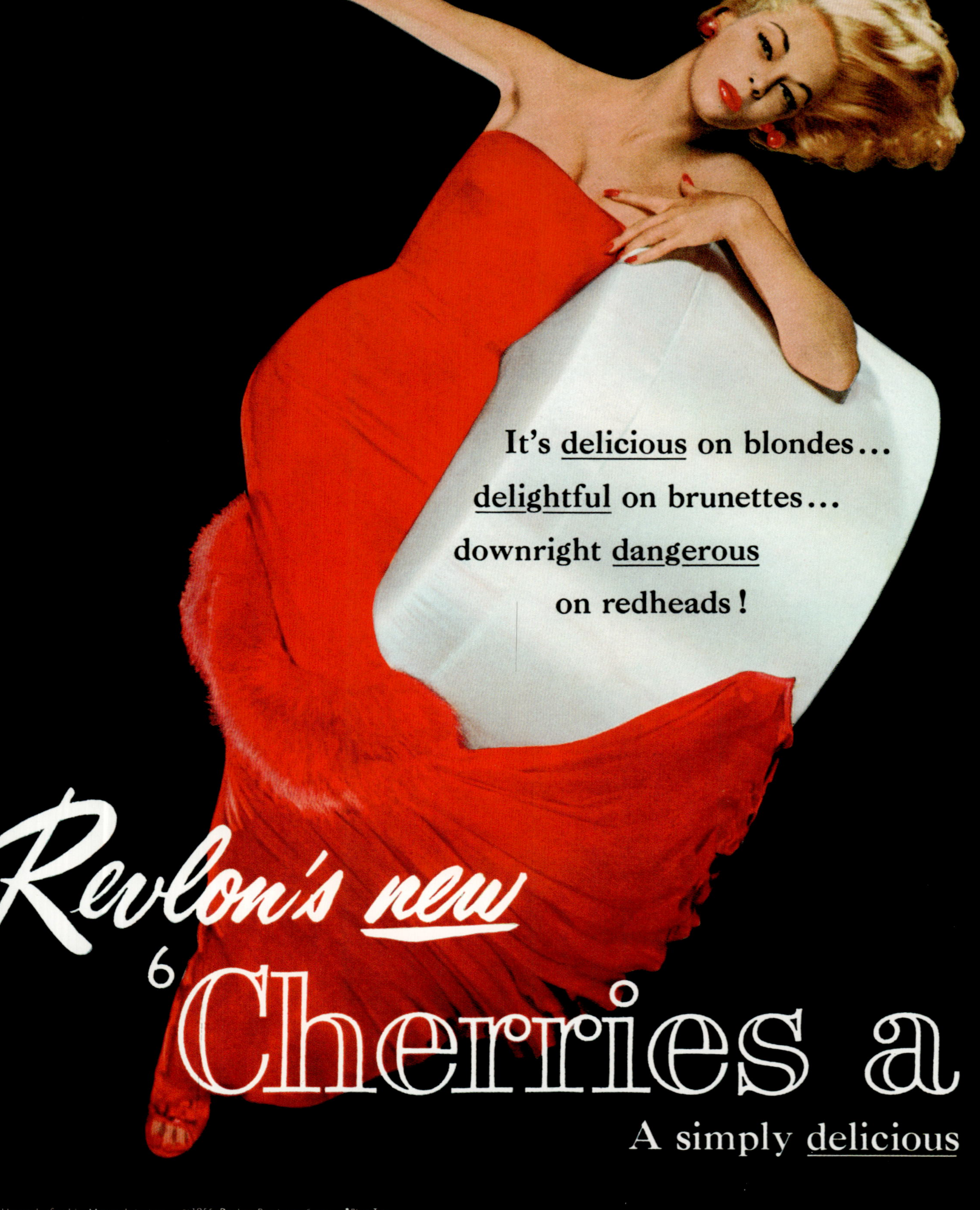
It's delicious on blondes...
delightful on brunettes...
downright dangerous
on redheads!
Revlon's new
'Cherries a
A simply delicious
Gown Galanos. Satin Hassock Sophie Mavro Interiors. ©1955 Revlon Products Corp *Plus Tax

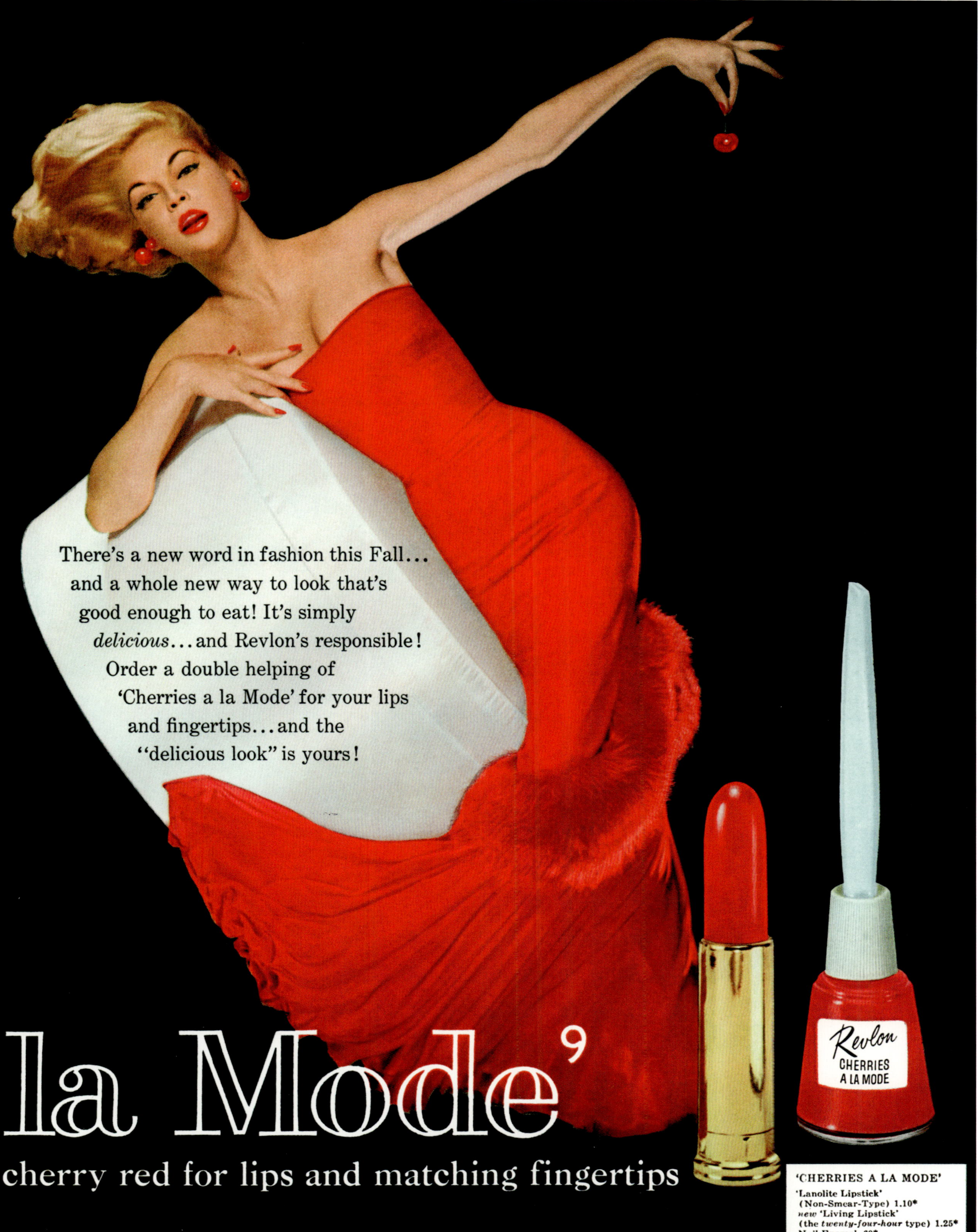
There's a new word in fashion this Fall... and a whole new way to look that's good enough to eat! It's simply *delicious*...and Revlon's responsible! Order a double helping of 'Cherries a la Mode' for your lips and fingertips...and the "delicious look" is yours!
Revlon
CHERRIES A LA MODE
la Mode'
cherry red for lips and matching fingertips
'CHERRIES A LA MODE'
'Lanolite Lipstick' (Non-Smear-Type) 1.10*
new 'Living Lipstick' (the *twenty-four-hour* type) 1.25*
Nail Enamel .60*

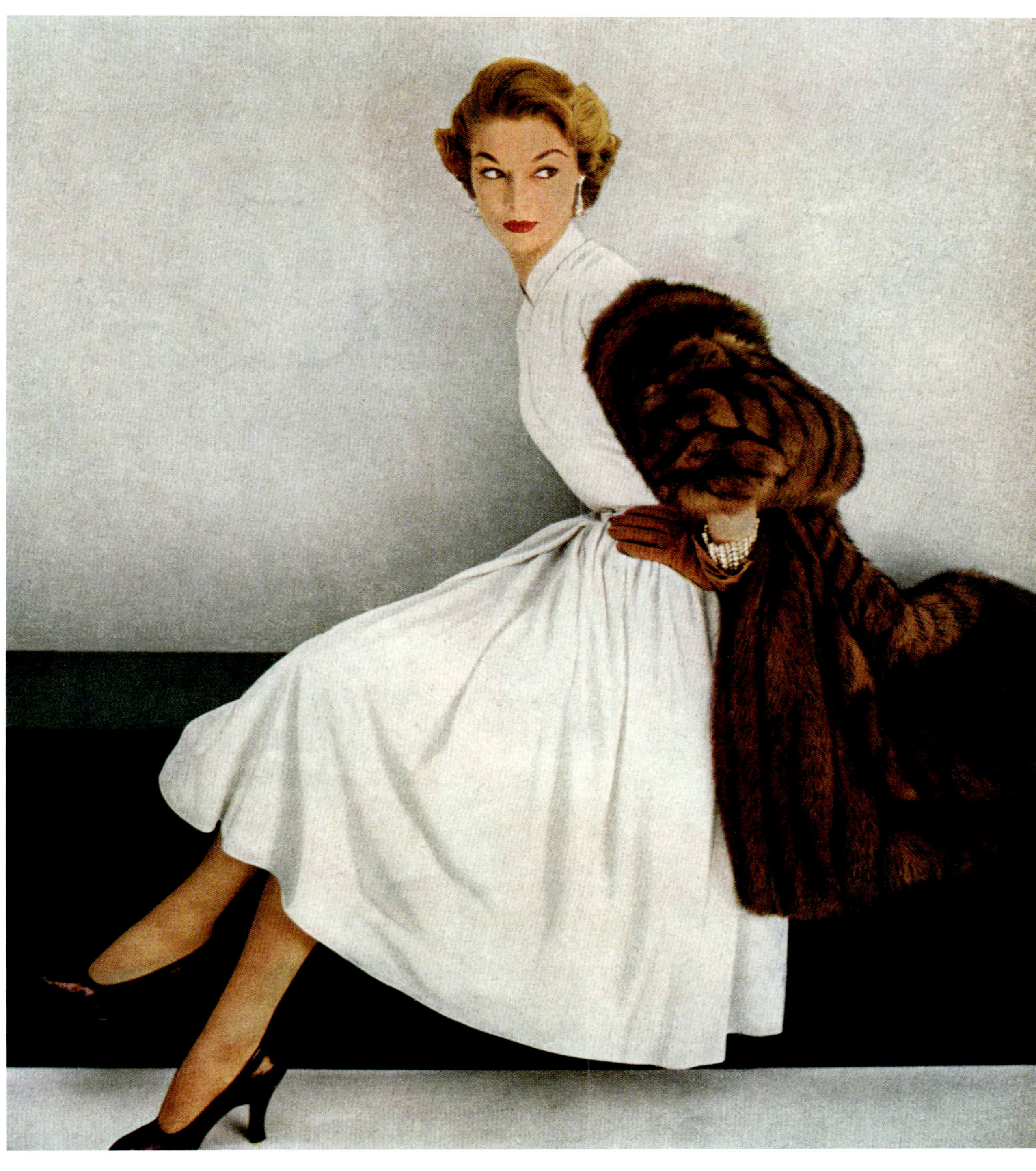

Opposite:
Black Crepe — the Color and the Cloth
Harper's Bazaar
August 1952
Photograph by
Lillian Bassman

Right:
Follow the Gleam
Harper's Bazaar
September 1952
Photograph by
Lillian Bassman

kept her from letting them show in any of the work they did together, including the editorial pictures they did for *Harper's Bazaar* towards the end of her career.

Those images, and others where Jean posed for *Bazaar* between 1952 and 1956, also contradict her assertion, to Michael Gross in *Model*, that she "belonged to *Vogue*" and "couldn't work for *Bazaar* and *Vogue* at the same time when I was working." Perhaps Jean was reflecting on the first years of her career, when she might have been discouraged from working for the blood rival of the magazine that helped launch her (though one of her very first editorial pictures was shot by Kay Bell Reynal and published in *Bazaar* in August 1948.) Or Jean might have felt a special loyalty to *Vogue*.

That being said, there were no rules against working for both. "It was unusual for photographers to cross over," according to Etheleen Staley, "but not for models. They worked for everybody—models were for hire." And working for *Bazaar* for Jean meant working with photographers Lillian Bassman and Louise Dahl-Wolfe, as well as Richard Avedon. Bassman's images of Patchett, as with other models with whom she worked, capture a delicate femininity without any trace of hauteur. Dahl-Wolfe enriched Patchett's portfolio with a series of images shot in 1953 at the Alhambra in Granada, Spain, that were among Jean's most distinctive since she flew home from Peru.

Jean's work for *Bazaar* came when the arc of her career was at its height. Seen through the frame of her years with the two industry leaders, starting midway through 1948

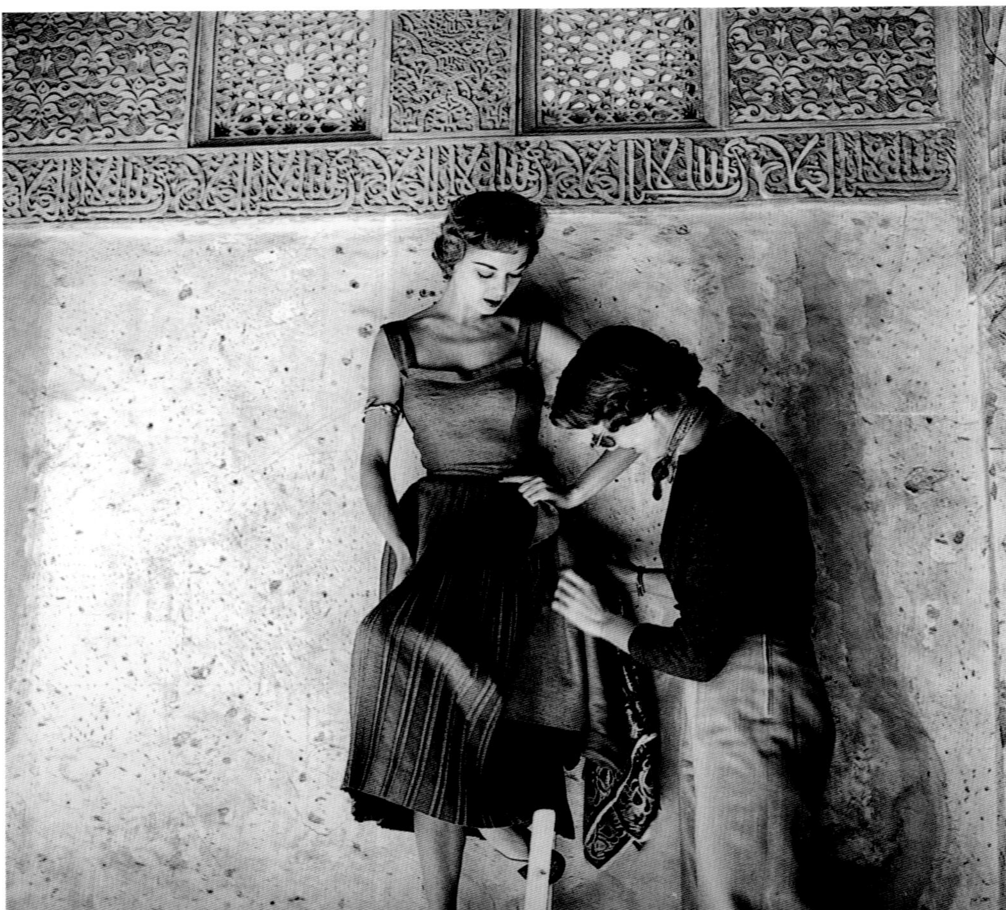

Patchett enjoyed extraordinary success with *Vogue,* which published her first cover, 23 editorial images, and eight ads, while sending her on the trip to Lima. By comparison, her appearances in *Bazaar* that year were limited to one editorial and two advertising images. The following year, Jean expanded her conquest of *Vogue*, with two more covers, 38 editorial images and 41 ads. *Bazaar* remained unconquered, with just two Patchett ads.

But by 1952, Patchett's ad and editorial pages in both magazines were roughly equivalent, with *Bazaar* in the lead. A rough parity between the two would continue through 1955, though that year also saw a sharp decline in Jean's total pages. That decline would continue into 1956, with 1957 marking Patchett's first year without an editorial image in either *Bazaar* or *Vogue*.

Photographer Jerry Schatzberg, who first met Patchett as Bill Helburn's assistant before making his own images of her for *Vogue*, recalled what it was like to work with Jean, as her career wound down. "First of all, she was amazing," said Schatzberg. "Because she was a real gal, you know? Little turn of her ankle, little legs. And, you know, I think for me she was a little intimidating. Because I was sort of at the end of her reign."

Commissioned by art director Alex Liberman to come up with new shapes "like the cha cha cha" for photos for a new Paris collection, Schatzberg brought Latin dancers from New York's Palladium dance hall to his studio and photographed them in "cha cha" dance poses he would adapt for his models. Patchett handled the new poses flawlessly and they were featured in *Vogue's* April 1 edition in 1958.

Three years later, Eileen Ford asked Schatzberg for an unusual favor. "She called me and said, 'Would you do some tests with Jean?' I guess her work was going down. I did what I thought was interesting—but I was too intimidated to really try and experiment with it." The images, of Jean in a pink hat and holding a red rose, show a model who turned 35 that year, with her trademark mole somewhat larger than it had been in her prime.

"I knew her as a goddess," said Schatzberg, "and I did the best I could. But you know—once you get past a certain point. . . and I think it's worse now, because the models start younger. They start at 15, 16. And they're finished when they're 21, 22."

Patchett would retire from her career the following year. She would do some catalog work for Saks Fifth Avenue in the 70s and continue to make occasional appearances in fashion magazines, including one of her "all-time favorite" images, shot in 1968 by photographer Marie Cosindas for Helena Rubinstein and showing Jean in graceful repose.

Jean did not miss modeling once she'd stopped, any more than she had taken it for granted as she started. Raising a family had always been her goal and she said she'd found combining the roles of wife, mother, and

Above:
Jean Patchett and Dresser
Granada, 1953
Photograph by
Louise Dahl-Wolfe

Right:
Cloths of 1953 in Granada
Harper's Bazaar
May 1953
Photograph by
Louise Dahl-Wolfe

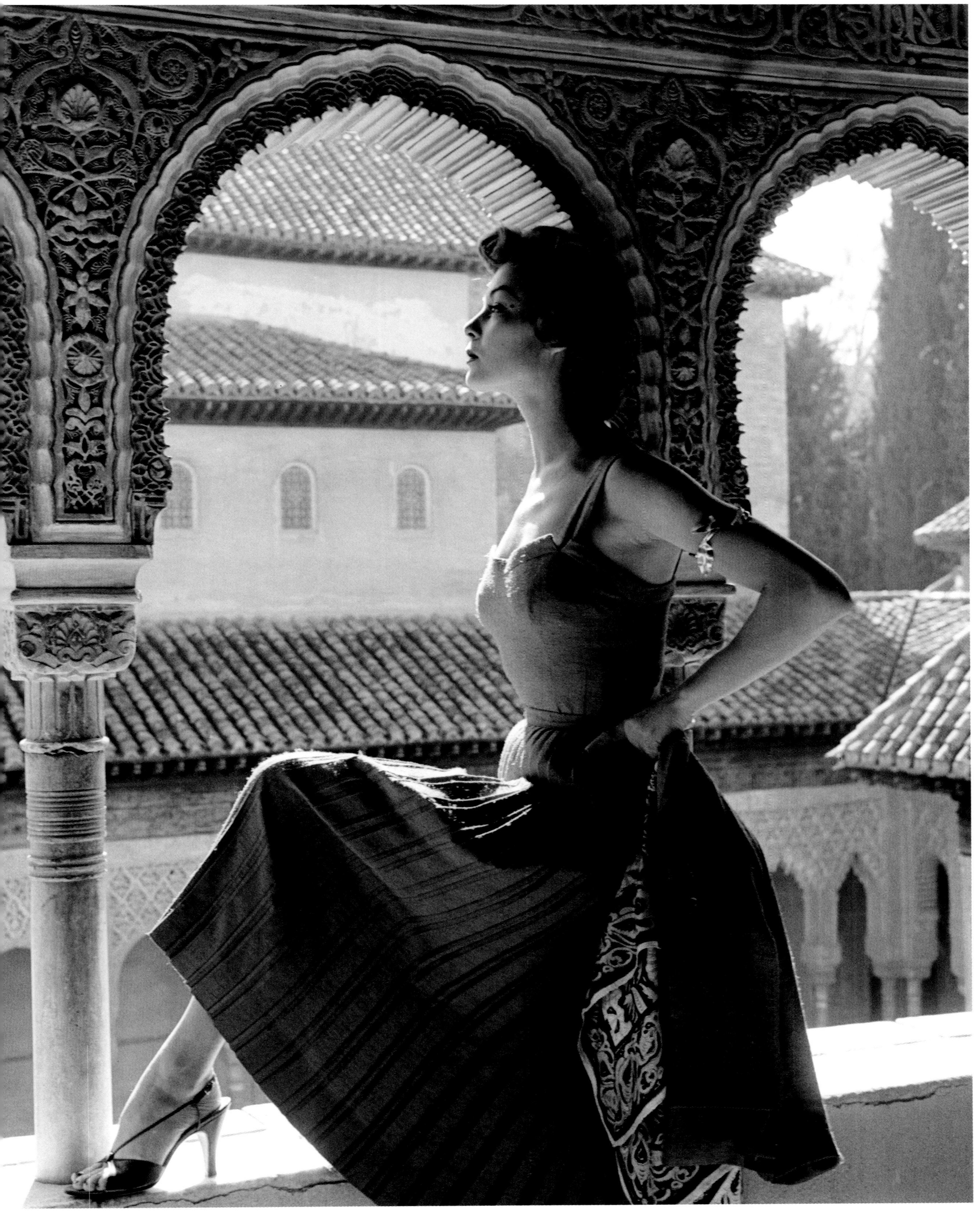

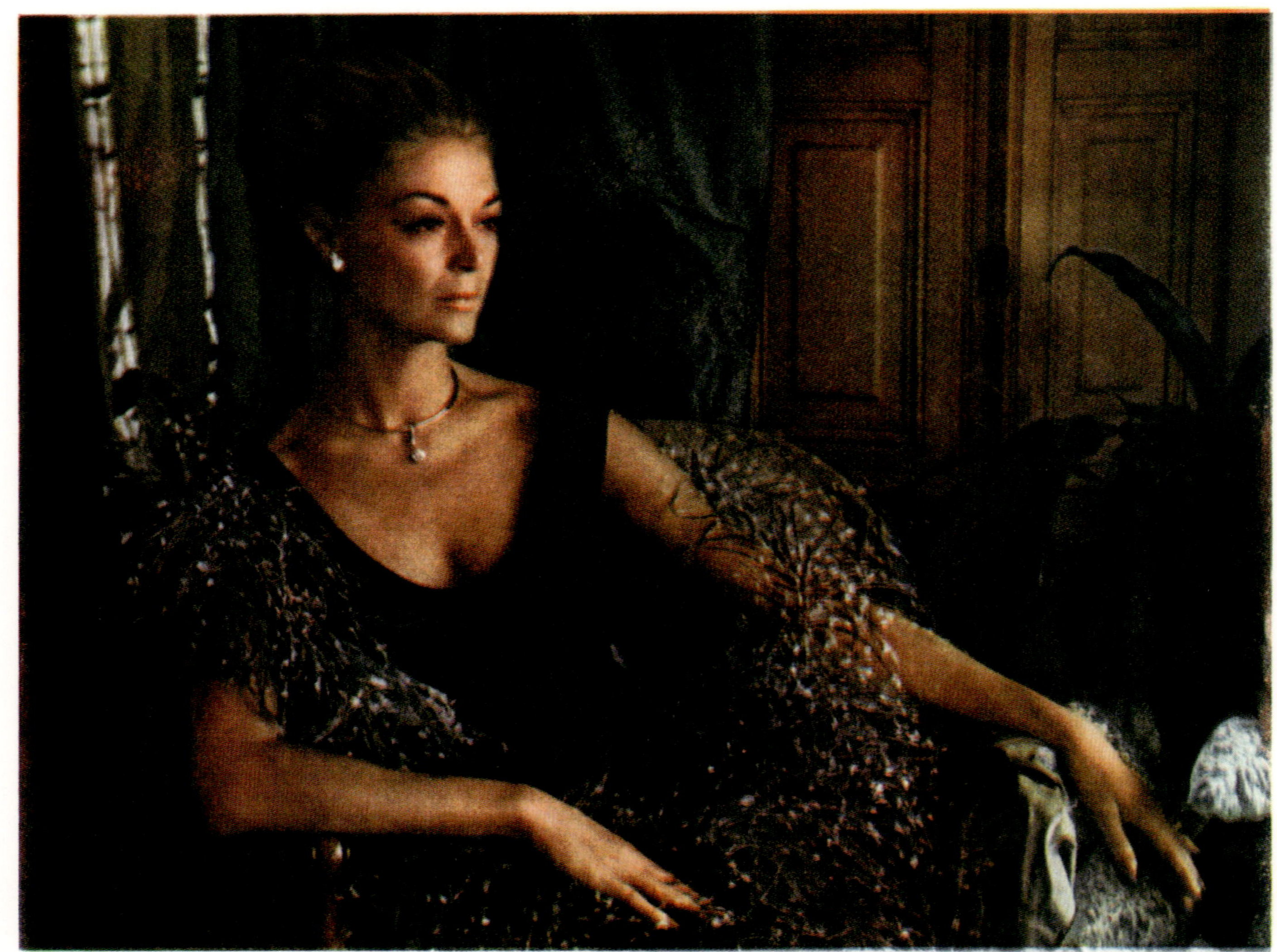

Polaroid portrait by Marie Cosindas commissioned by Helena Rubinstein, Inc., 1968. Dress and jewels by Pauline Trigère. © 1968 Helena Rubinstein, Inc.

A special sort of elegant woman has always used the world's
most luxurious beauty preparations, Herbessence® by Helena Rubinstein.
Many of the formulas using rare herbals and natural extracts were
created to pamper and protect the most beautiful women in the world.

These rich moisturizers, cleansers, special creams and lotions now can be yours.

Just go to any fine store and whisper, "Herbessence."

Herbessence Beauty Preparations

Helena Rubinstein

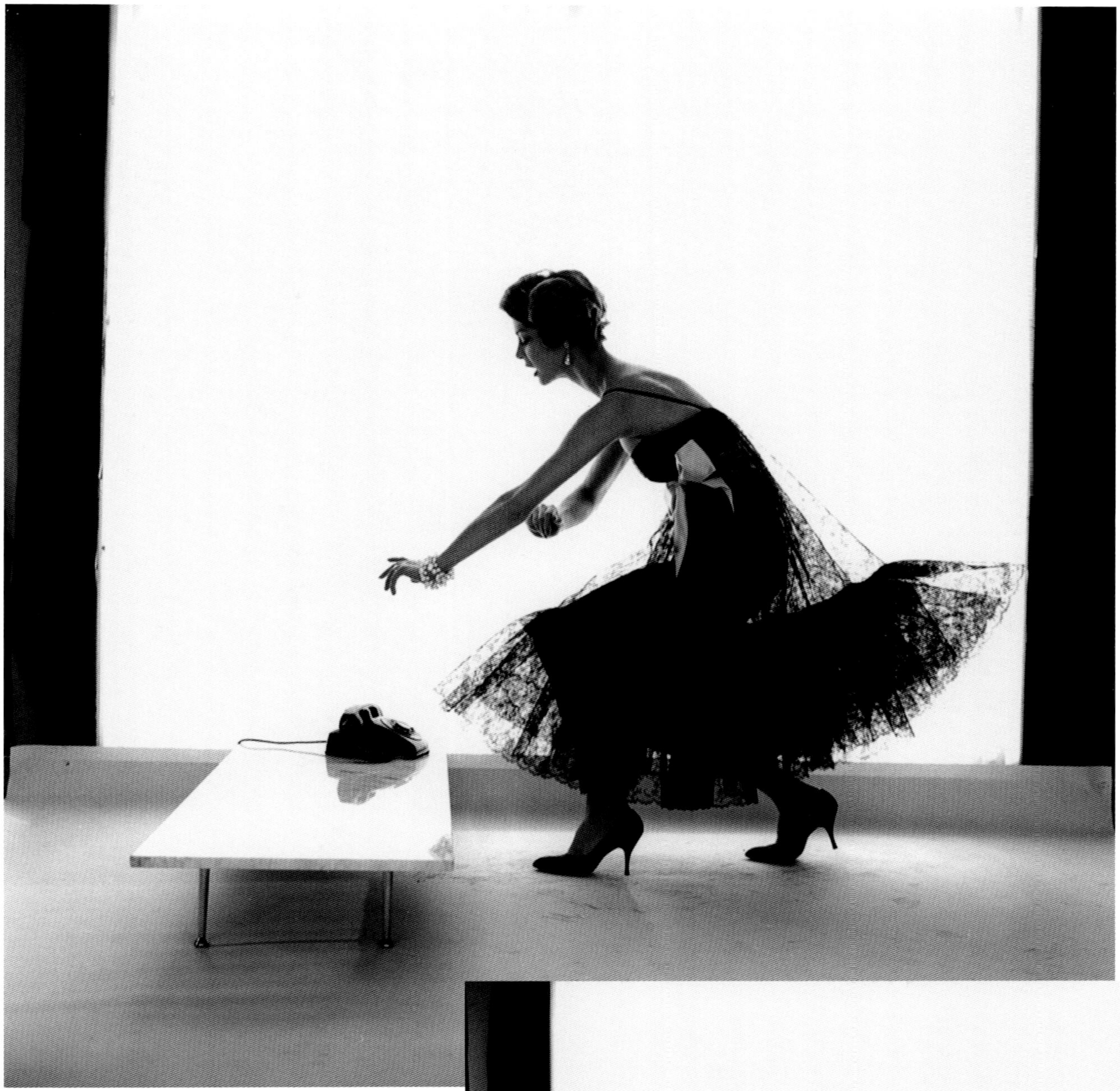

This page:
Cha Cha Cha Series
Vogue
February 17, 1958
Photographs by
Jerry Schatzberg

Opposite:
Ad for "Herbessence"
by Helena Rubenstein
1968
Photograph by
Marie Cosindas

model all but impossible. "There was never a sense of 'Ah, I gave it up. I wish I hadn't,'" said Jean's daughter Amy. When the famous mole continued to grow, Patchett had it removed, "with no loss of identity."

Jean and Louis continued to enjoy an active social life, at their homes in Manhattan and Westhampton Beach, Long Island. They played golf at local country clubs and Jean satisfied her artistic drive with needlepoint and painting. She maintained her weight and looks throughout and kept some of her most iconic pictures on display. A scrapbook assembled by her older sister would be brought out occasionally—but only if Jean was asked.

After Jean Patchett died on January 22, 2002, the *New York Times* asked Irving Penn to comment. He sent back a slip of lined paper. On it he wrote, "A Young American Goddess in Paris Couture." ■

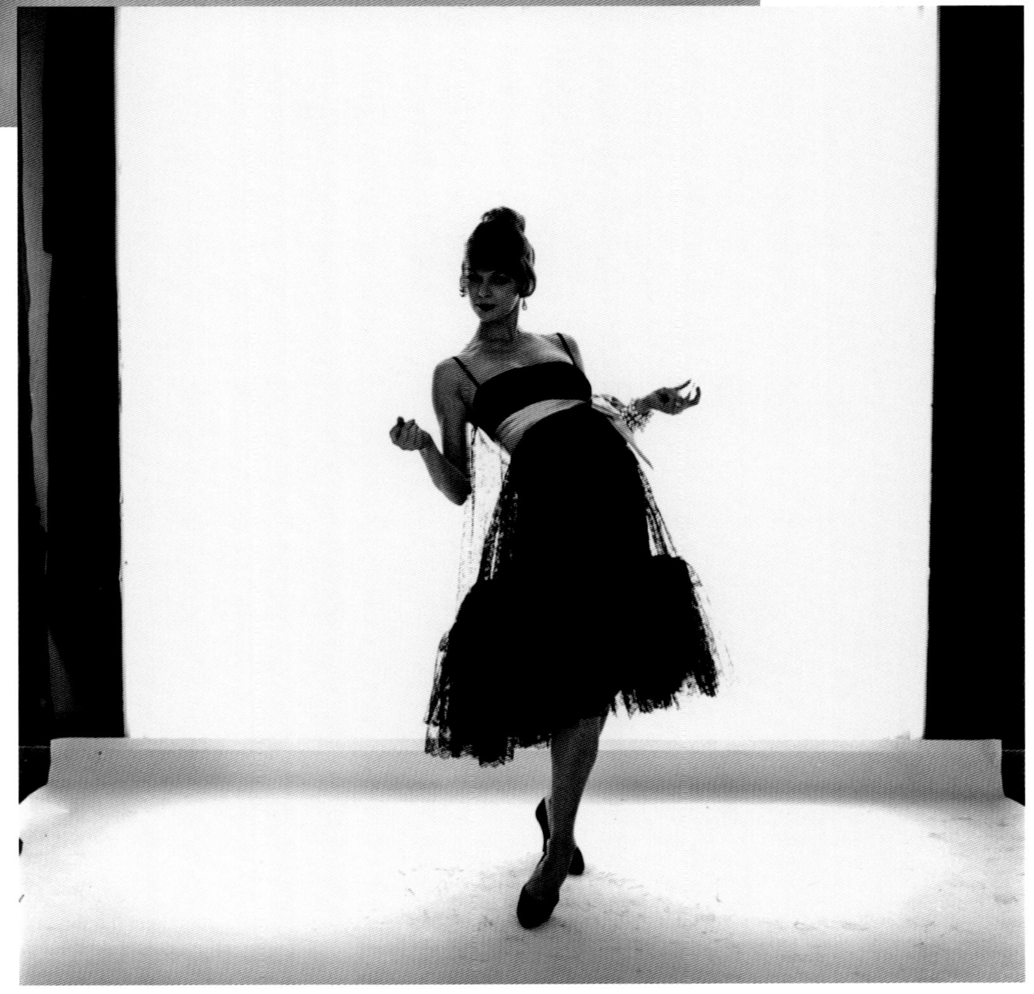

"Flying Down to Lima"
Jean Patchett in
Bullfighter's Hat
Vogue
February 15, 1949
Photograph by Irving Penn

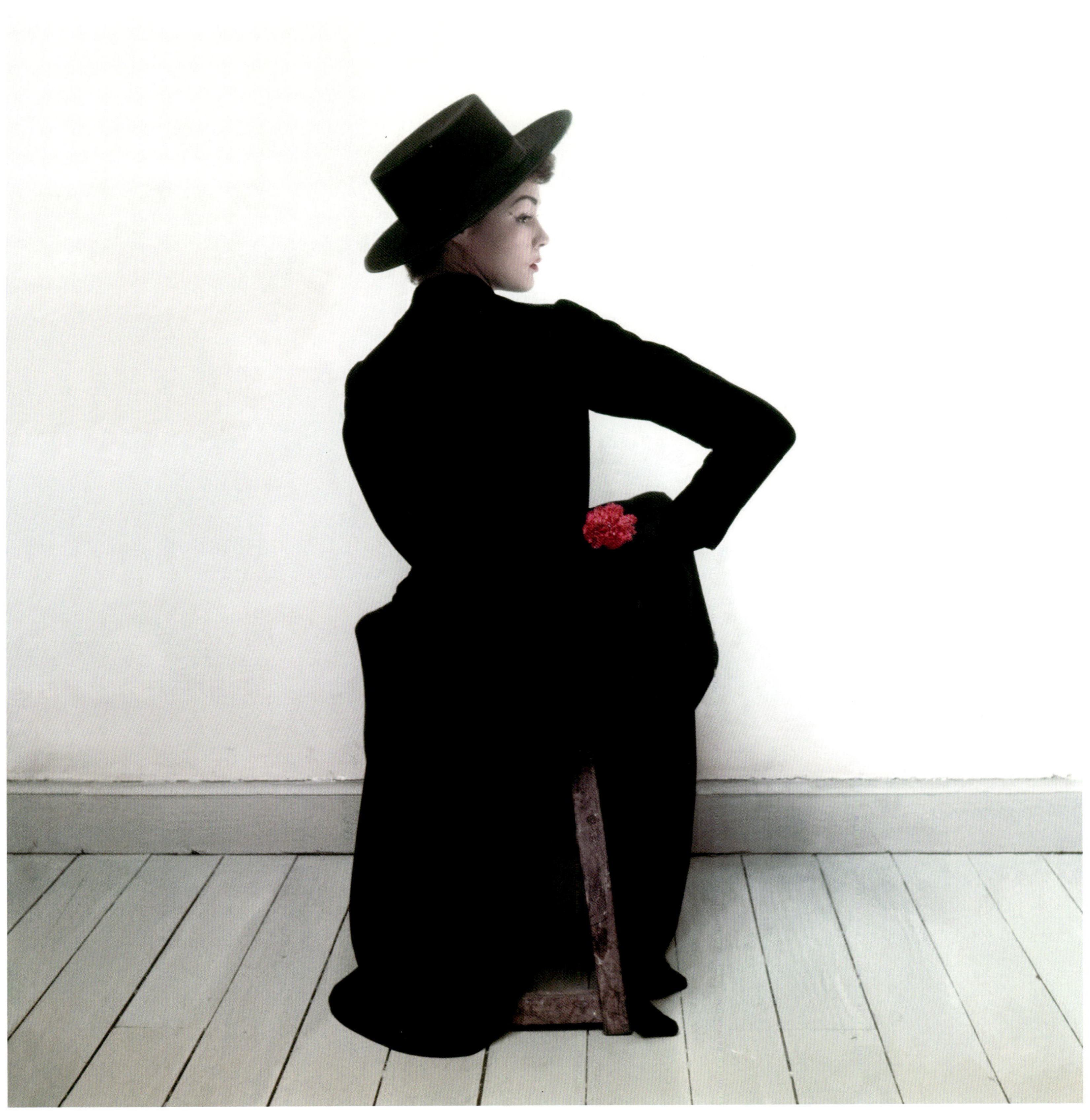

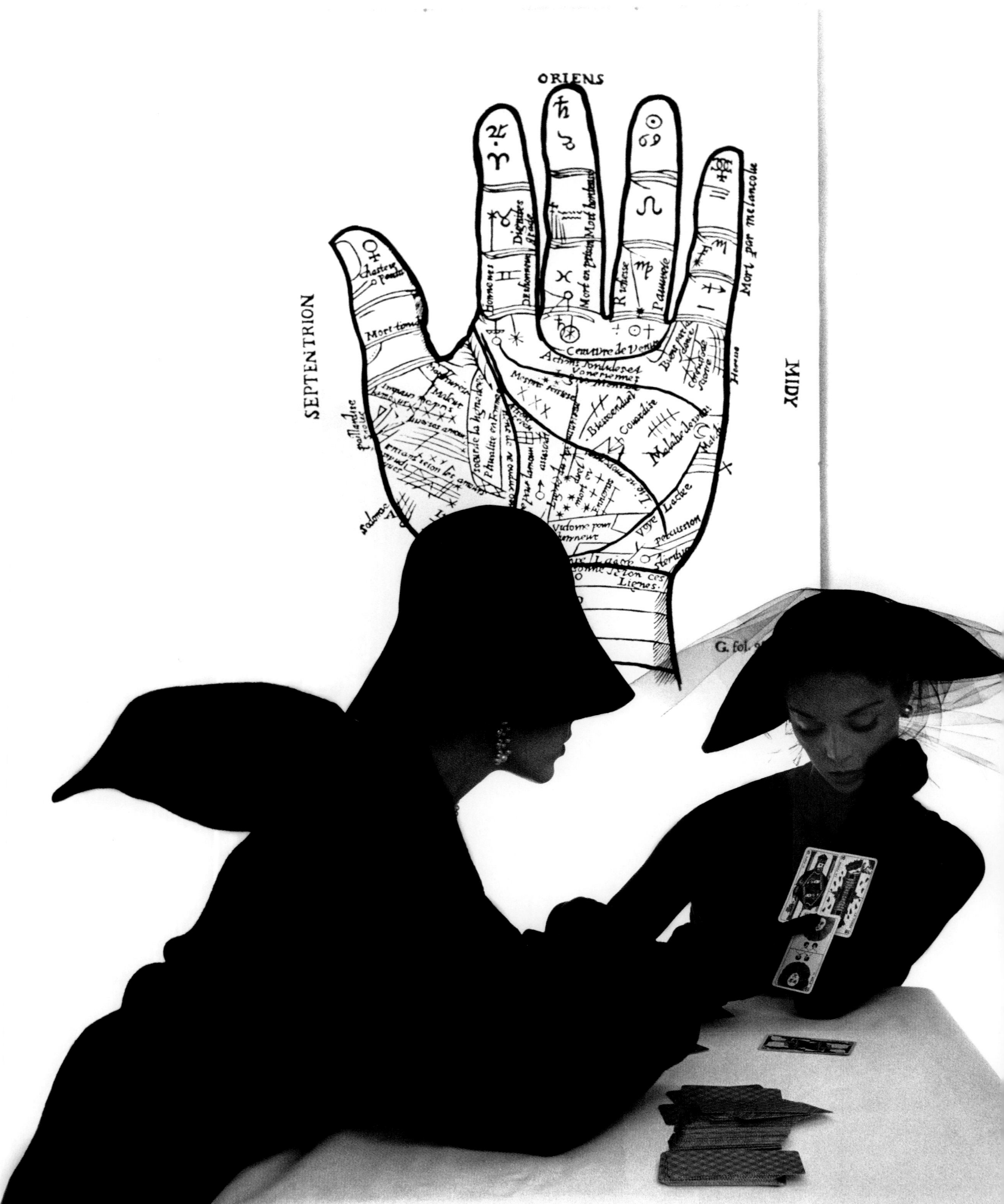
ORIENS
SEPTENTRION
MIDY

The Tarot Reader
Vogue
October 15, 1949
Photograph by Irving Penn

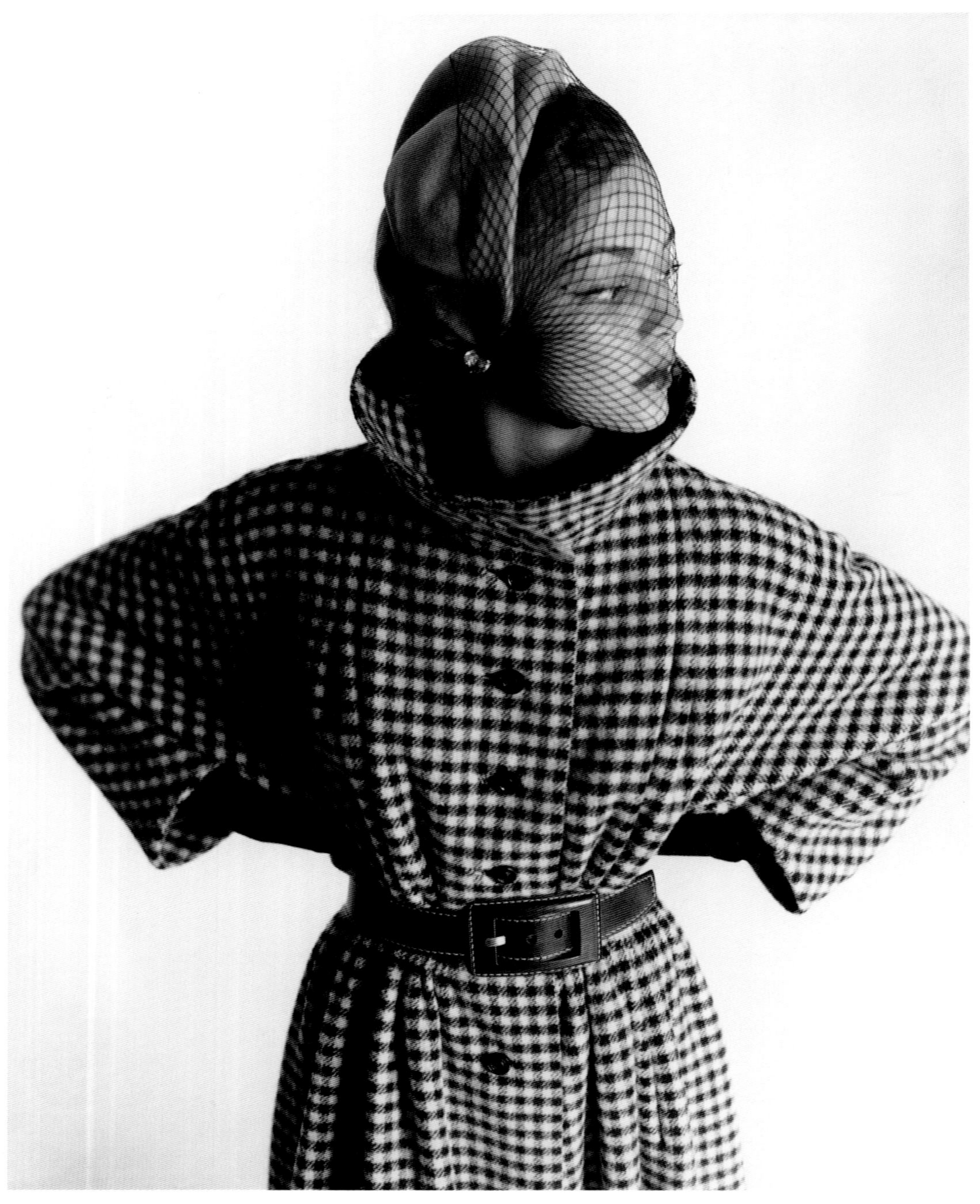

Above:
American Collections —
Fashion Stars Coming In
Vogue
September 1, 1948
Turban by Mr. John,
coat by Monte-Sano
Photograph by Horst P. Horst

Opposite:
Pale satin, cut to a low,
lovely line in the new
tradition of great ball dresses
Vogue
September 15, 1948
Photograph by John Rawlings

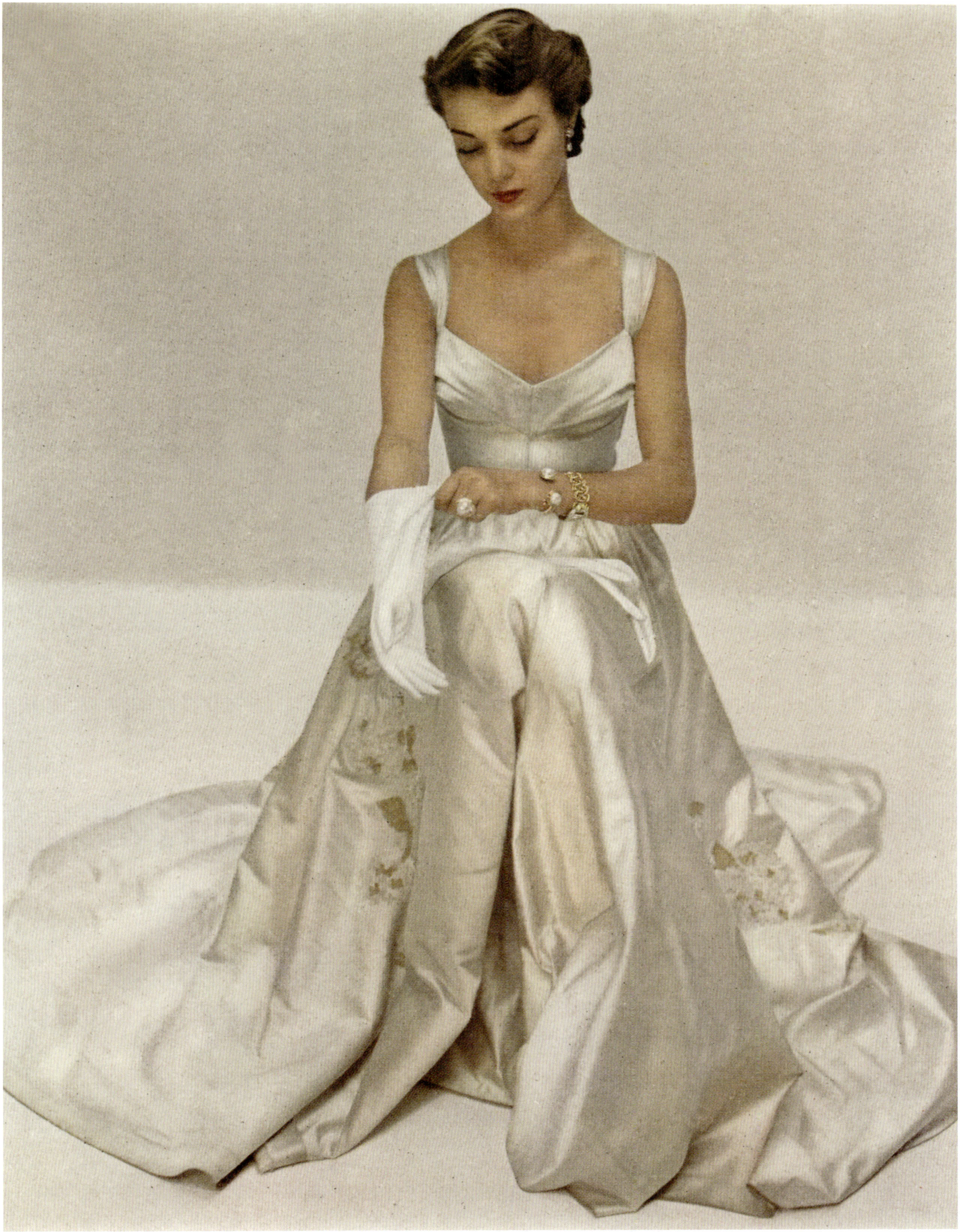

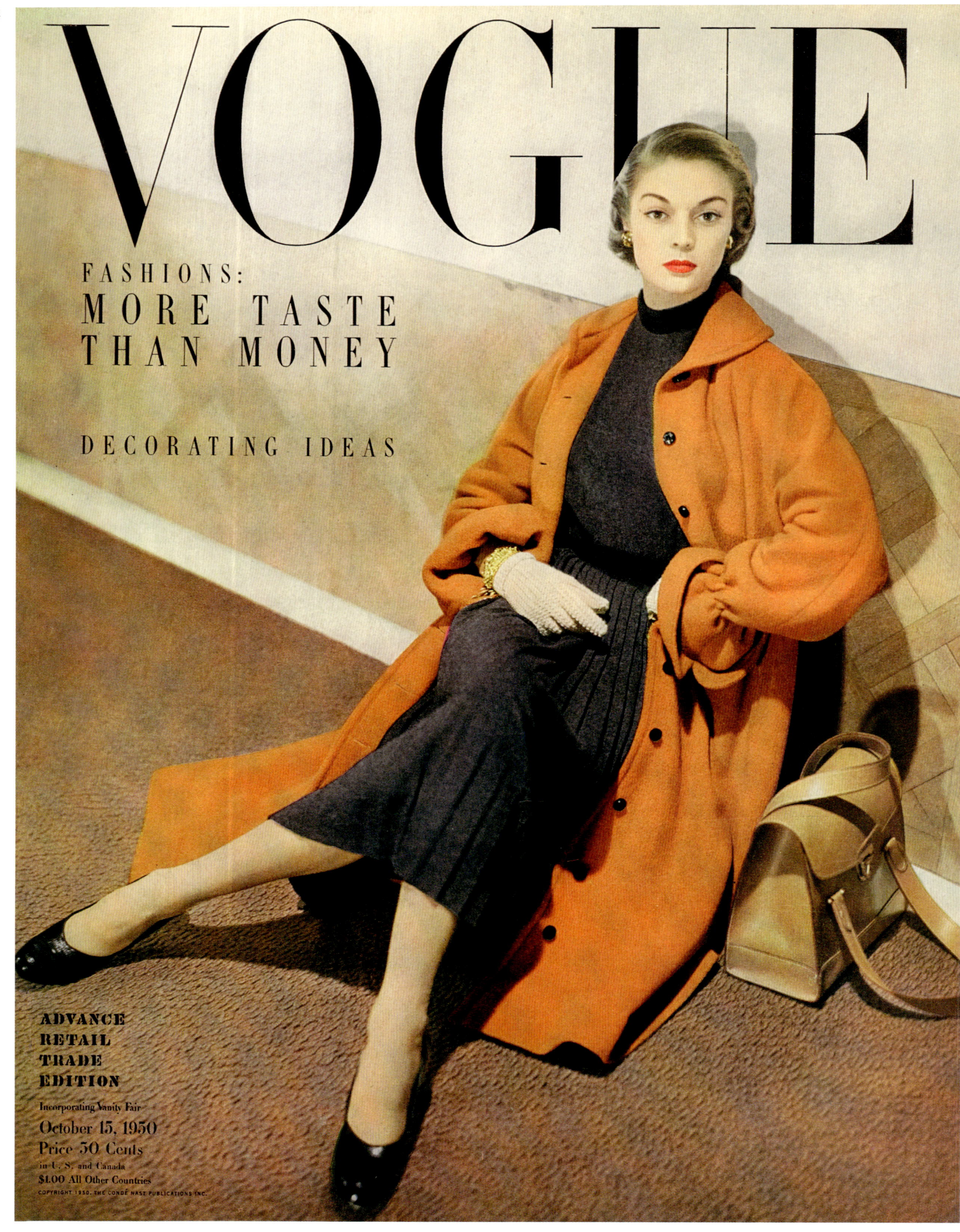
VOGUE
FASHIONS:
MORE TASTE
THAN MONEY
DECORATING IDEAS
ADVANCE
RETAIL
TRADE
EDITION
Incorporating Vanity Fair
October 15, 1950
Price 50 Cents
in U. S. and Canada
$1.00 All Other Countries
COPYRIGHT 1950, THE CONDÉ NAST PUBLICATIONS INC.

Vogue
October 15, 1950
Photograph by Horst P. Horst

New question: How Long is an Evening Dress?
Vogue
November 1, 1949
Dress by Ben Gam
Photograph by Horst P. Horst

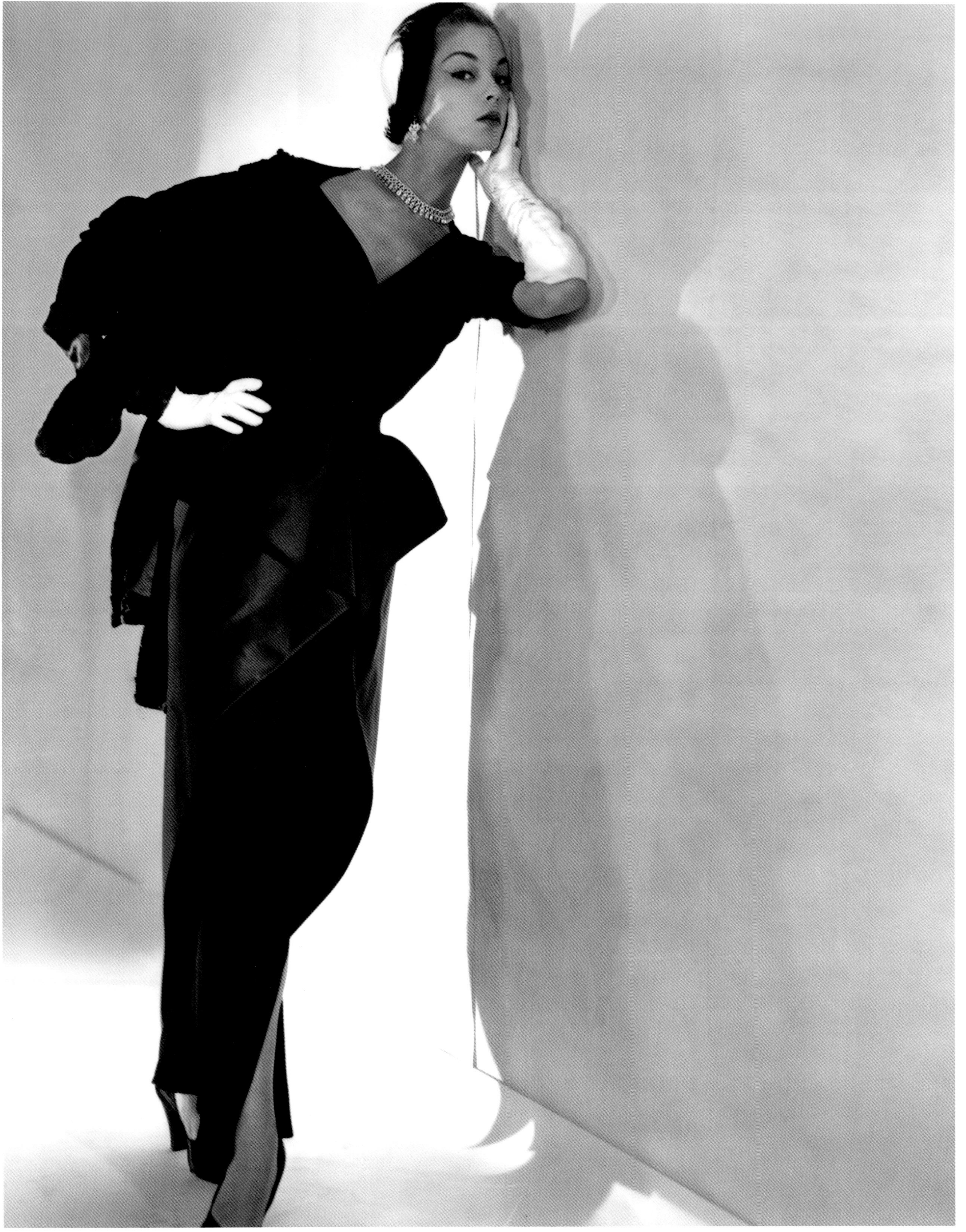

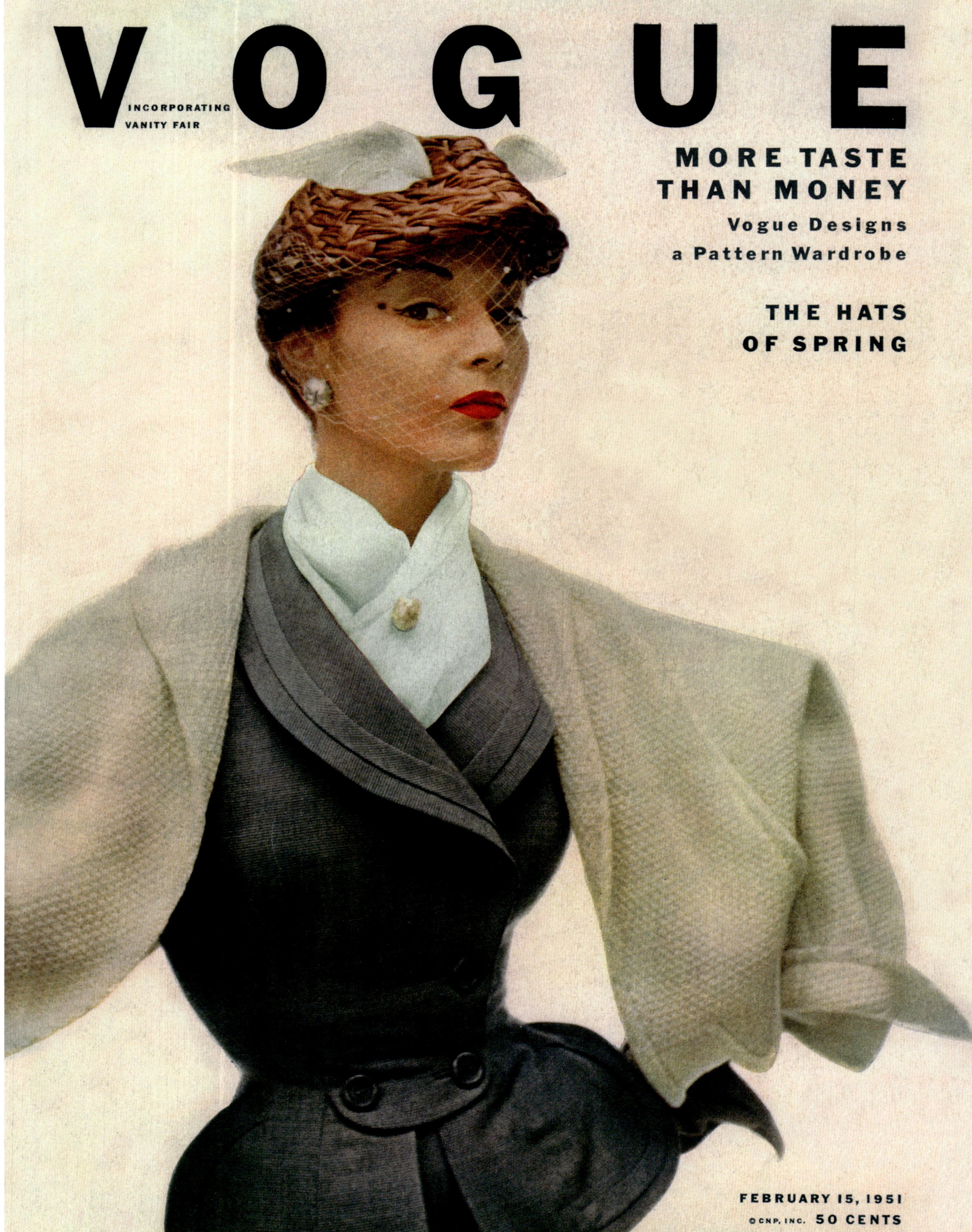
VOGUE
INCORPORATING
VANITY FAIR
MORE TASTE
THAN MONEY
Vogue Designs
a Pattern Wardrobe
THE HATS
OF SPRING
FEBRUARY 15, 1951
© CNP, INC. 50 CENTS

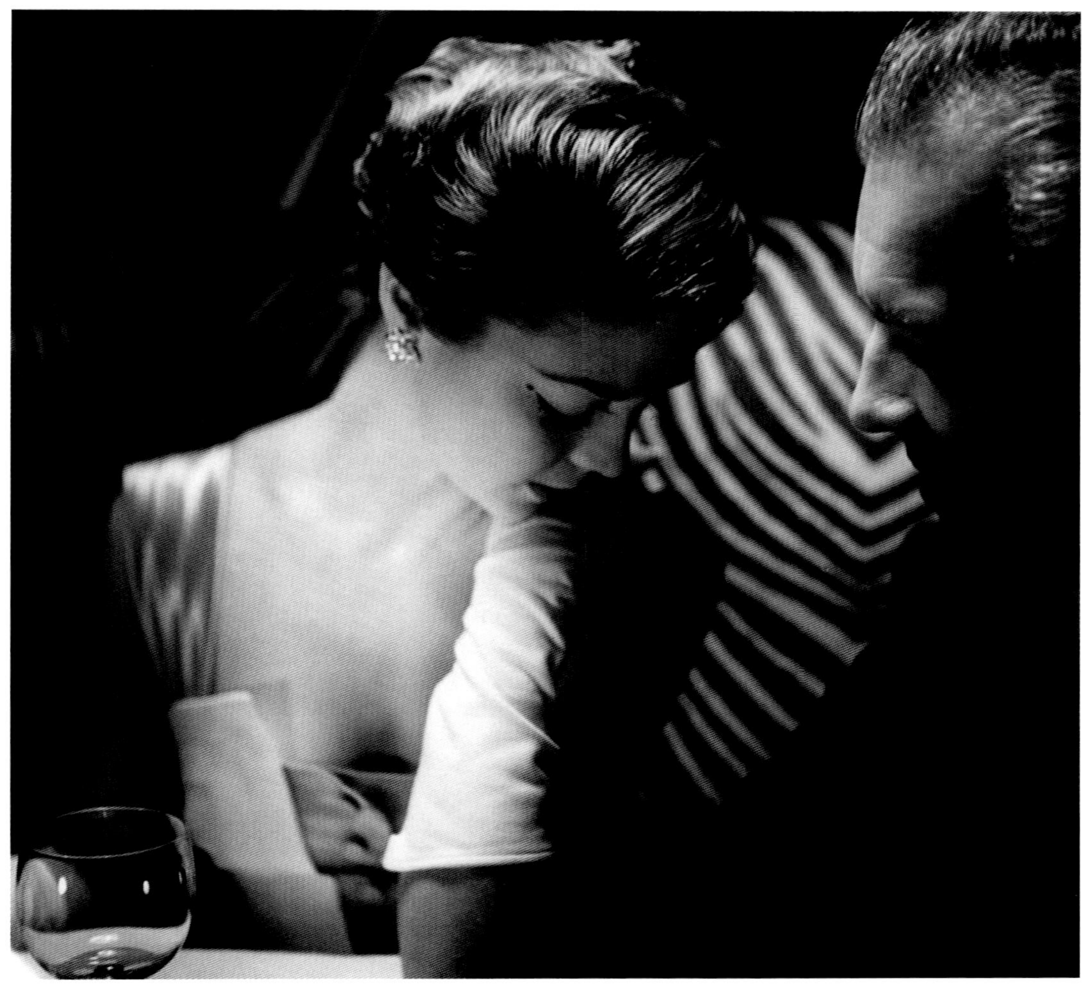

Above:
Jean Patchett at the El Morocco, New York
Advertising photograph for Charbert "Consent" perfume
1953
Photograph by Peter Basch

Opposite:
Vogue
February 15, 1951
Photograph by Irving Penn

"Flying Down to Lima"
. . . the Coat and Suit that Went to Lima, to Come Back in Time for Spring
Vogue
February 15, 1949
Photograph by Irving Penn

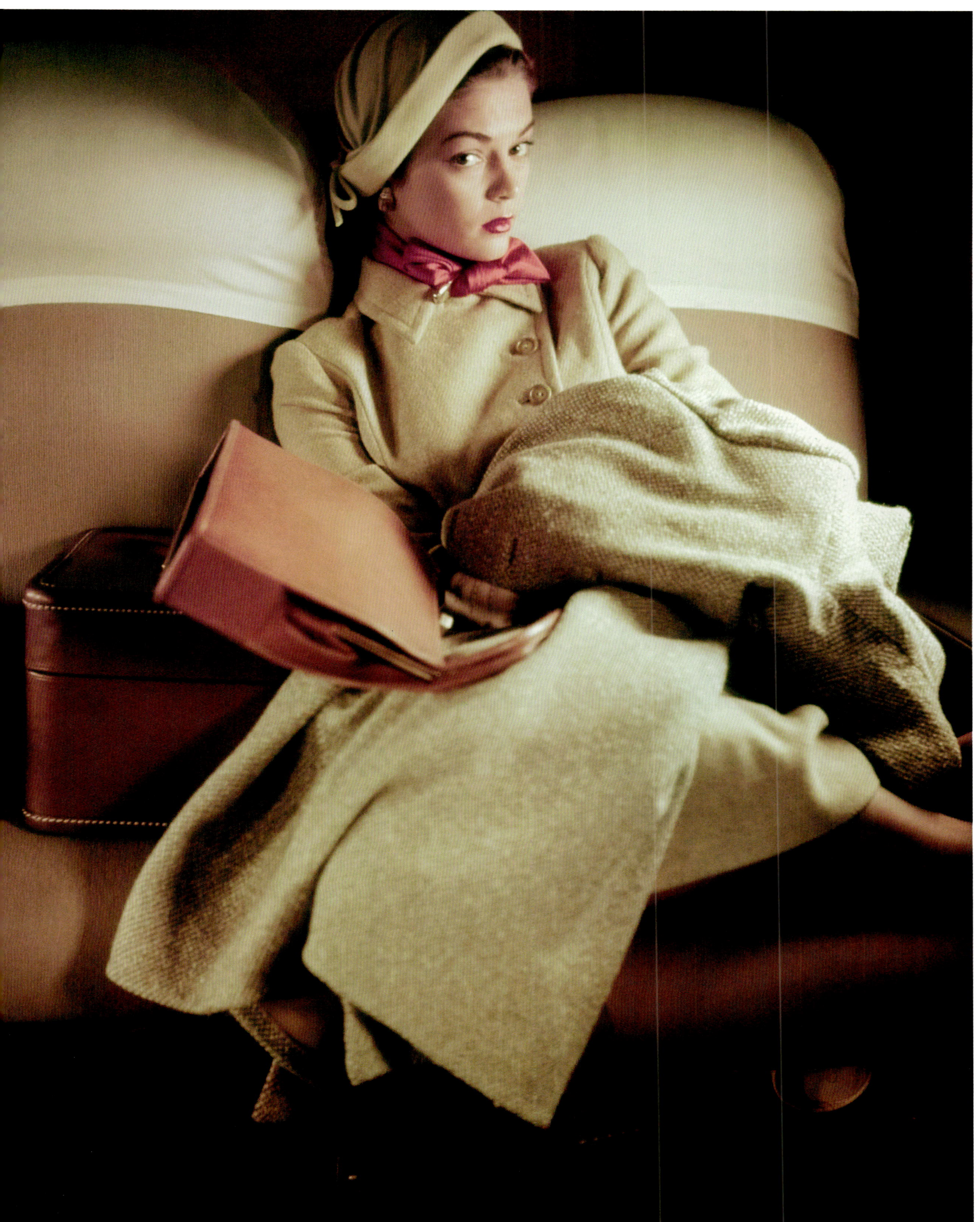

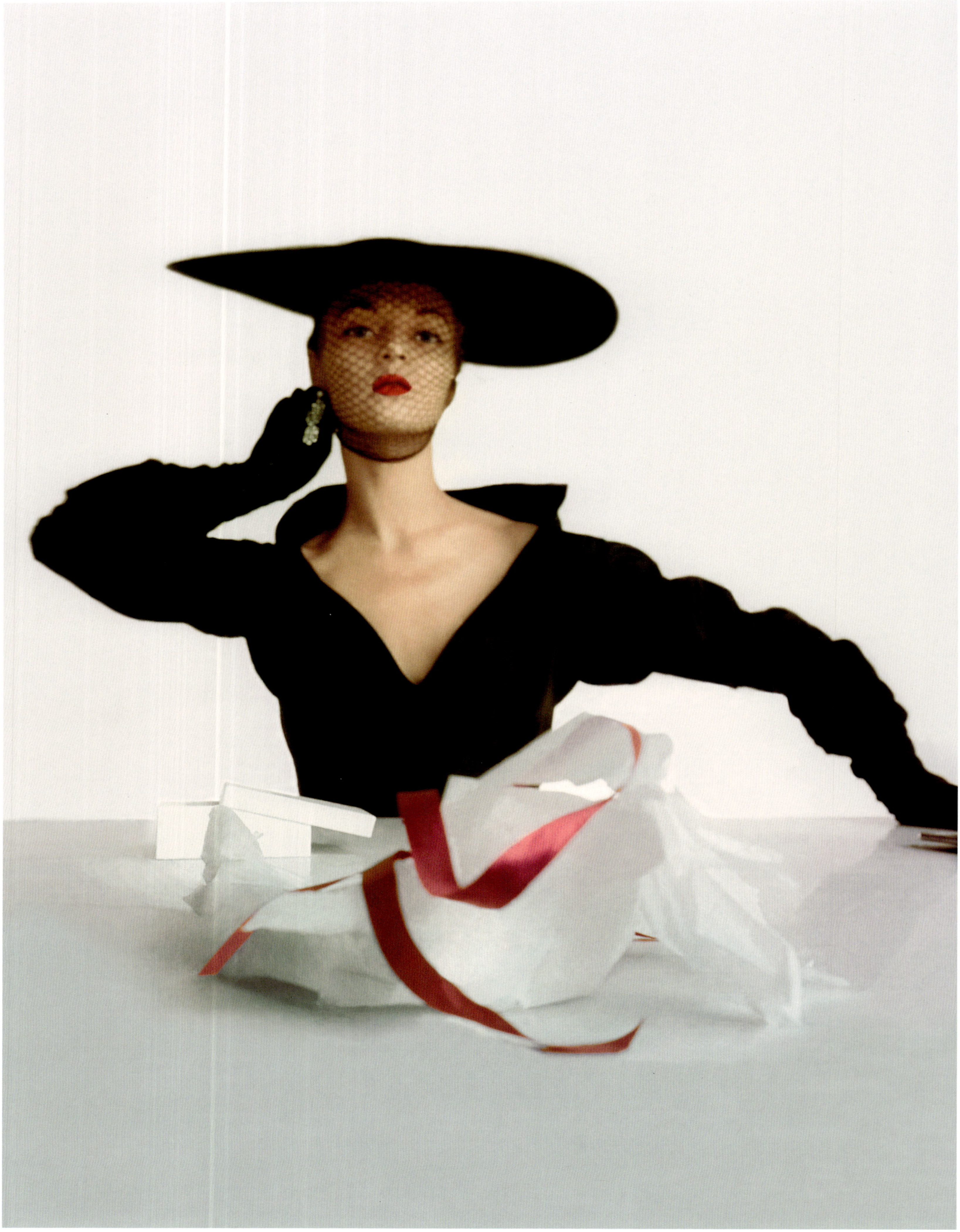

Vogue
Cover image
November 15, 1949
Photograph by Irving Penn

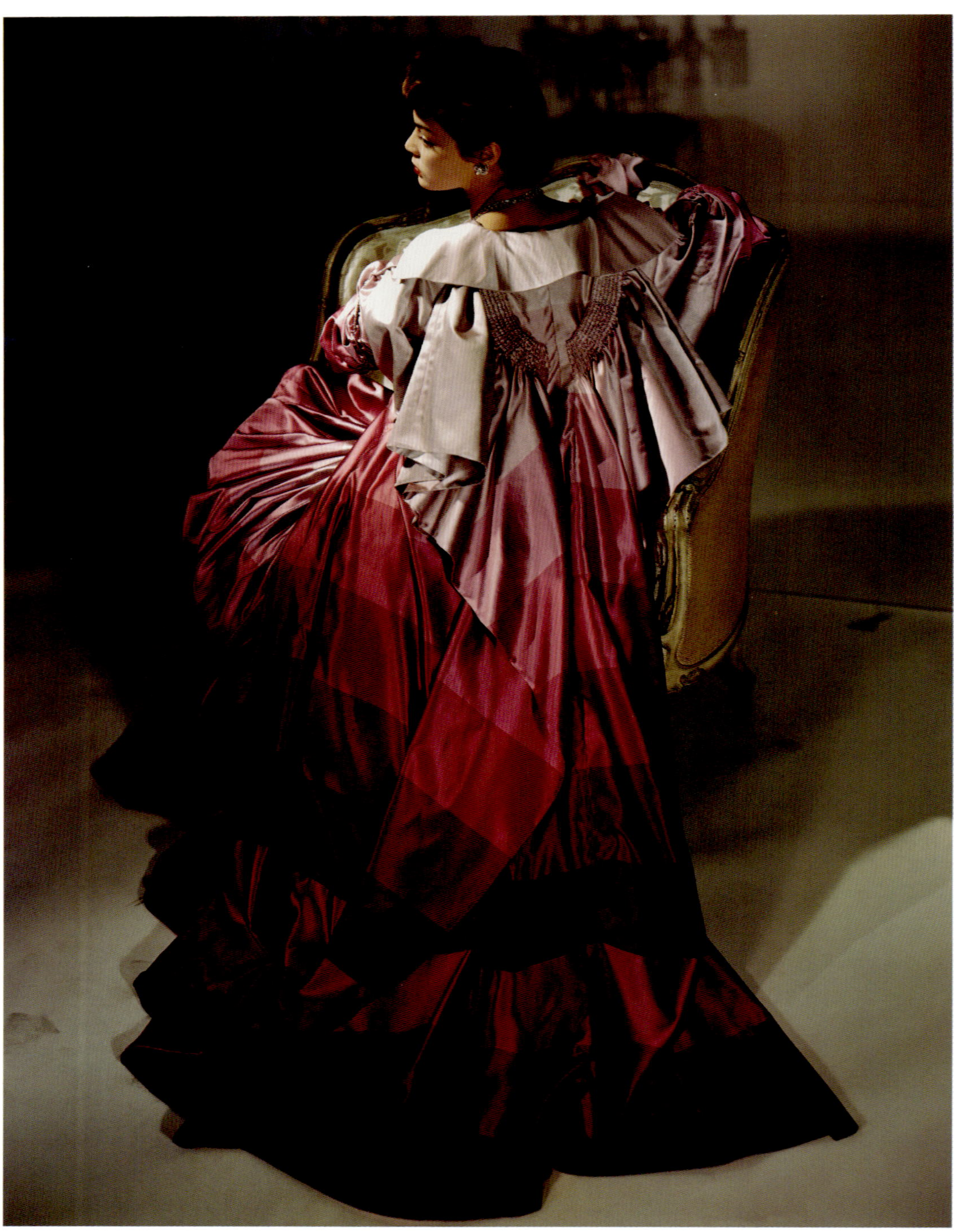

Above:
The Venetian Idea (variant)
Vogue
1948
Evening coat by Adrian
Photograph by
Horst P. Horst

Opposite:
The Venetian Idea
Vogue
November 1, 1948
Evening coat by Adrian
Photograph by Horst P. Horst

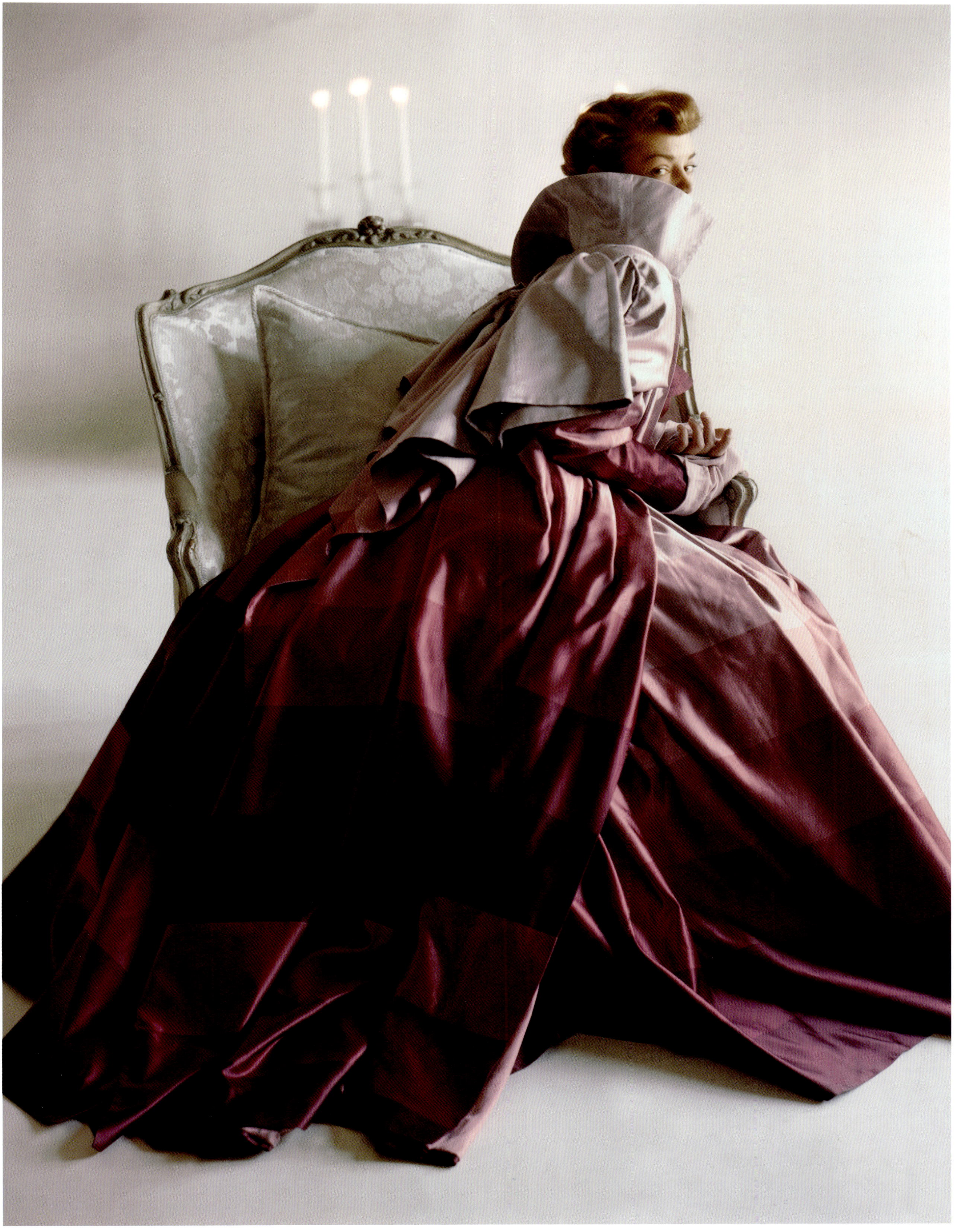

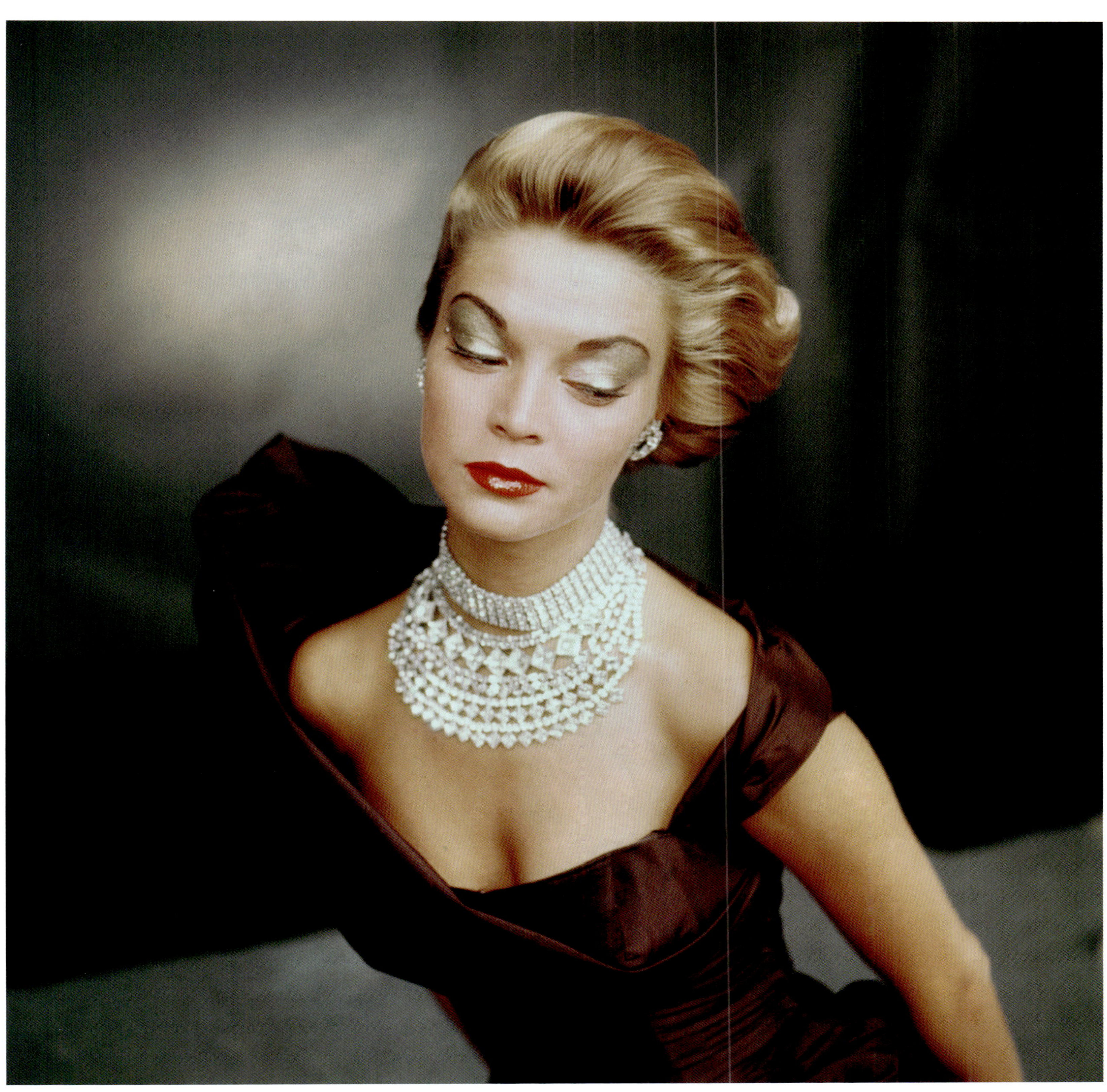

Vogue
August 1, 1951
Photograph by John Rawlings

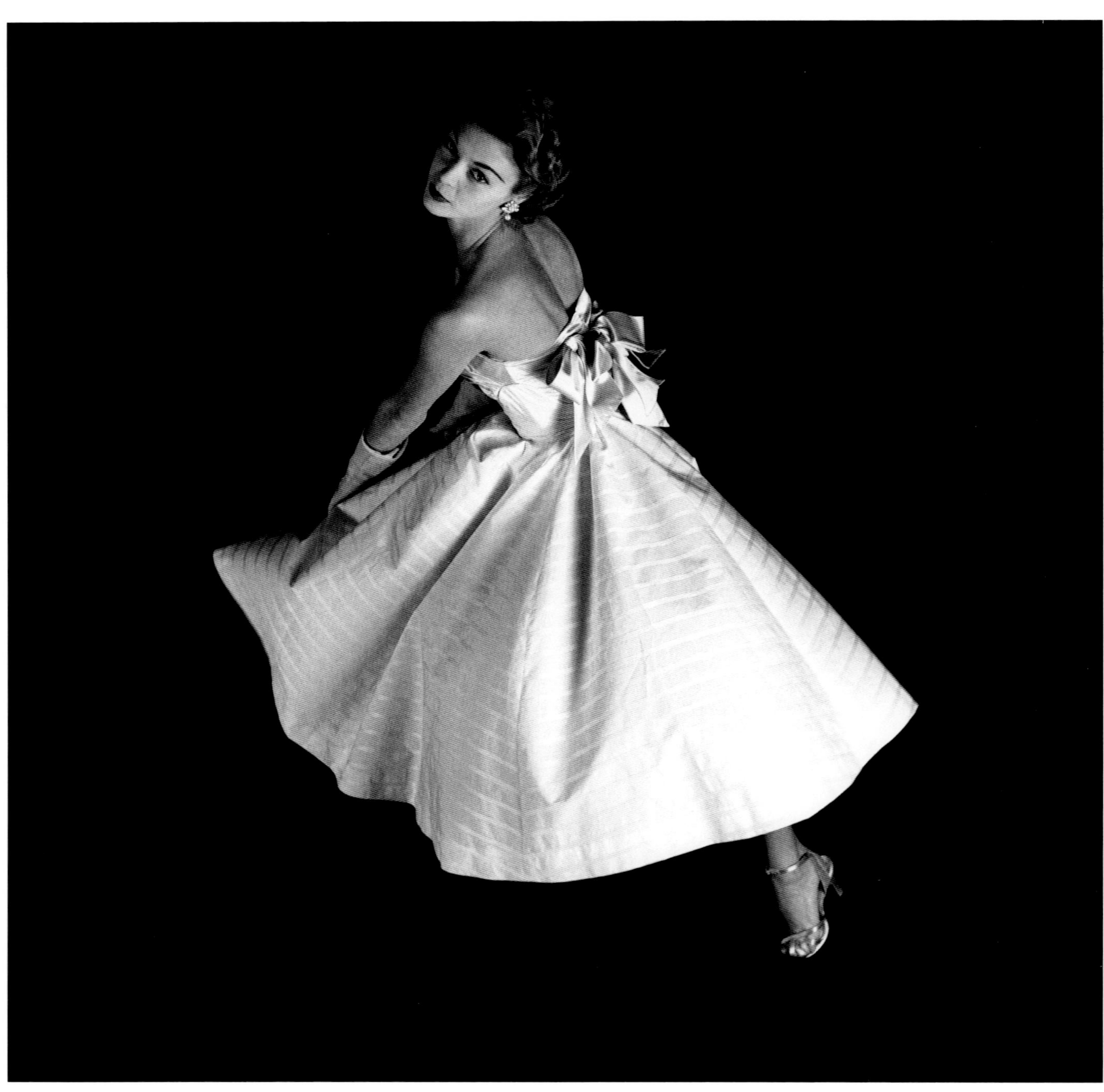

Above:
Town & Country
February 1952
Photograph by
Milton H. Greene

Opposite:
Glamour
July 1950
Photograph by
Clifford Coffin

Photograph by Milton H. Greene © 2019 Joshua Greene. www.archiveimages.com

GLAMOUR

for the girl with a job

ANNUAL
BEAUTY
ISSUE,
featuring:

*How
An Average Girl
Became A Beauty*

*Her 7 Day Diet
and
Beauty Plan*

*6 Pages
of
New Coiffures*

July 1950
Price 25 Cents

COPYRIGHT 1950, THE CONDÉ NAST PUBLICATIONS INC.

Paris Spectaculars
Vogue
April 1, 1950
Gown by Balenciaga
Photograph by
Norman Parkinson

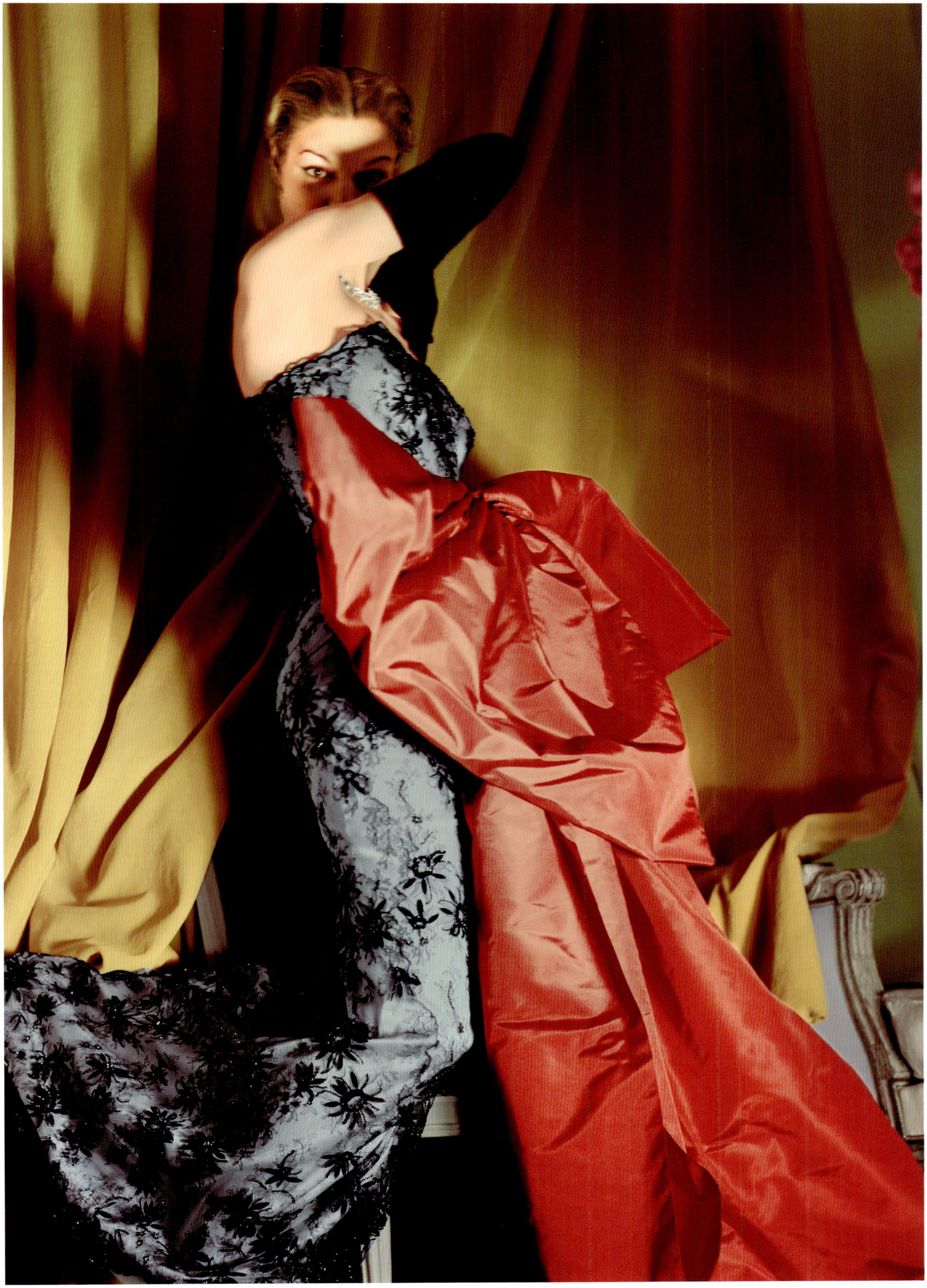

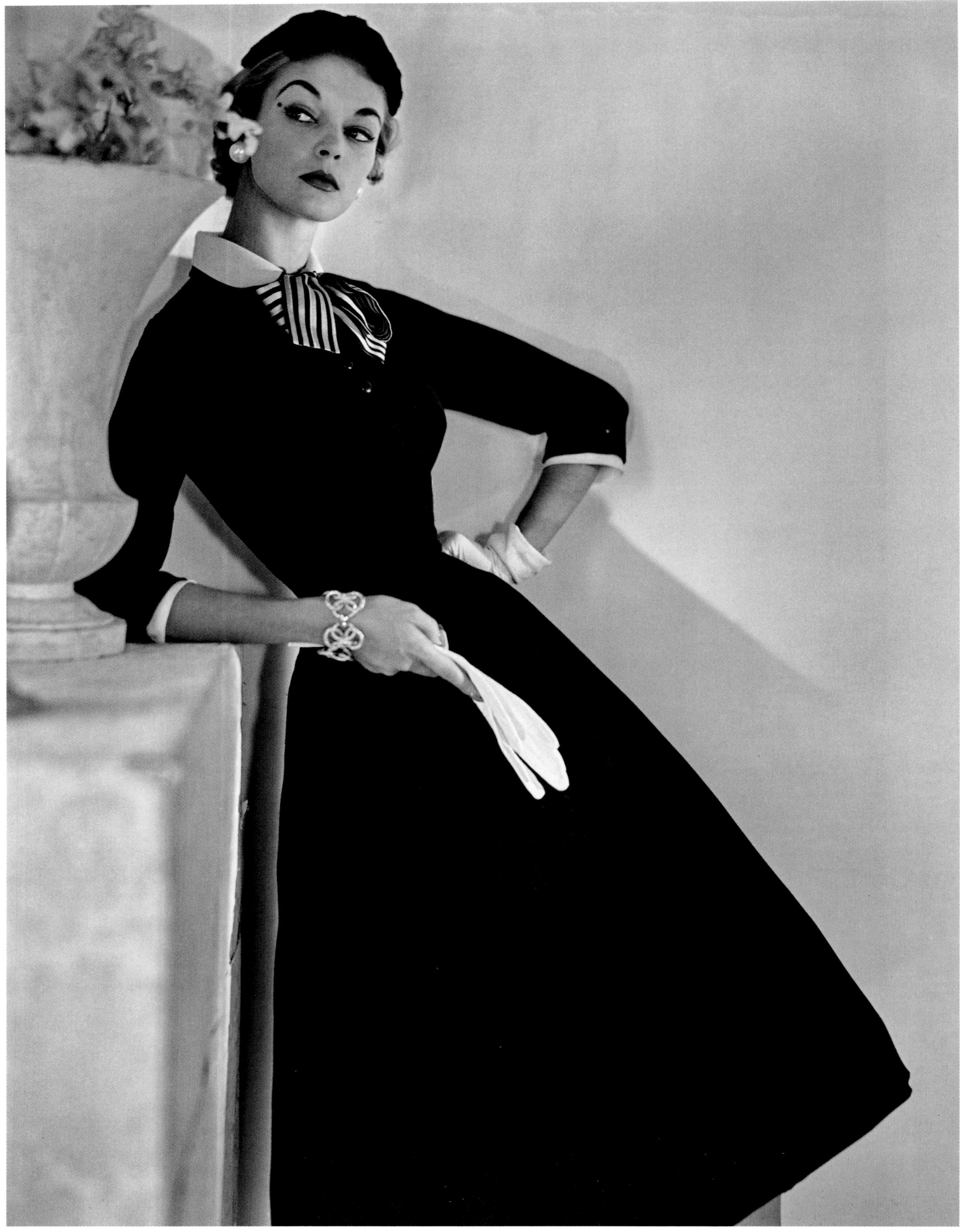

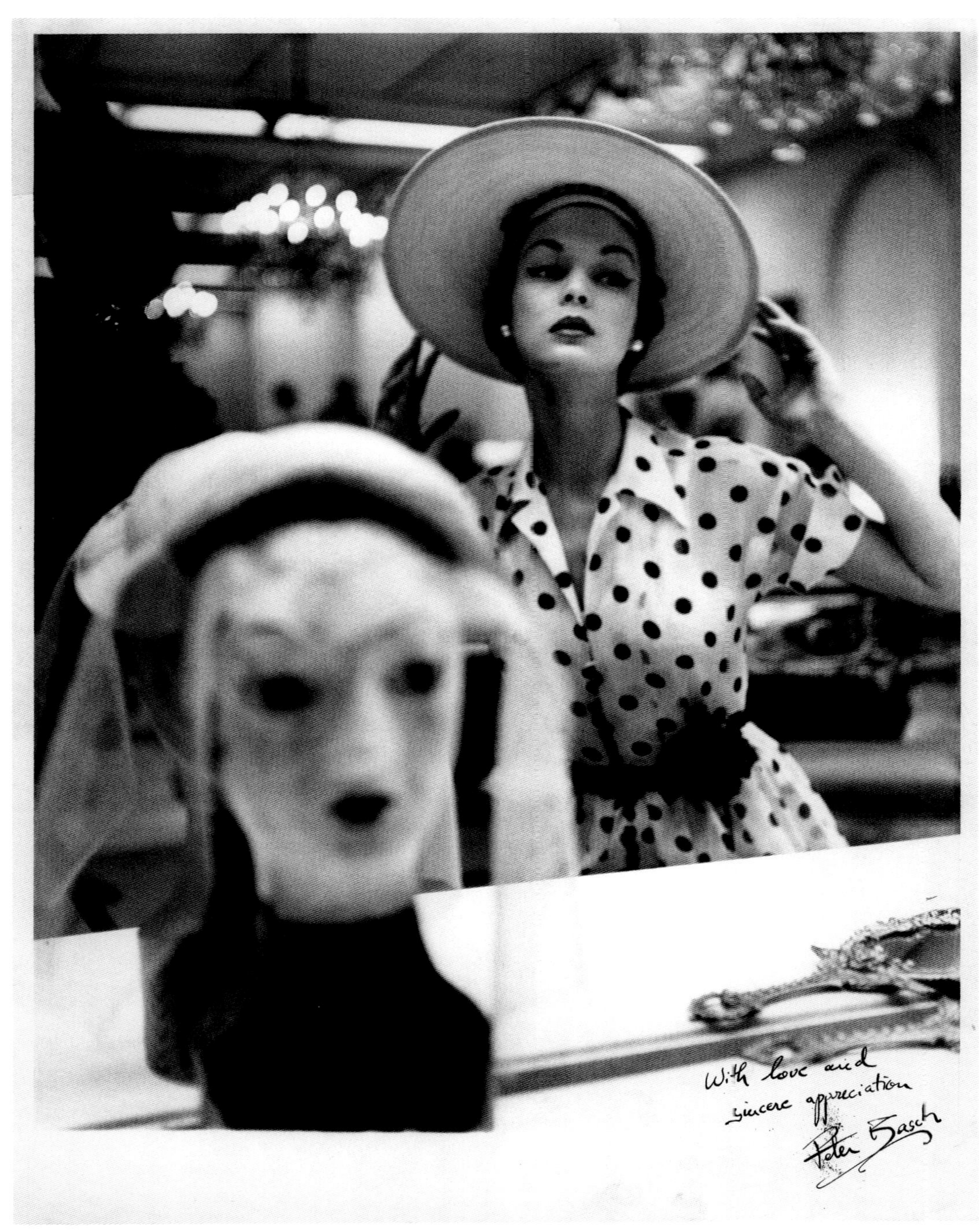

Above:
Pageant
1950
Photograph by Peter Basch

Opposite:
Second wind for
a winter wardrobe
Vogue
November 1, 1953
Dress by Mollie Parnis,
hat by Lilly Daché,
bracelets by Sperry
Photograph by Horst P. Horst

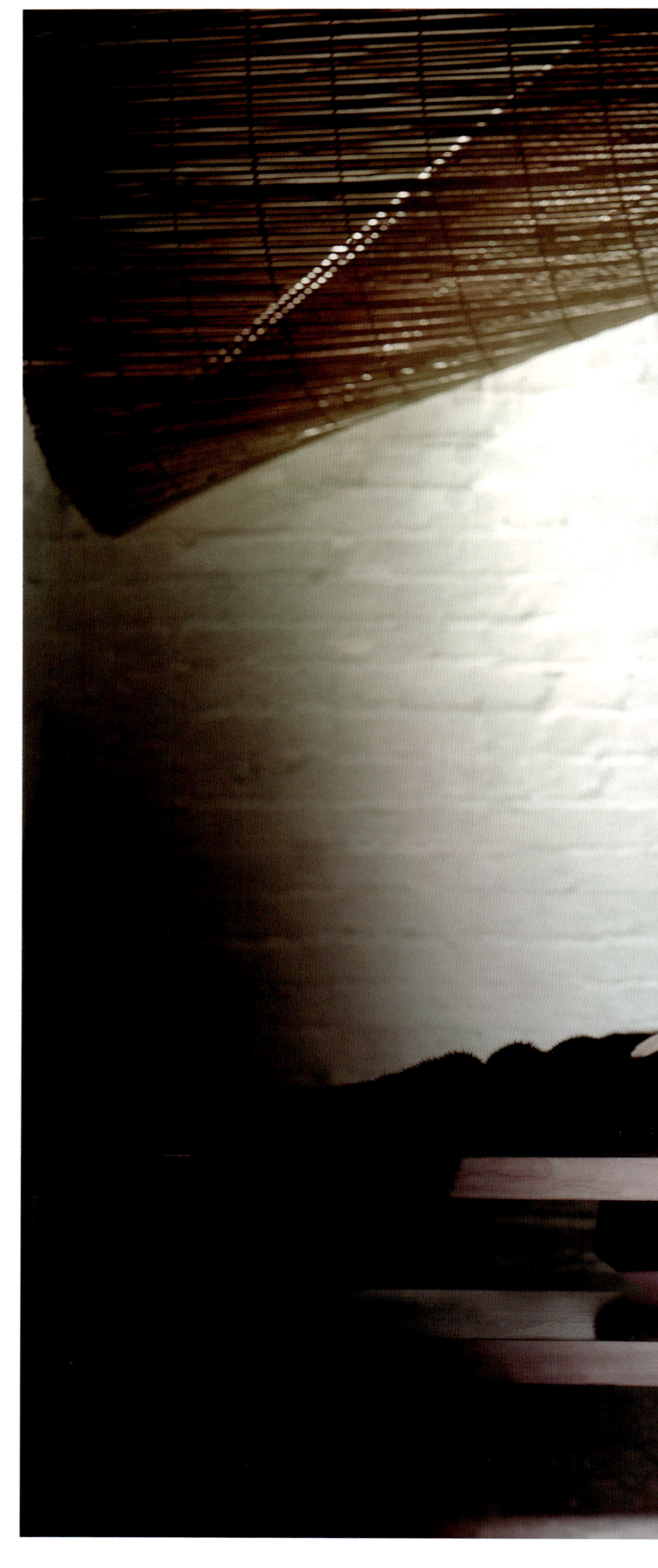

More taste than money
Vogue
February 15, 1950
Photograph by
John Rawlings

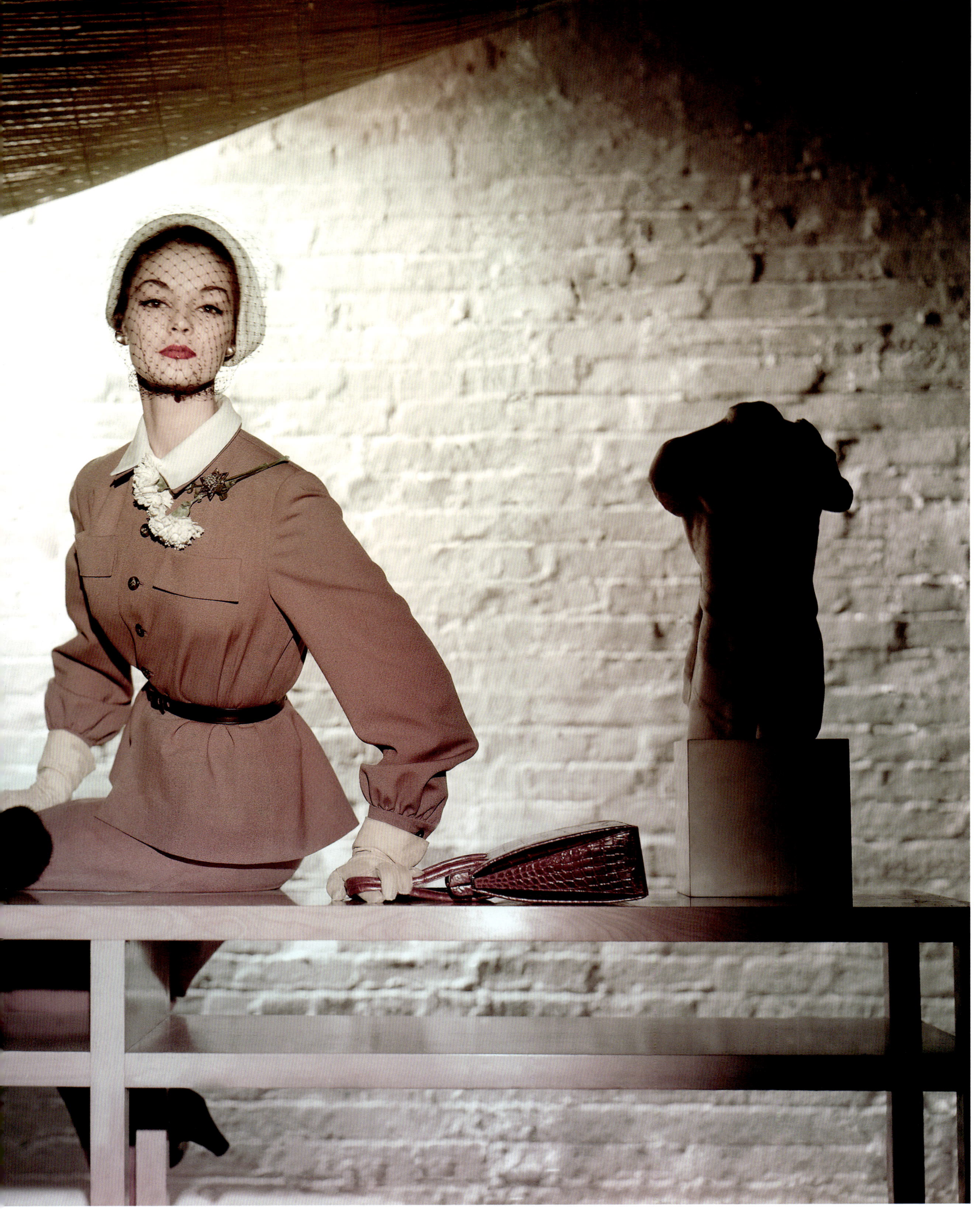

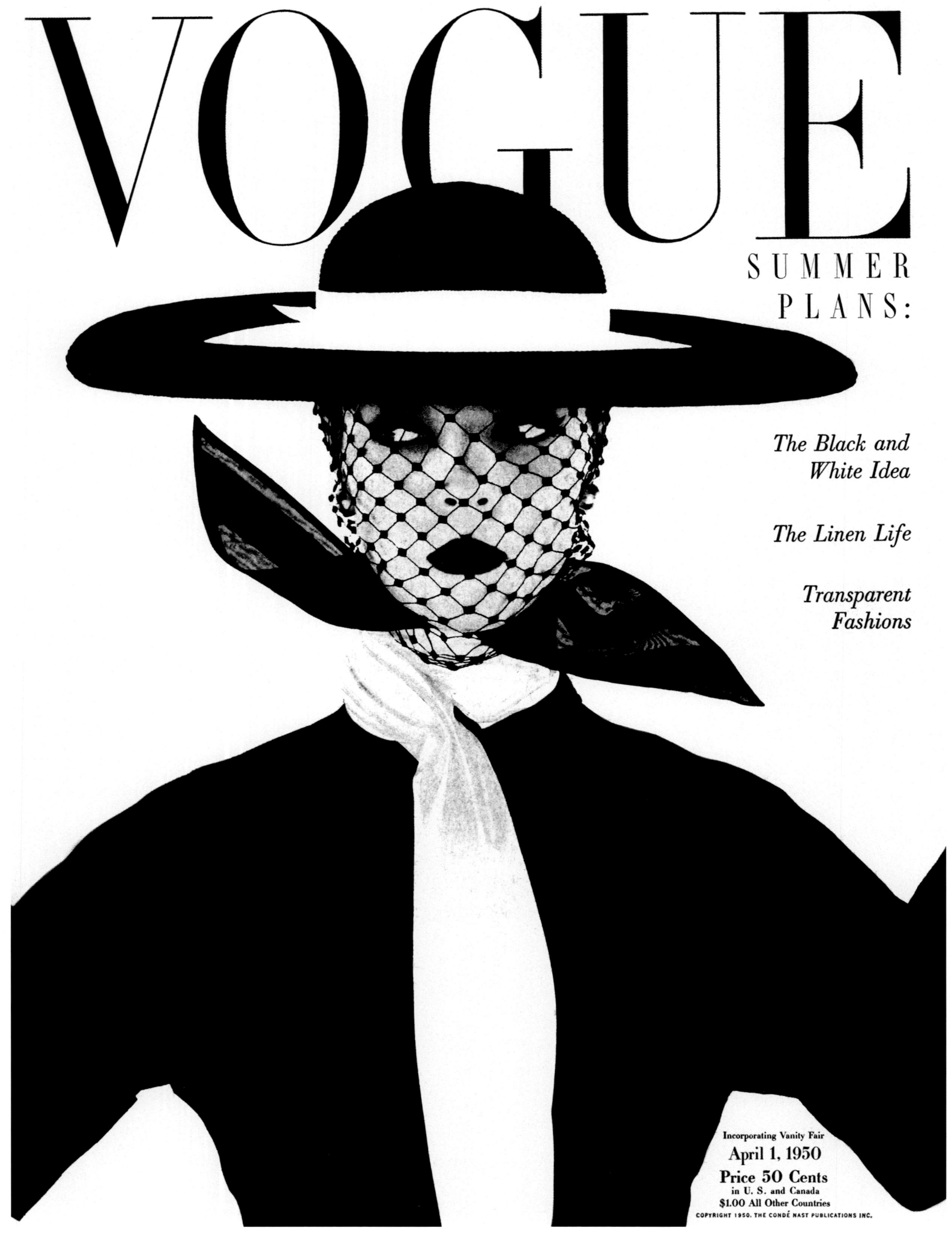
VOGUE
SUMMER
PLANS:
The Black and
White Idea
The Linen Life
Transparent
Fashions
Incorporating Vanity Fair
April 1, 1950
Price 50 Cents
in U. S. and Canada
$1.00 All Other Countries
COPYRIGHT 1950. THE CONDÉ NAST PUBLICATIONS INC.

Vogue
April 1, 1950
Photograph by Irving Penn

Vogue
July 1950
Photograph by Irving Penn

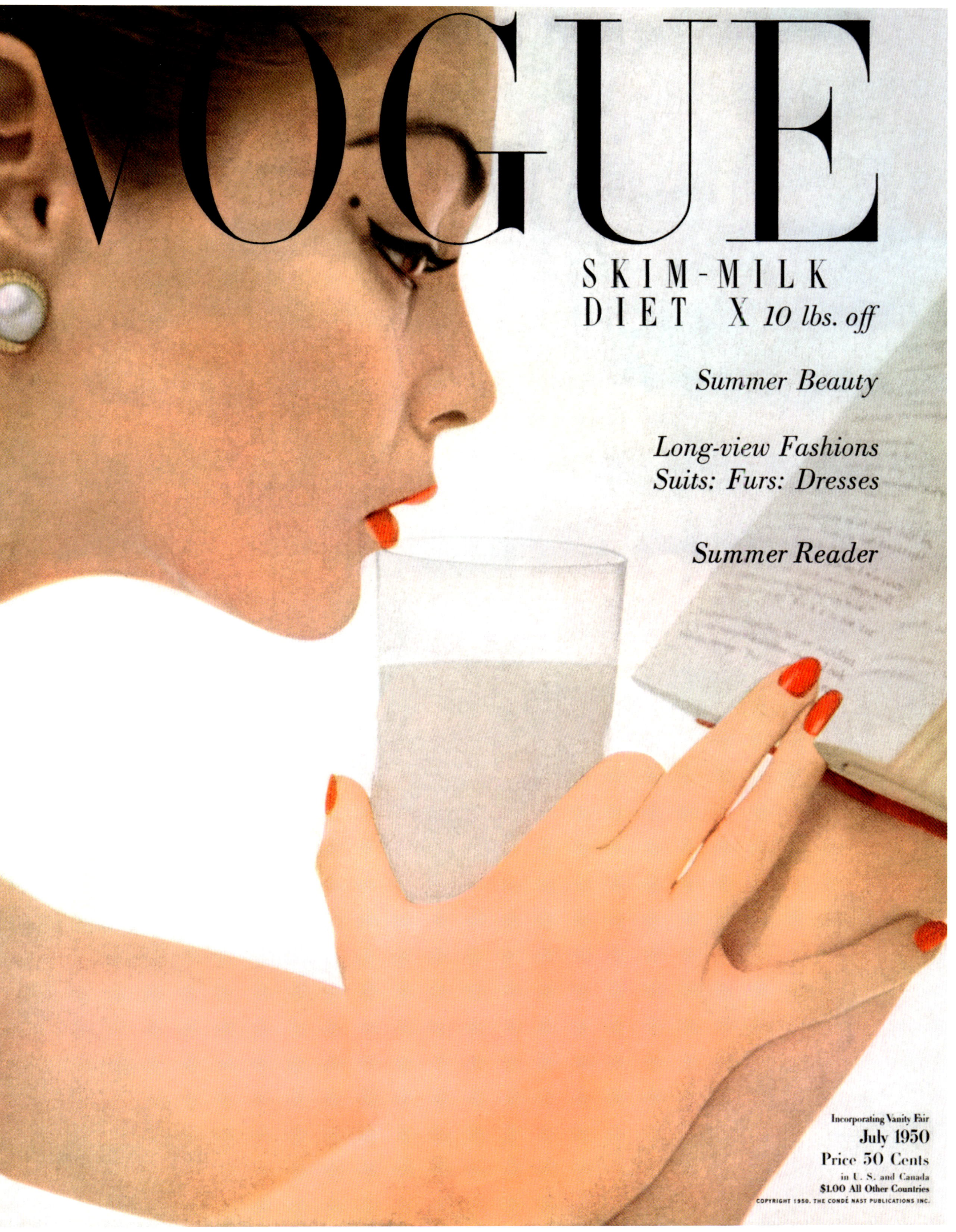
VOGUE
SKIM-MILK
DIET X 10 lbs. off
Summer Beauty
Long-view Fashions
Suits: Furs: Dresses
Summer Reader
Incorporating Vanity Fair
July 1950
Price 50 Cents
in U. S. and Canada
$1.00 All Other Countries
COPYRIGHT 1950. THE CONDÉ NAST PUBLICATIONS INC.

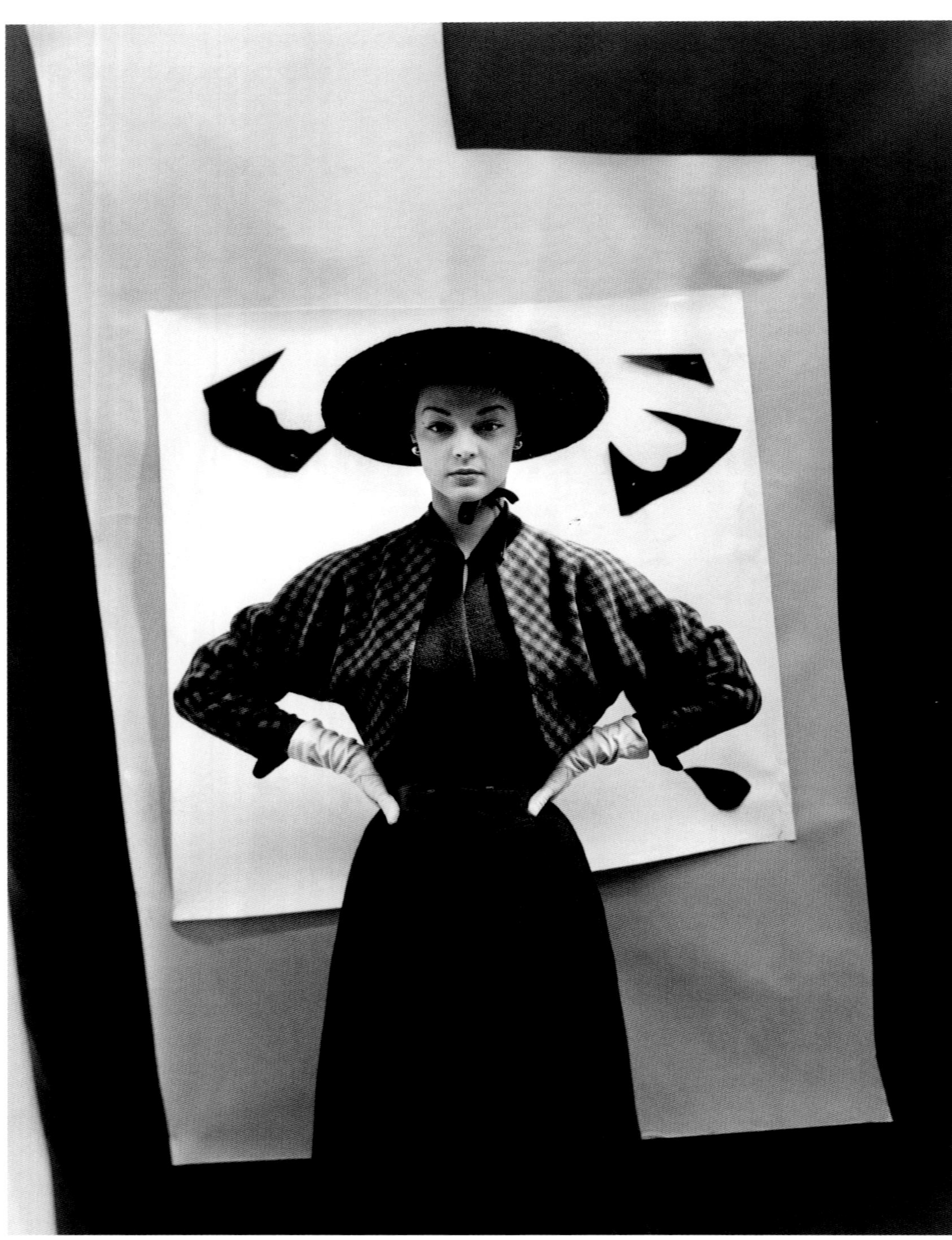

Above:
Check Dash
Vogue
March 14, 1949
Photograph by
Cecil Beaton

Opposite:
Coral Orange
Vogue
March 15, 1950
Photograph by
Norman Parkinson

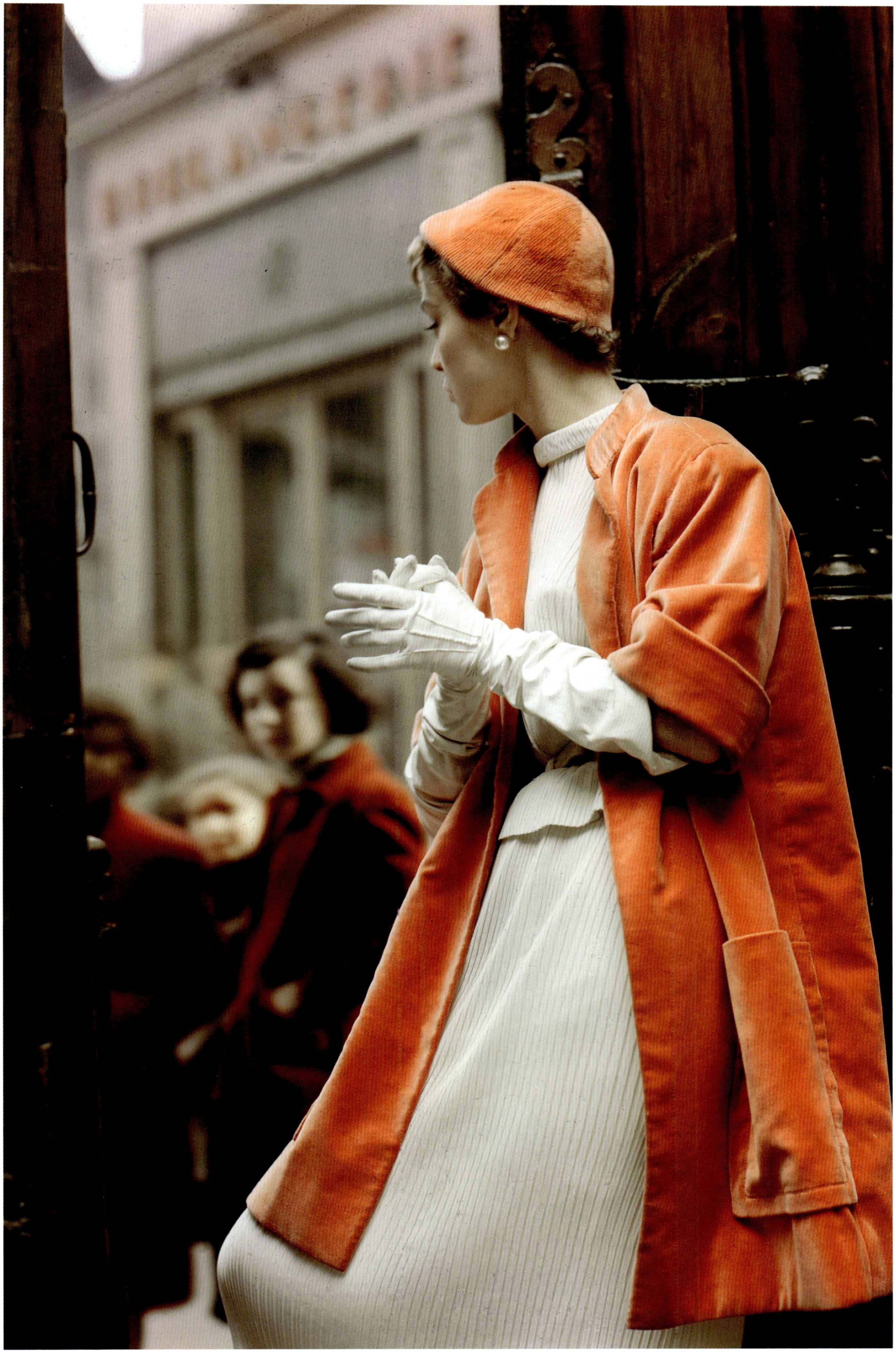

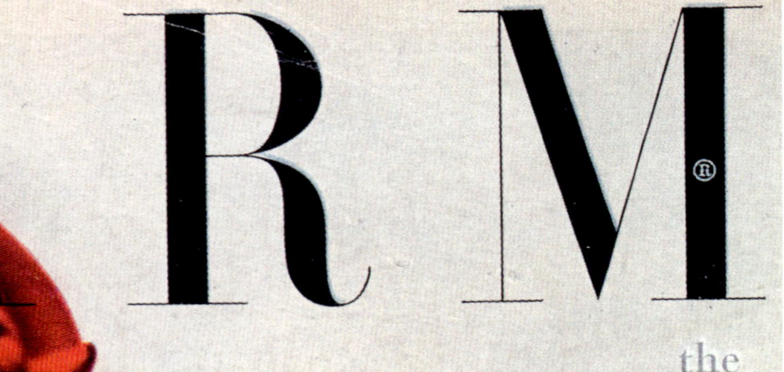

CHARM®

the magazine for women who work

IN THE HOLIDAY MOOD

PART 1 . . . this issue

fashions for fun

10 pages of shop-early-gifts

coming in December PART 2

NOVEMBER 1951 · 25 CENTS

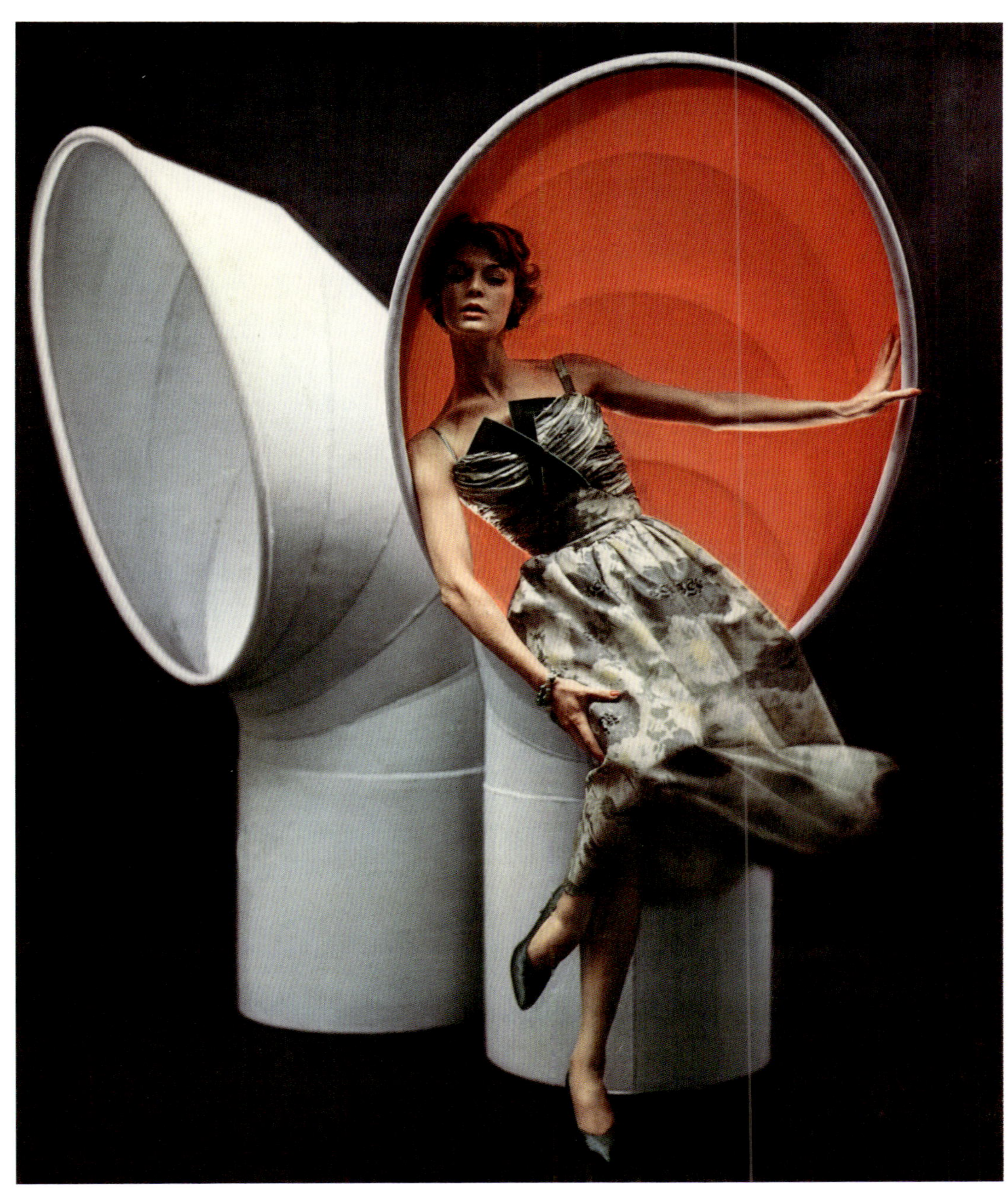

Above:
Seascape
Advertising photograph
for Supima
The New Yorker
December 1958
Photograph by
William Helburn

Opposite:
Charm
November 1951
Photograph by
William Helburn

Doe Eye
Vogue
Cover image
January 1950
Photograph by
Erwin Blumenfeld

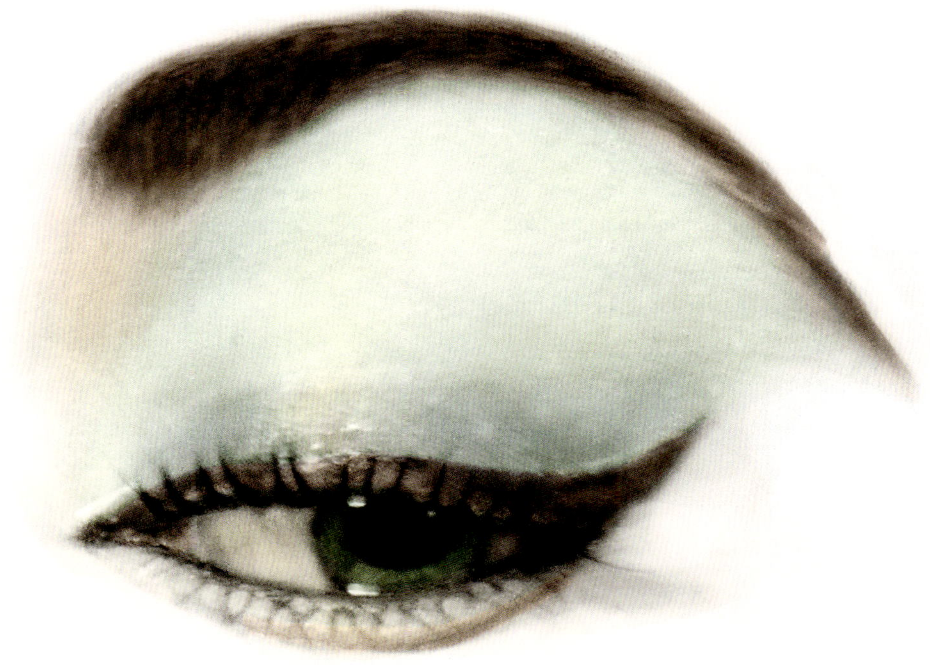

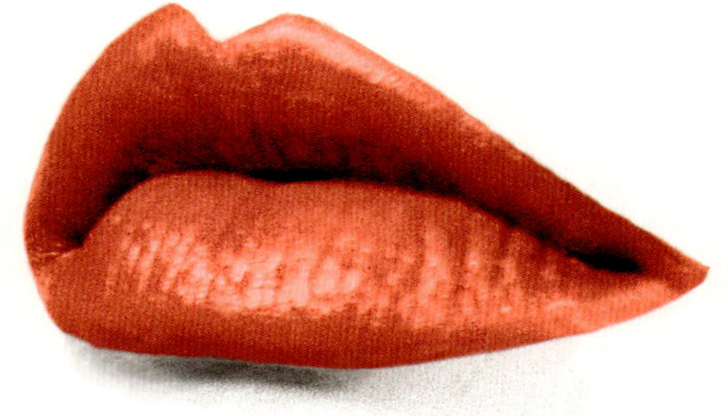

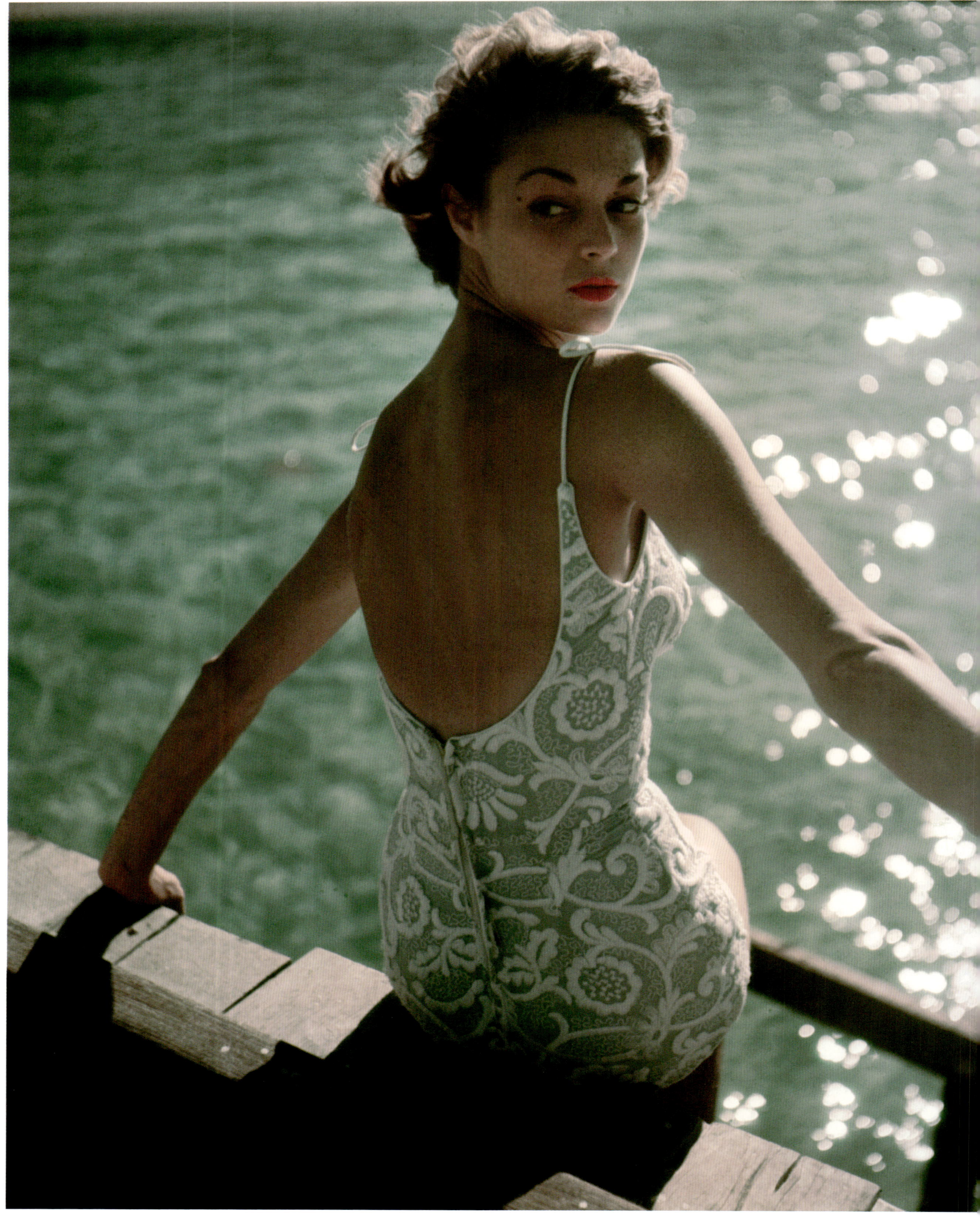

The Embroidered Bathing Suit
Vogue
November 15, 1950
Photograph by
Clifford Coffin

Lace — The Most Eligible Evening Partner
Harper's Bazaar
October 1952
Photograph by
Louise Dahl-Wolfe

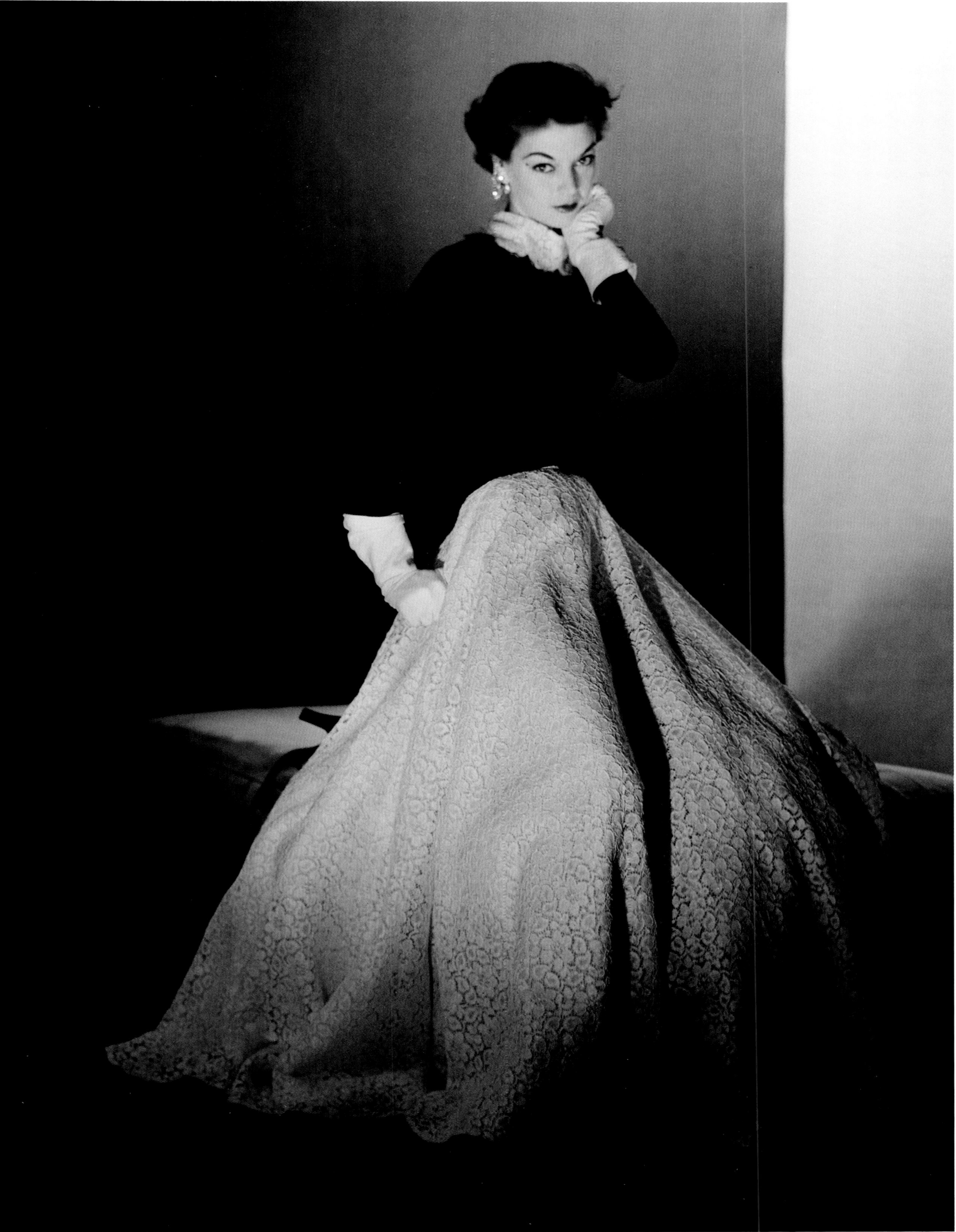

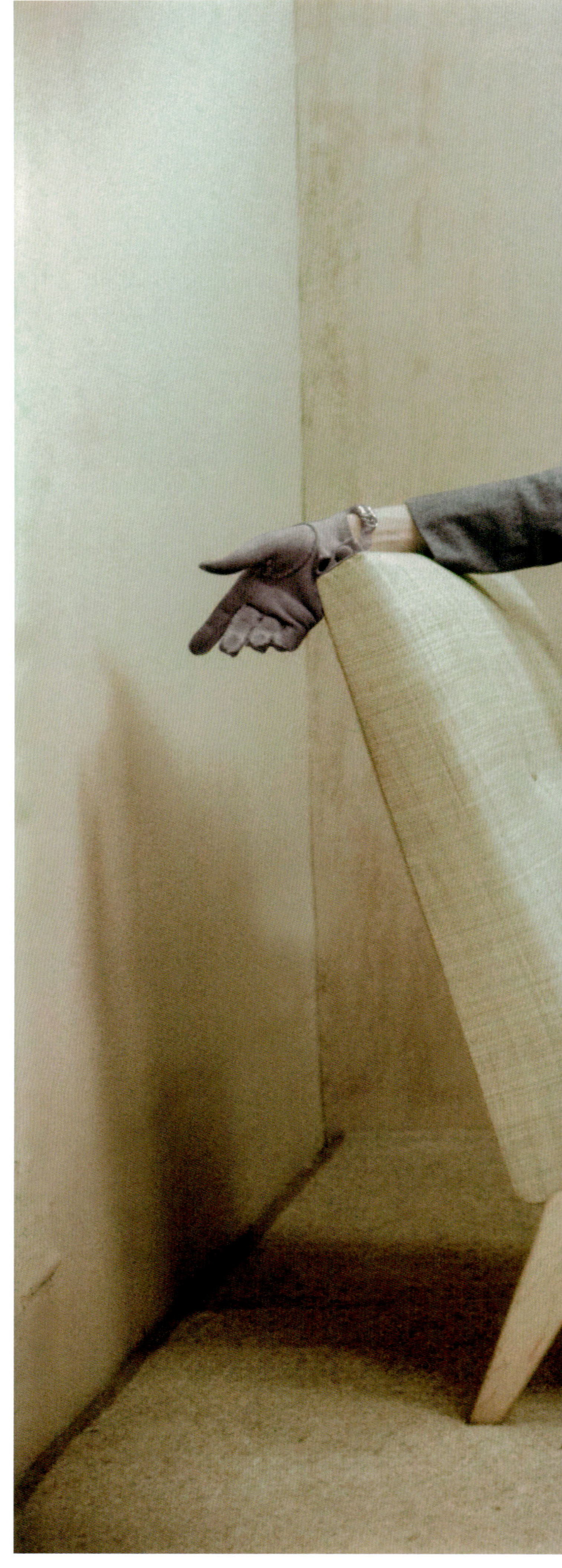

With the silk suit, the pretty shoe
Vogue
March 1, 1951
Suit by Trigère
Photograph by
Frances McLaughlin-Gill

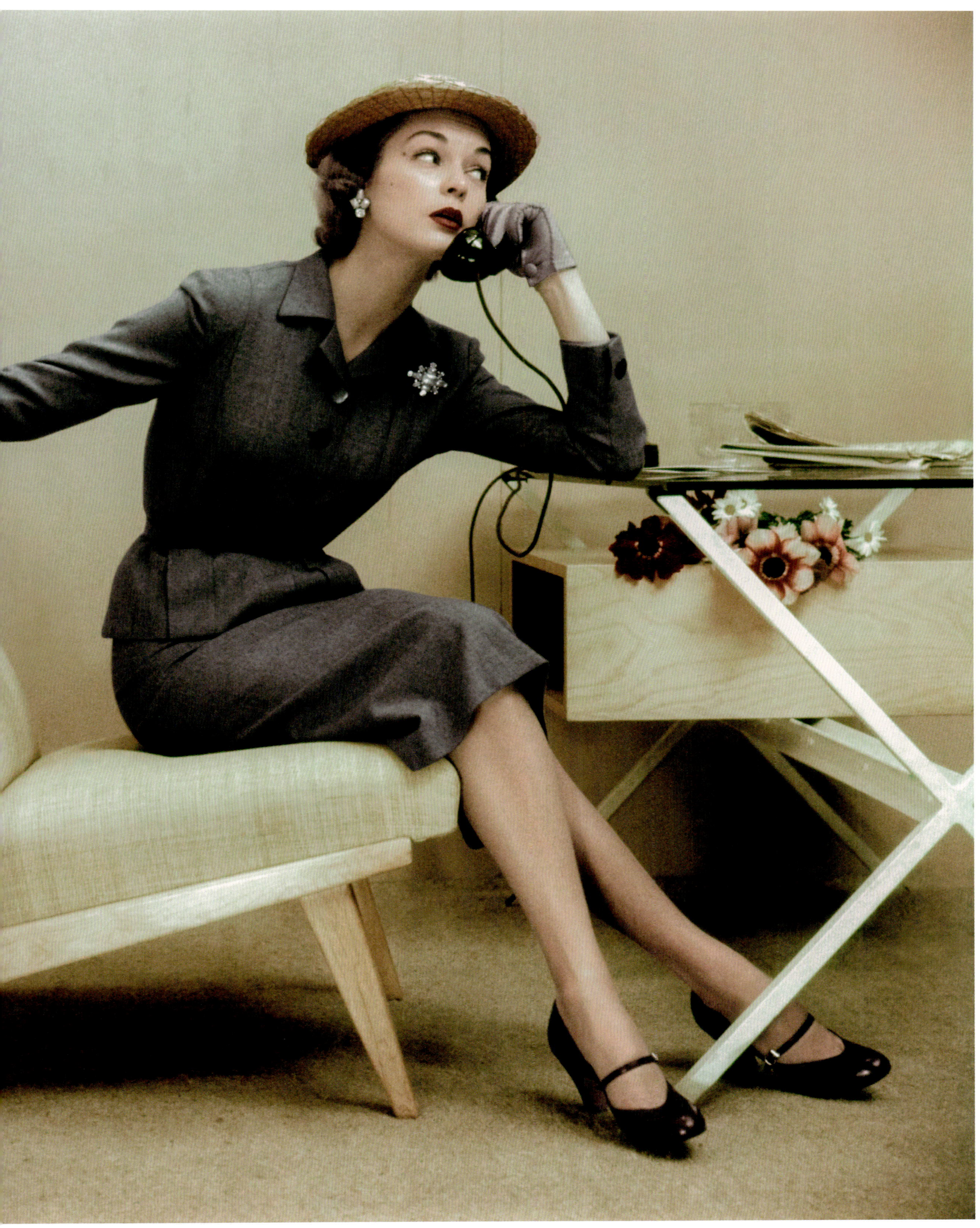

JULIUS GARFINCKEL & CO.

IN THE NATION'S CAPITAL

JACQUES FATH (PARIS-NEW YORK) DESIGNS IN AMERICA FOR JOSEPH HALPERT A SIDE-SWEPT GREY WOOLEN, WITH FLOWING SATIN PANEL.

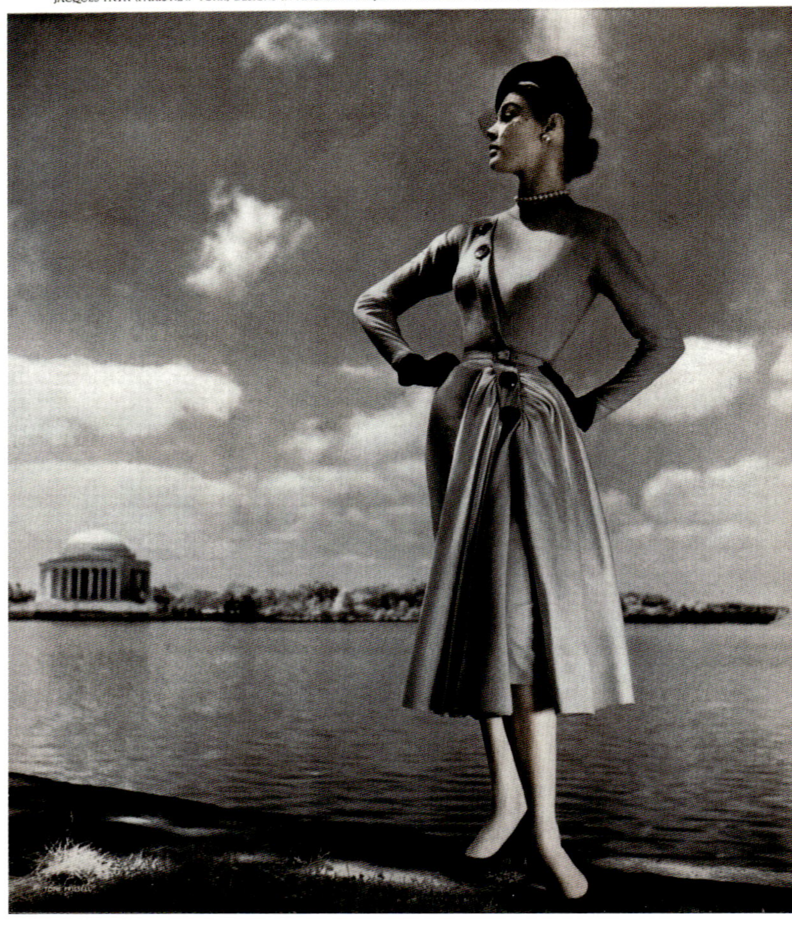

HAT BY MR. JOHN

RAWLINGS

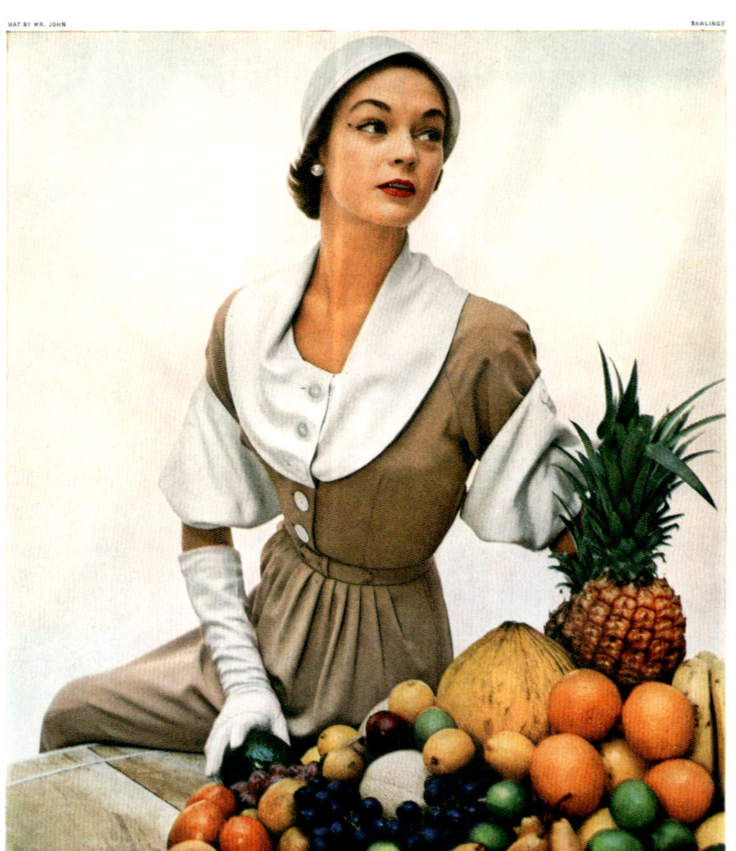

Pattullo . . . Jo Copeland dress—with important nuances that mark it 1951: the deep cowl-draped collar—wide cuffs—a softer narrowness—the gentle drape and fine texture of Onondaga's Monastique. Like so many of the important new fashion fabrics, Monastique is woven with Enka Rayon. Saks Fifth Avenue, New York; Neiman-Marcus, Dallas; Harzfeld's, Kansas City; Ransohoffs, San Francisco.

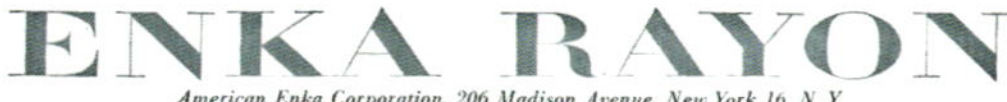

American Enka Corporation, 206 Madison Avenue, New York 16, N. Y.

This page, from top:
Ad for Julius Garfinckel & Co.
1951
Photograph by
Toni Frissell

Ad for Enka Rayon
1951
Photograph by
John Rawlings

Opposite:
Follow the Gleam
Harper's Bazaar
September 1952
Photograph by
Lillian Bassman

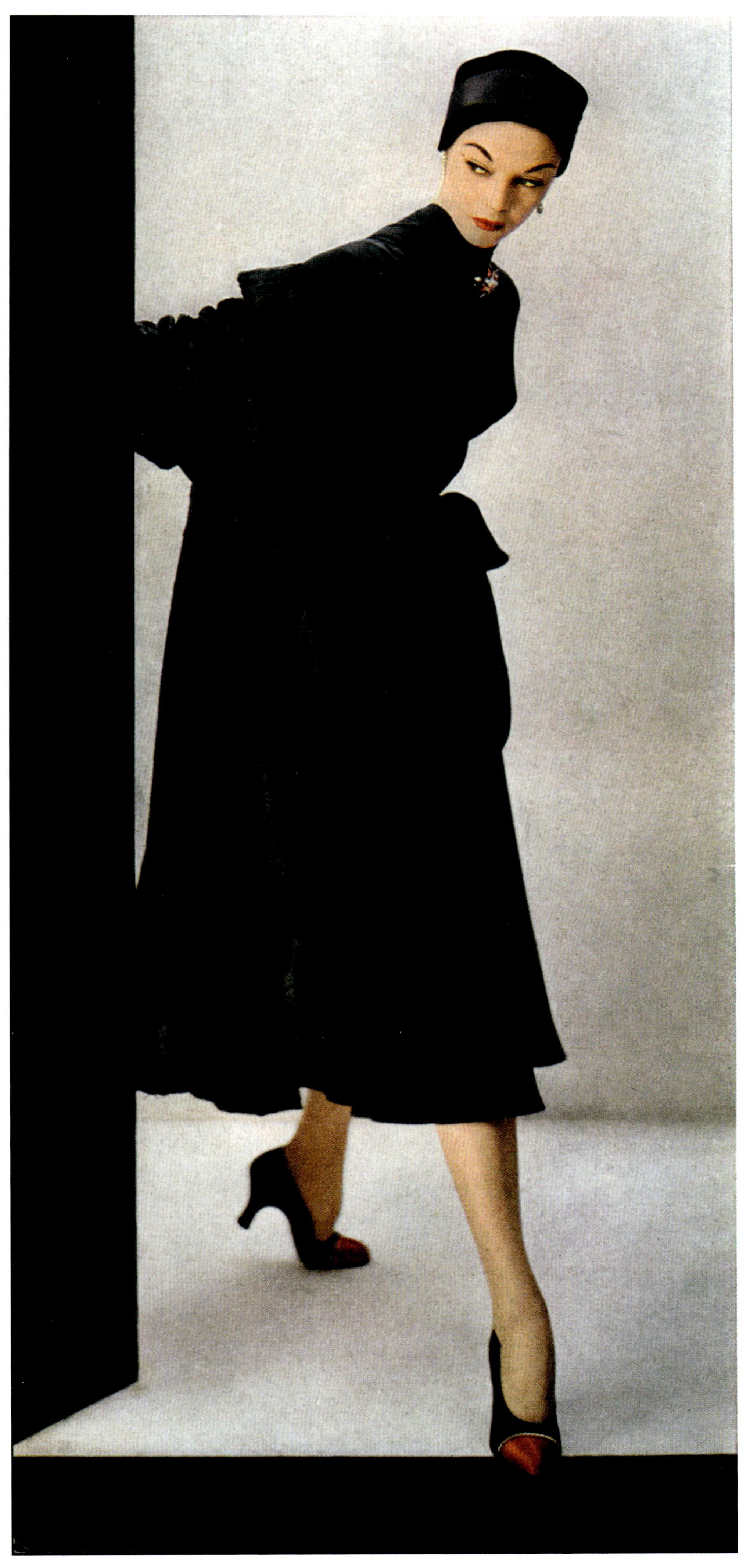

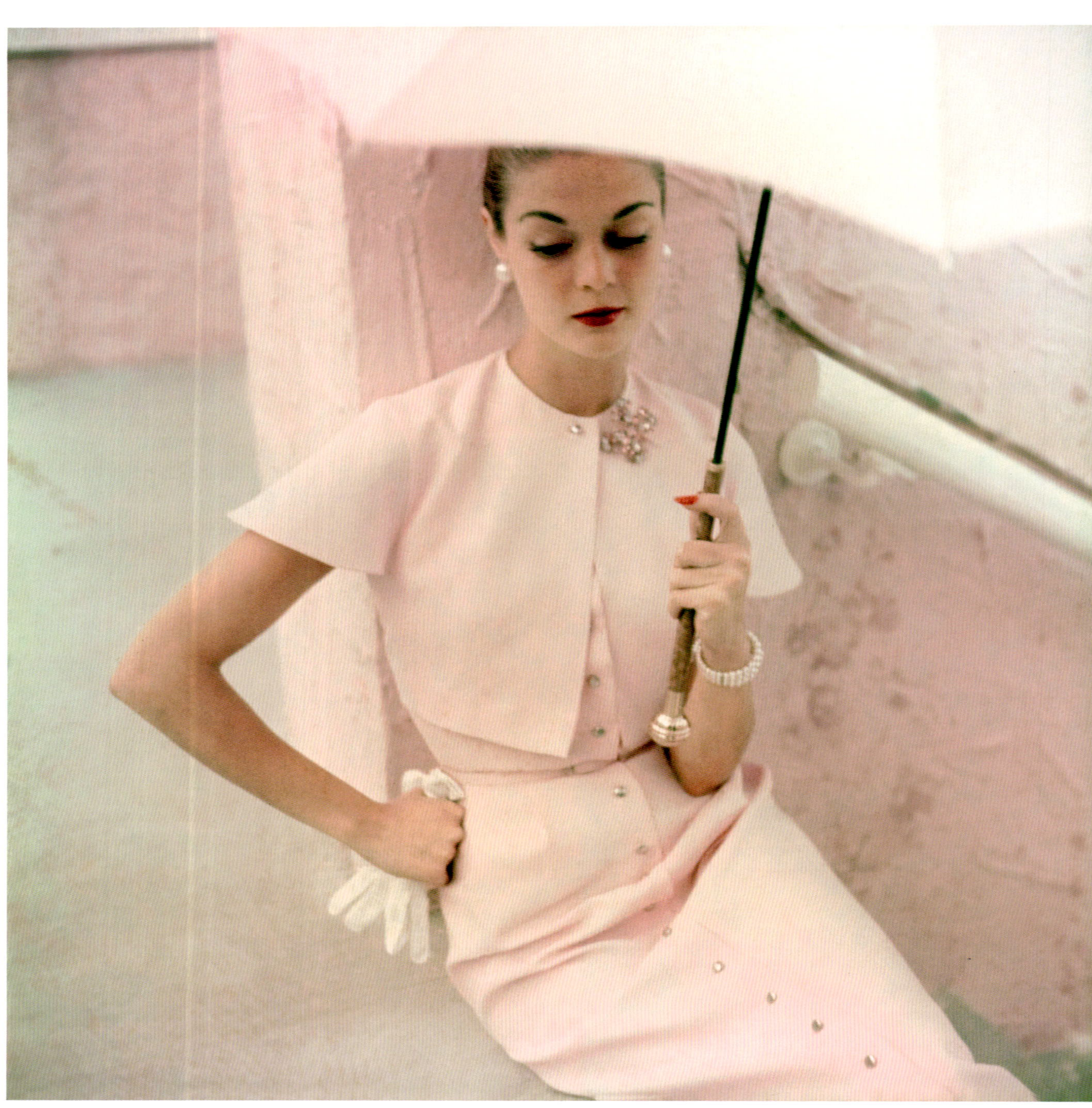

Above:
Frosted Summer Colors
Vogue
May 1, 1951
Photograph by
Clifford Coffin

Opposite:
Heading South:
Brigance's beach ideas
Vogue
December 1951
Photograph by
Horst P. Horst

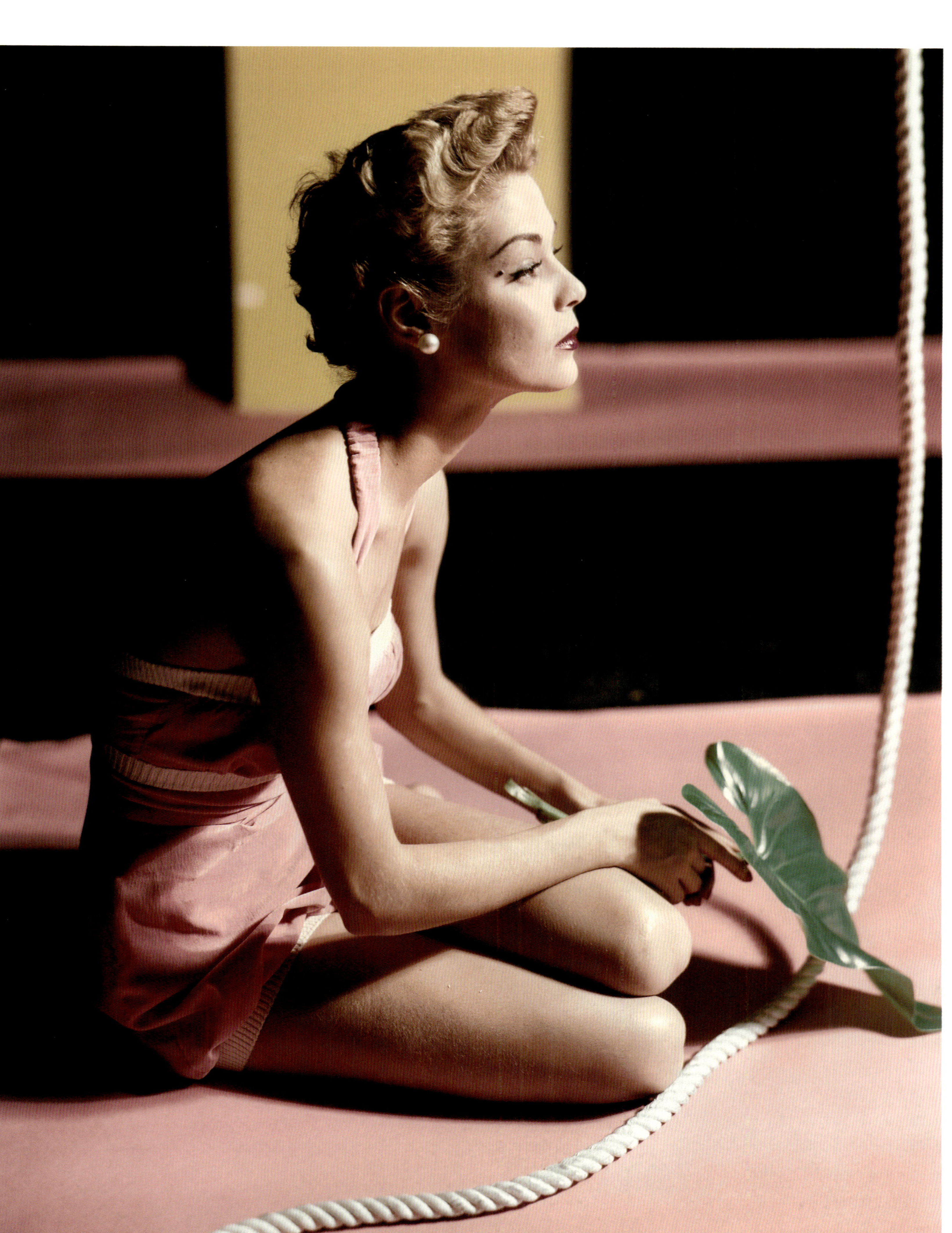

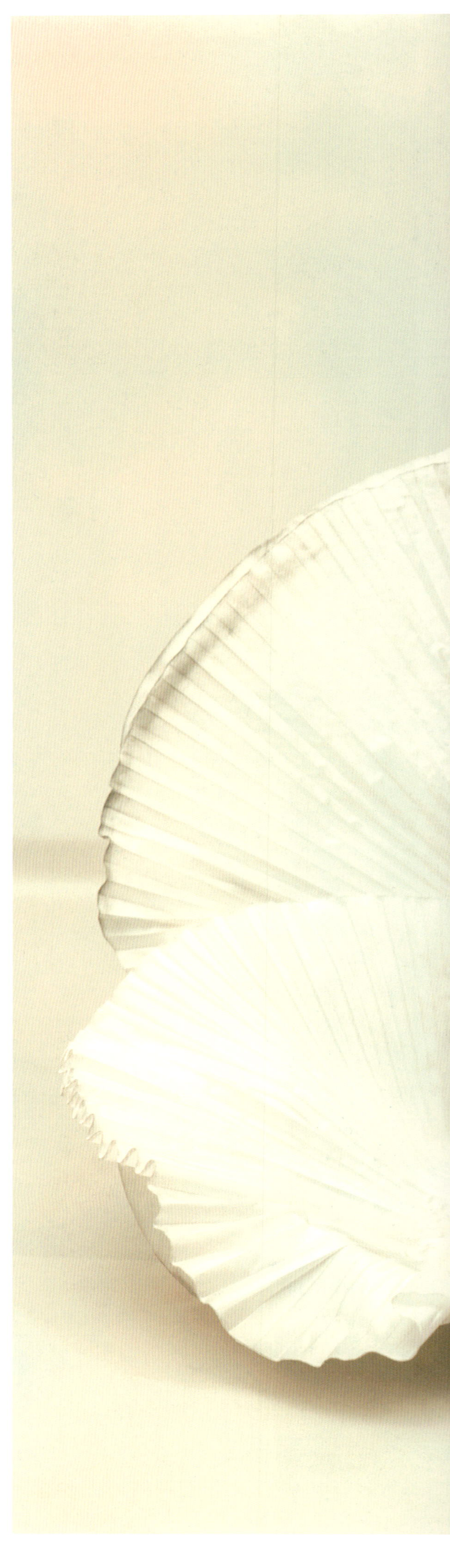

British Vogue
May 1950
Gown by Dior
Photograph by
Norman Parkinson

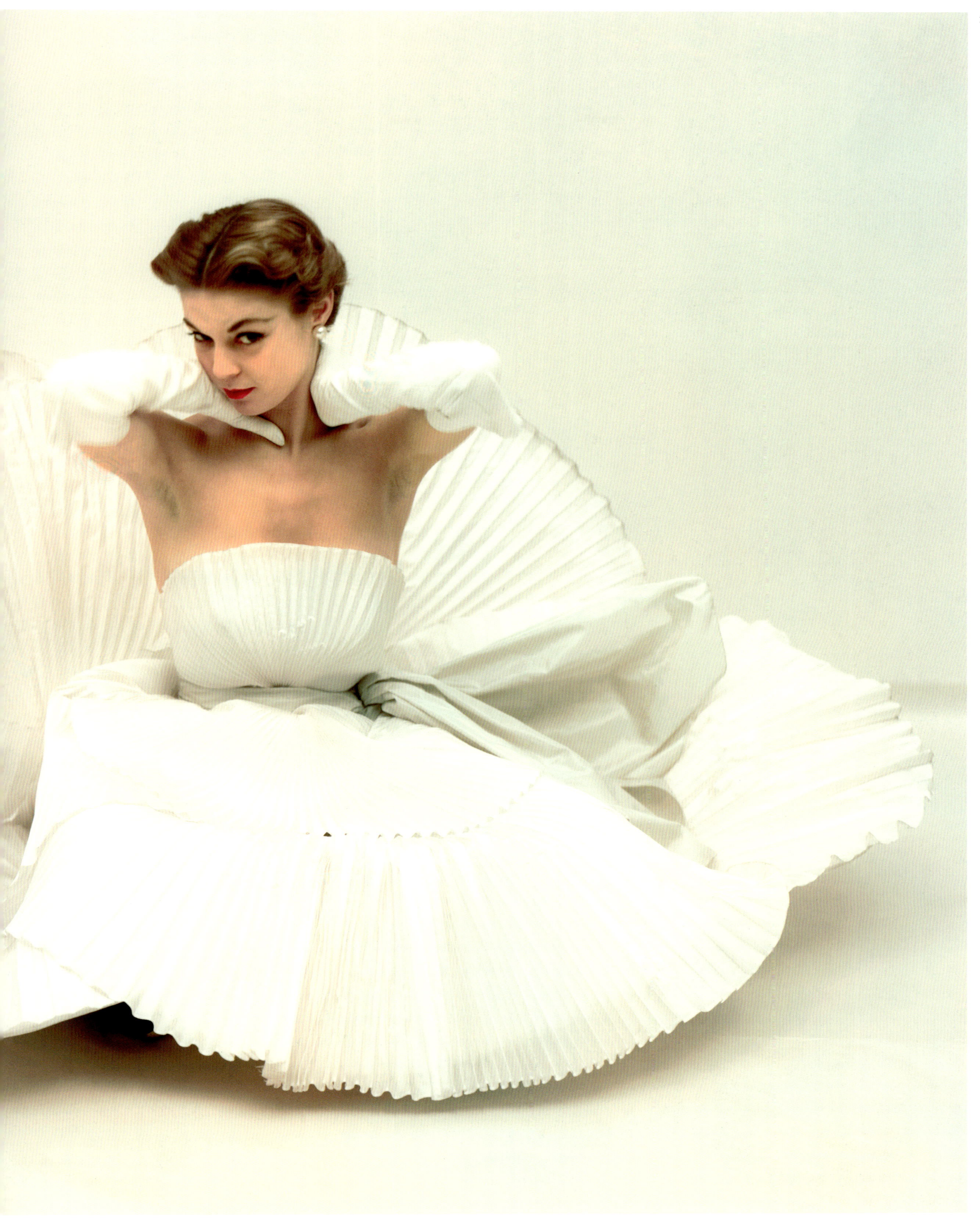

How to Make a Suit
Glamour
February 1951
Photograph by
Clifford Coffin

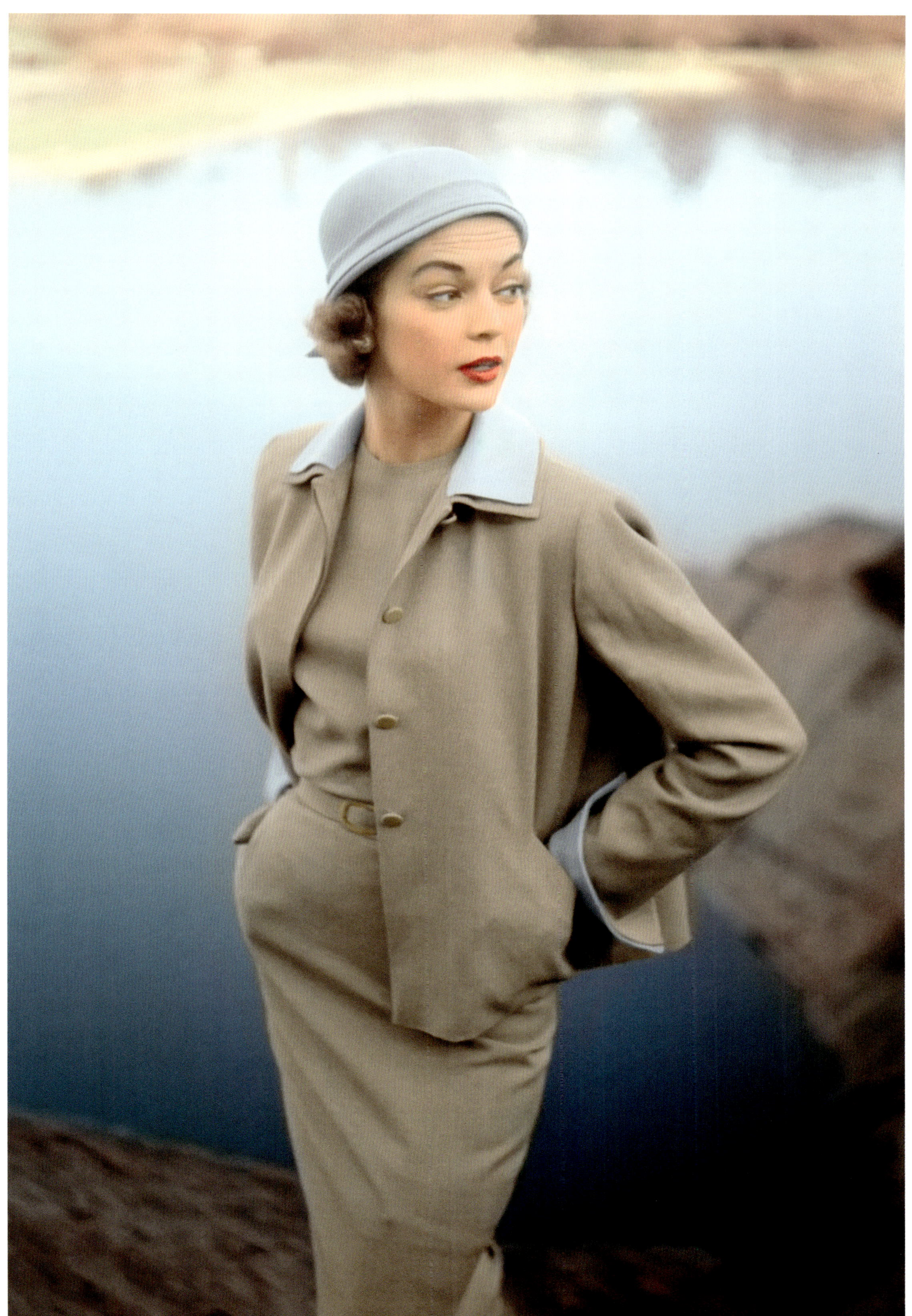

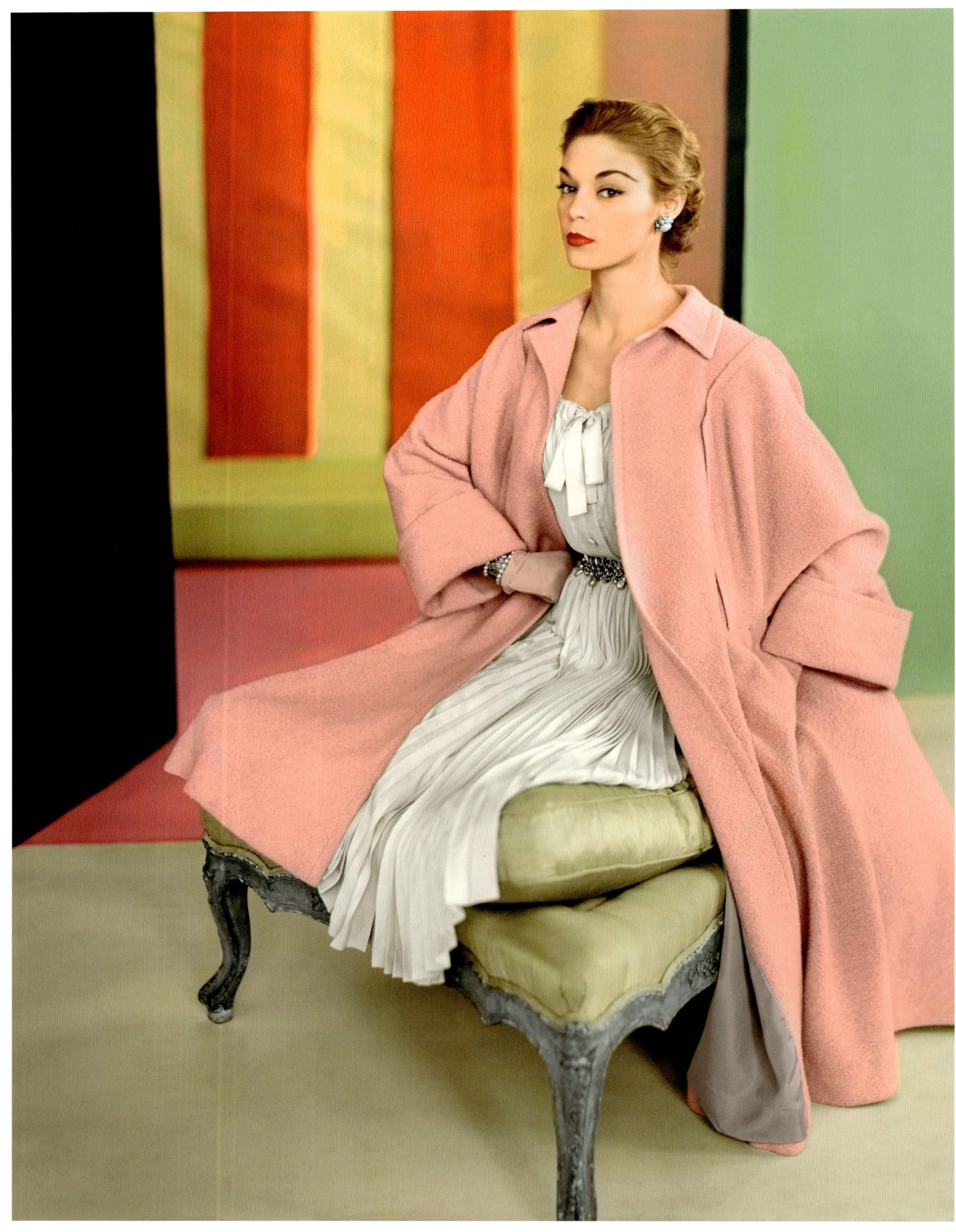

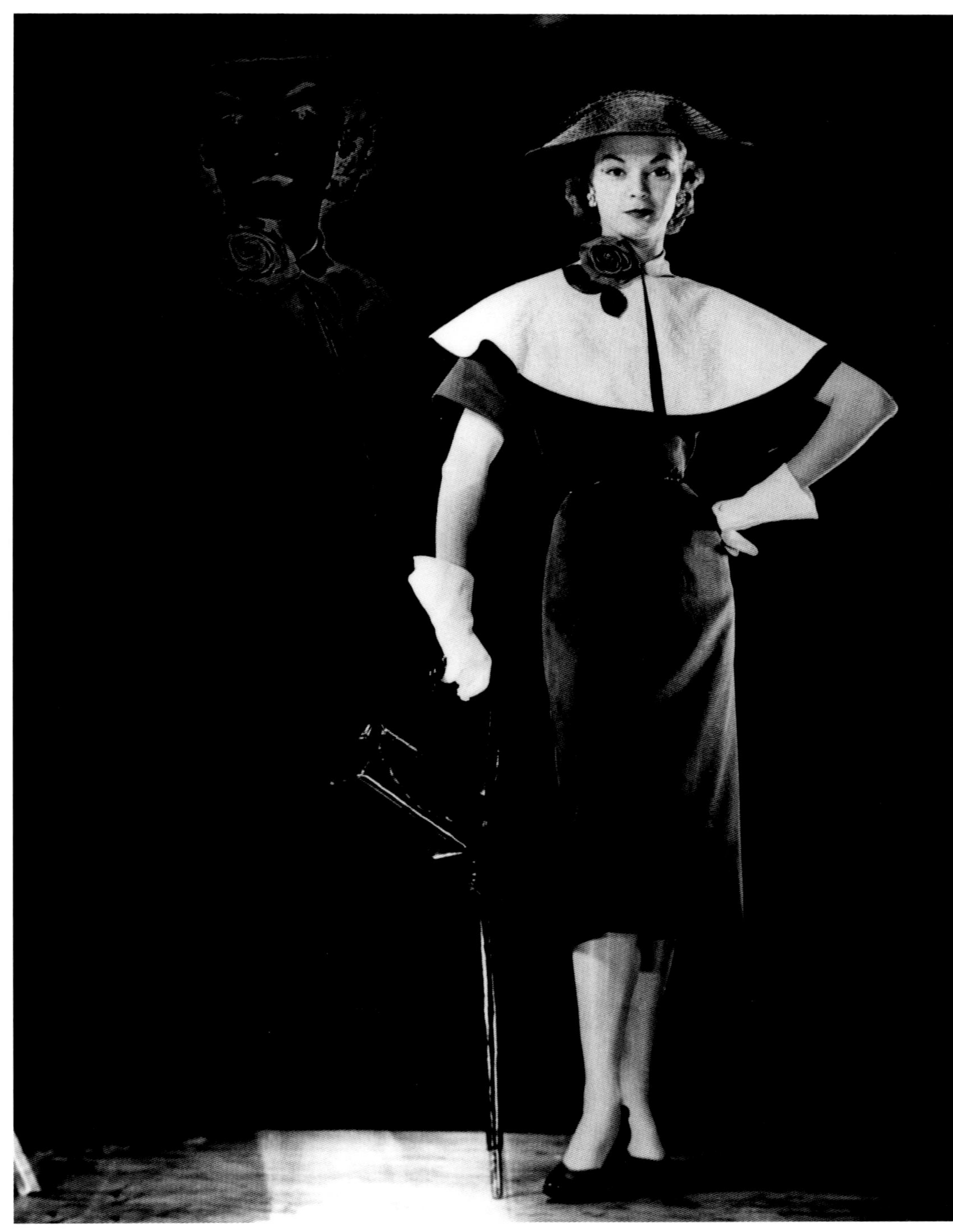

Above:
Advertising Photograph
for Saks Fifth Avenue
Circa 1951
Photograph by Gjon Mili

Opposite:
The Pink Coat South
Vogue
January 1952
Dress by Mollie Parnis
Photograph by
Horst P. Horst

New Bloom: New Pinks
Vogue
May 15, 1950
Photograph by
John Rawlings

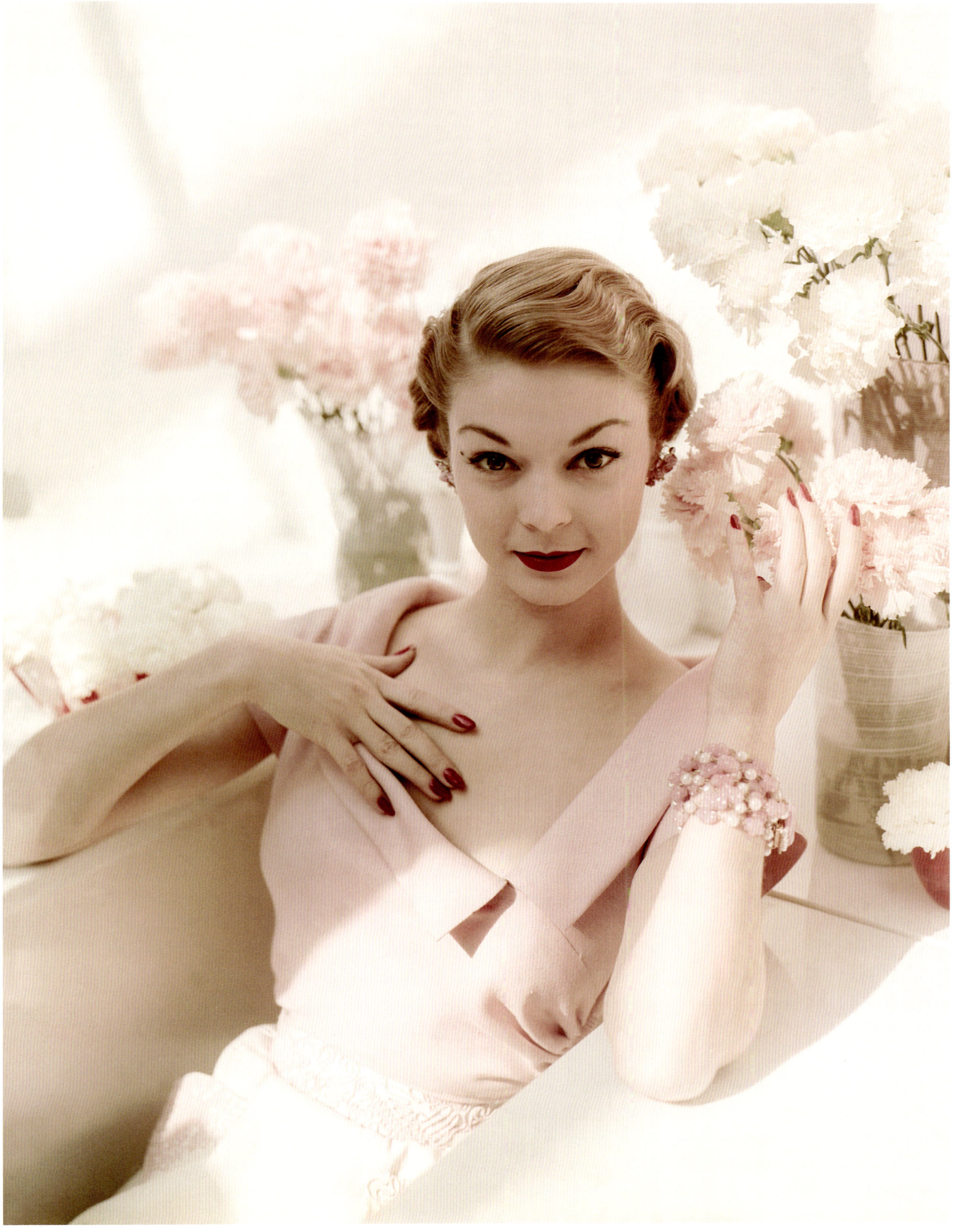

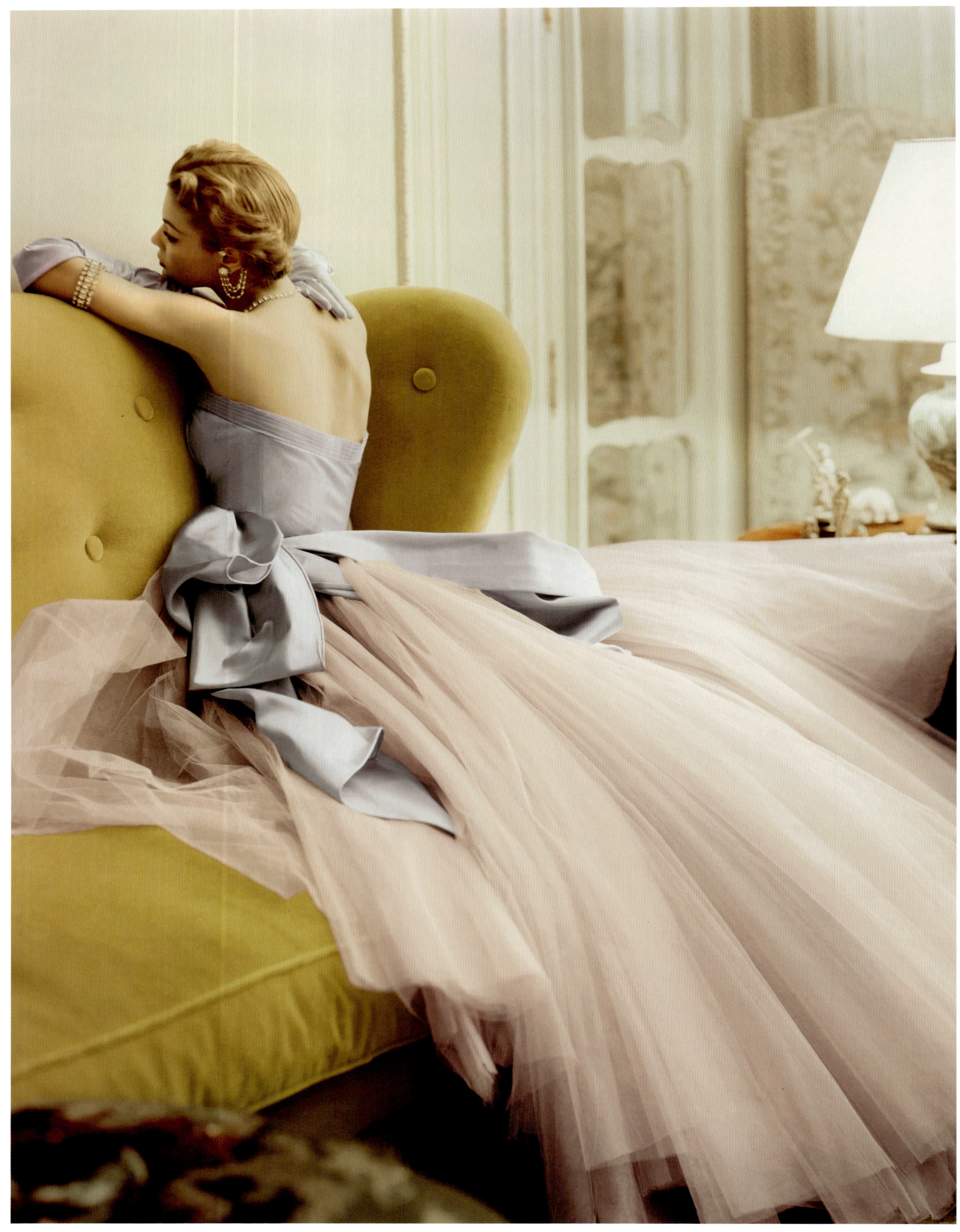

Paris Spectaculars
Vogue
April 1, 1950
Evening gown by
Jean Dessès
Photograph by
Norman Parkinson

Circa 1950
Photograph by
Norman Parkinson

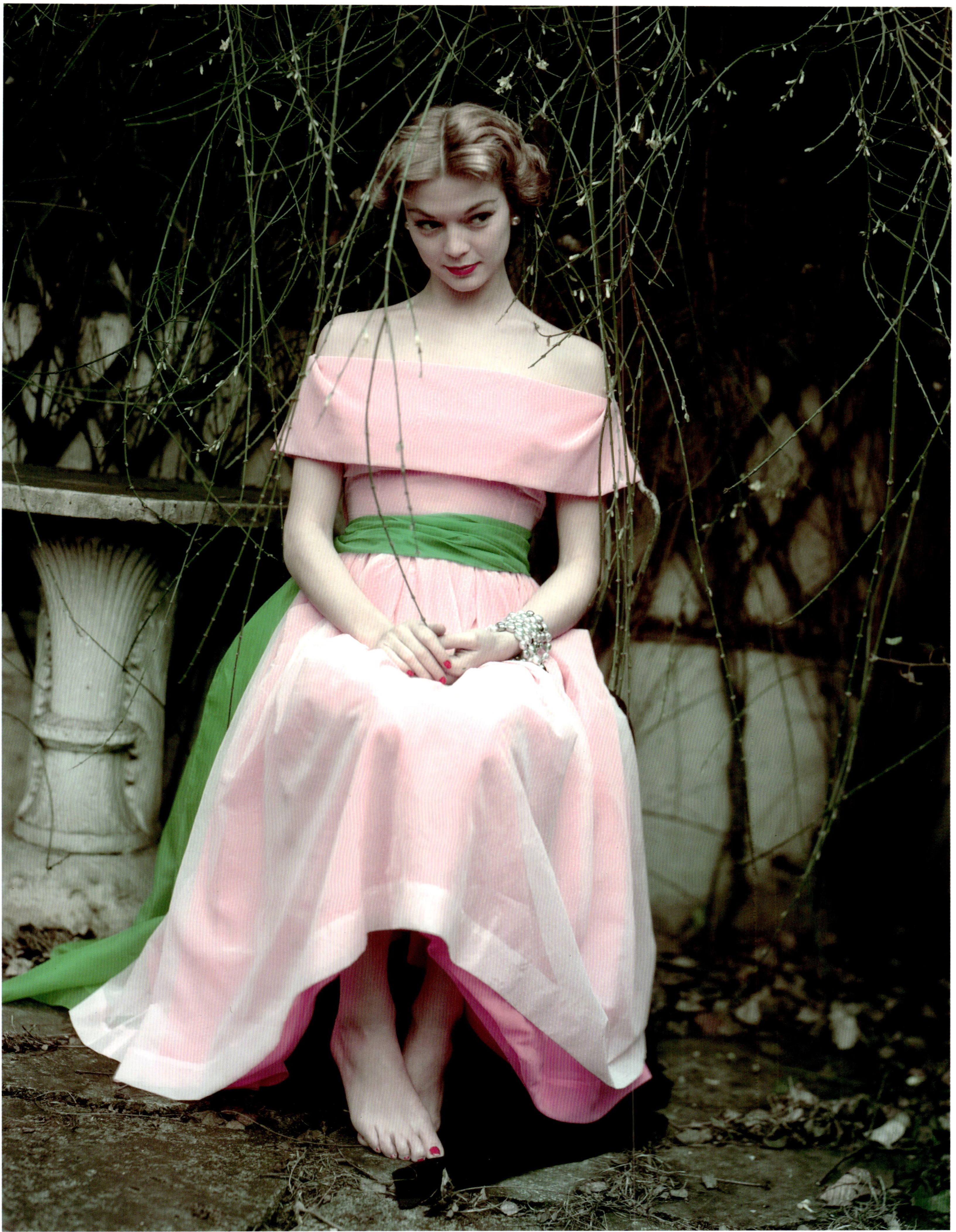

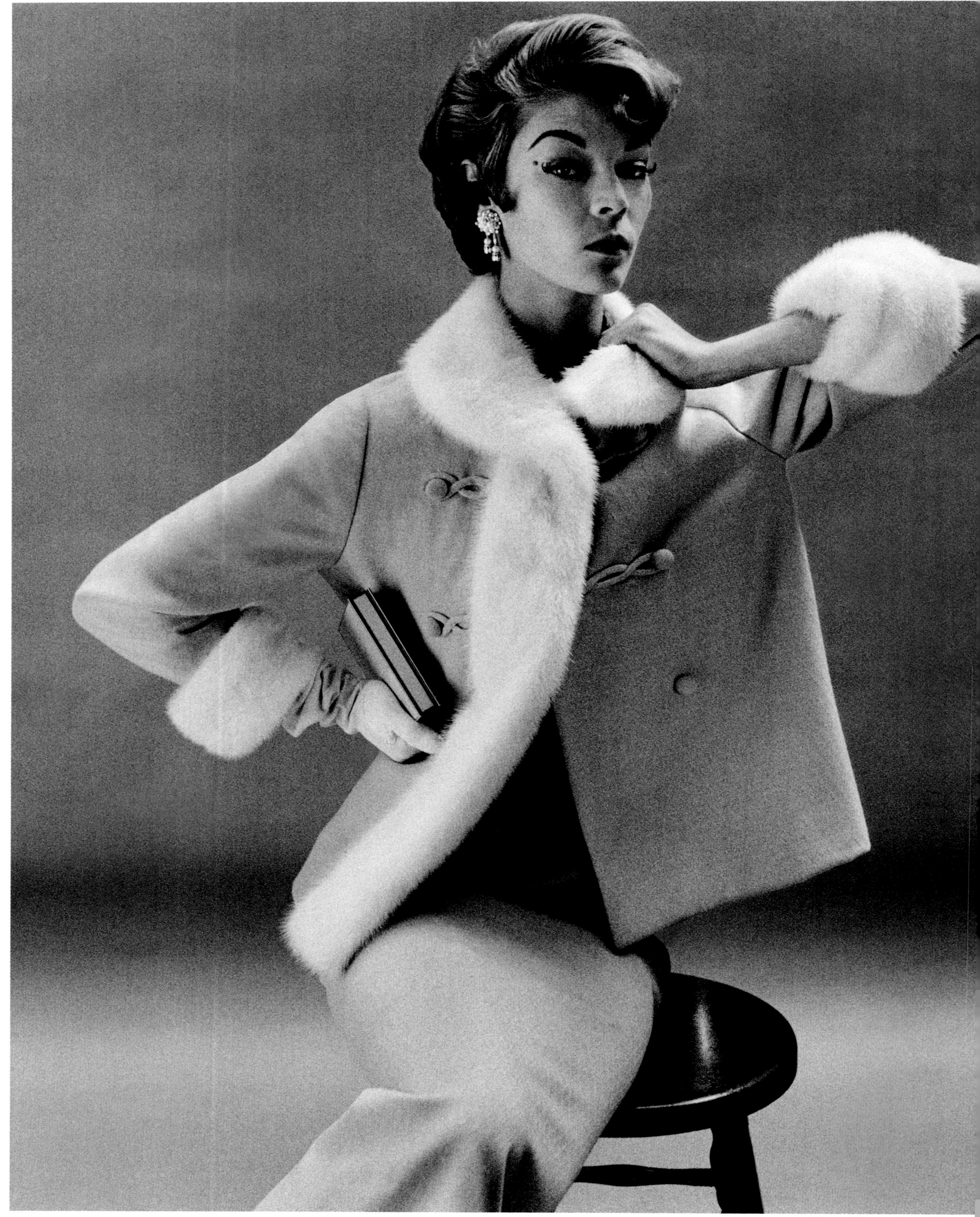

Suit by Mainbocher
Harper's Bazaar
January 1, 1952
Photograph by
Richard Avedon

Ad for Bergdorf Goodman
May 26, 1951
Photograph by
Richard Avedon

Heavenly Homebody–Exclusive

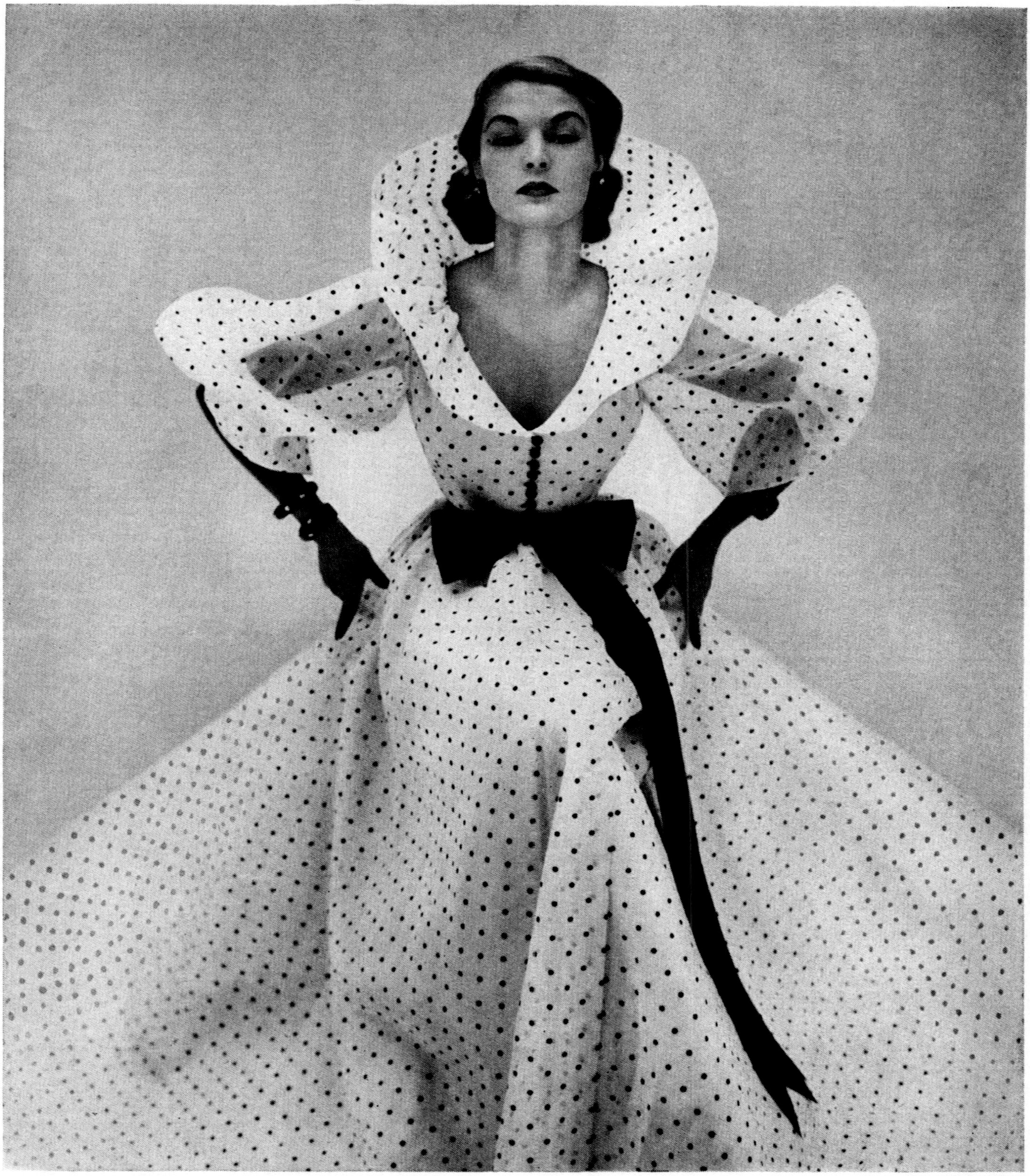

RICHARD AVEDON

Angels will entertain "at home" this summer in our cloud-drift of organdy with airborne sleeves.
White dotted, buttoned and bowed and sashed with black velvet, sizes 10 to 18, $40
A short version (just as angelic with its collarless, heart-neckline) in sizes 10 to 16, is $35

In our Beautiful New Negligée Salon *Second Floor*

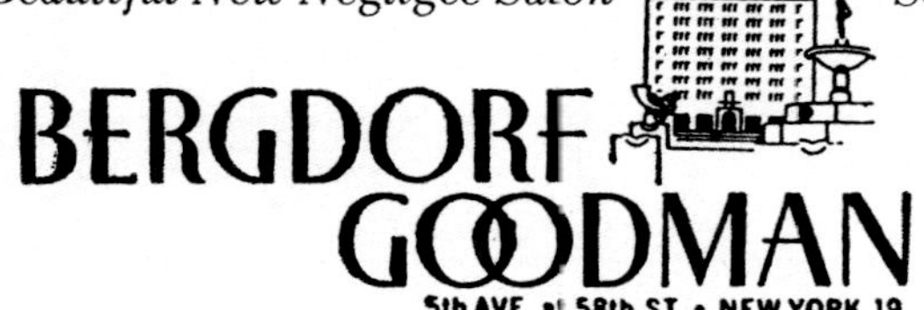

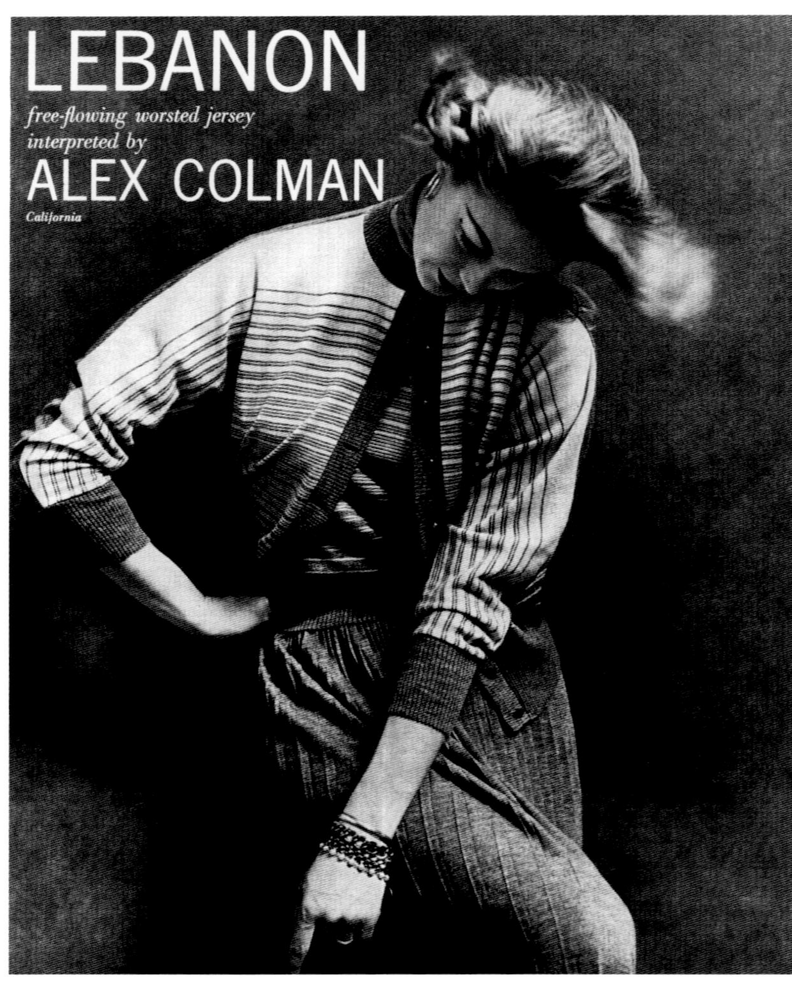

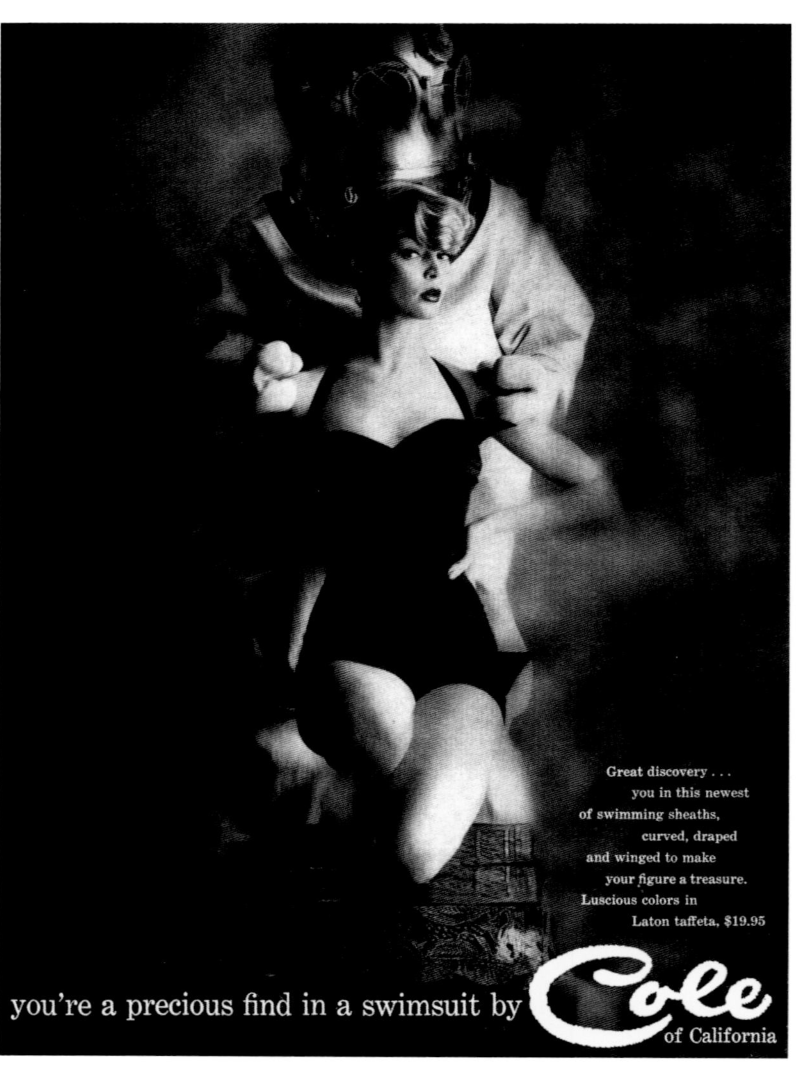

This page, from top:
Ad for Lebanon
for Alex Colman
1952

Ad for Cole of California
1954
Photograph by
William Helburn

Opposite:
Ad for Sag-No-Mor
by Wyner
1952
Photograph by
Maria Martell

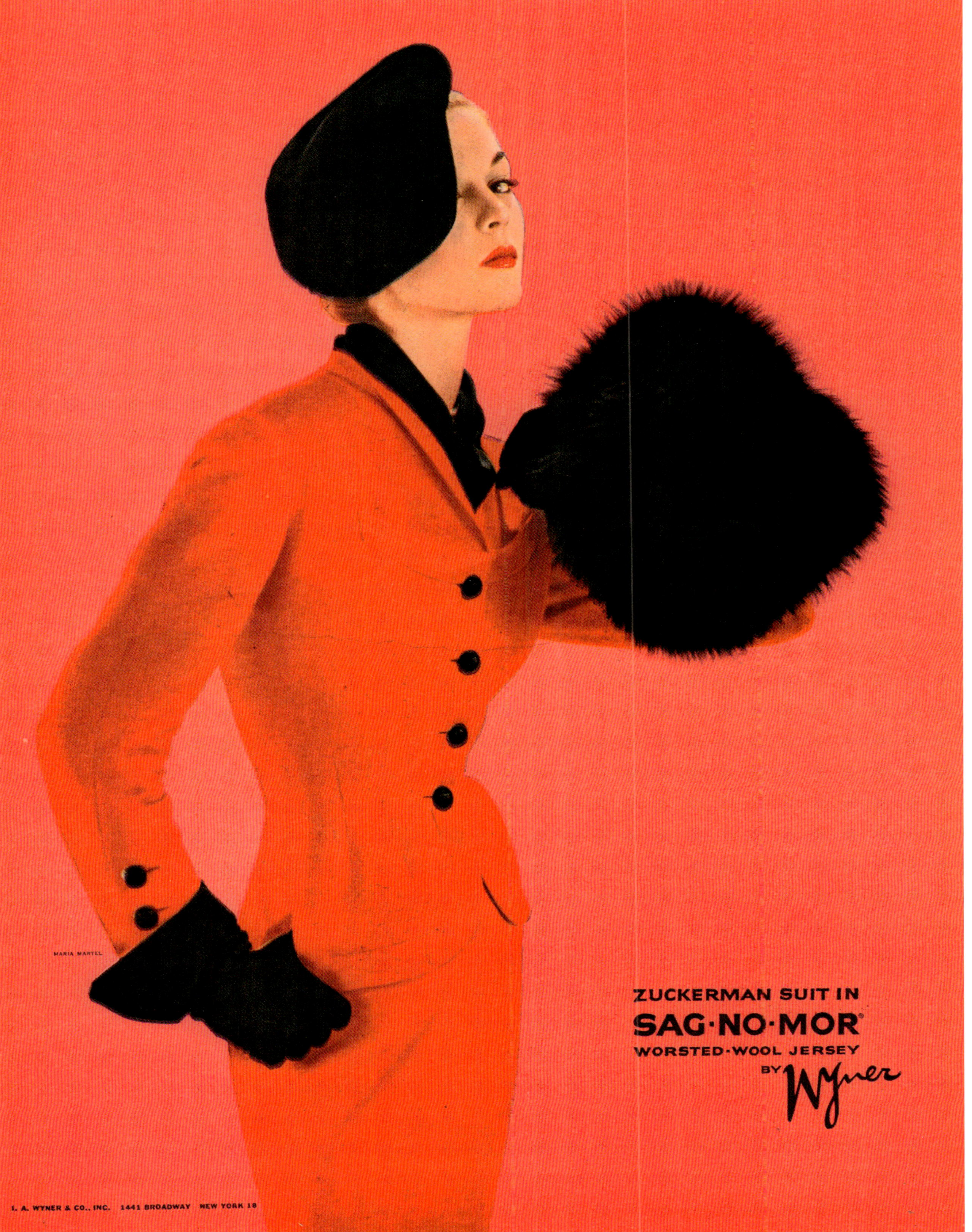
MARIA MARTEL
ZUCKERMAN SUIT IN
SAG·NO·MOR®
WORSTED-WOOL JERSEY
BY Wyner
I. A. WYNER & CO., INC. 1441 BROADWAY NEW YORK 18

Look
October 1953
Bathing suit by Jantzen
Photograph by
Milton H. Greene

Photograph by Milton H. Greene. © 2019 Joshua Greene. www.archiveimages.com

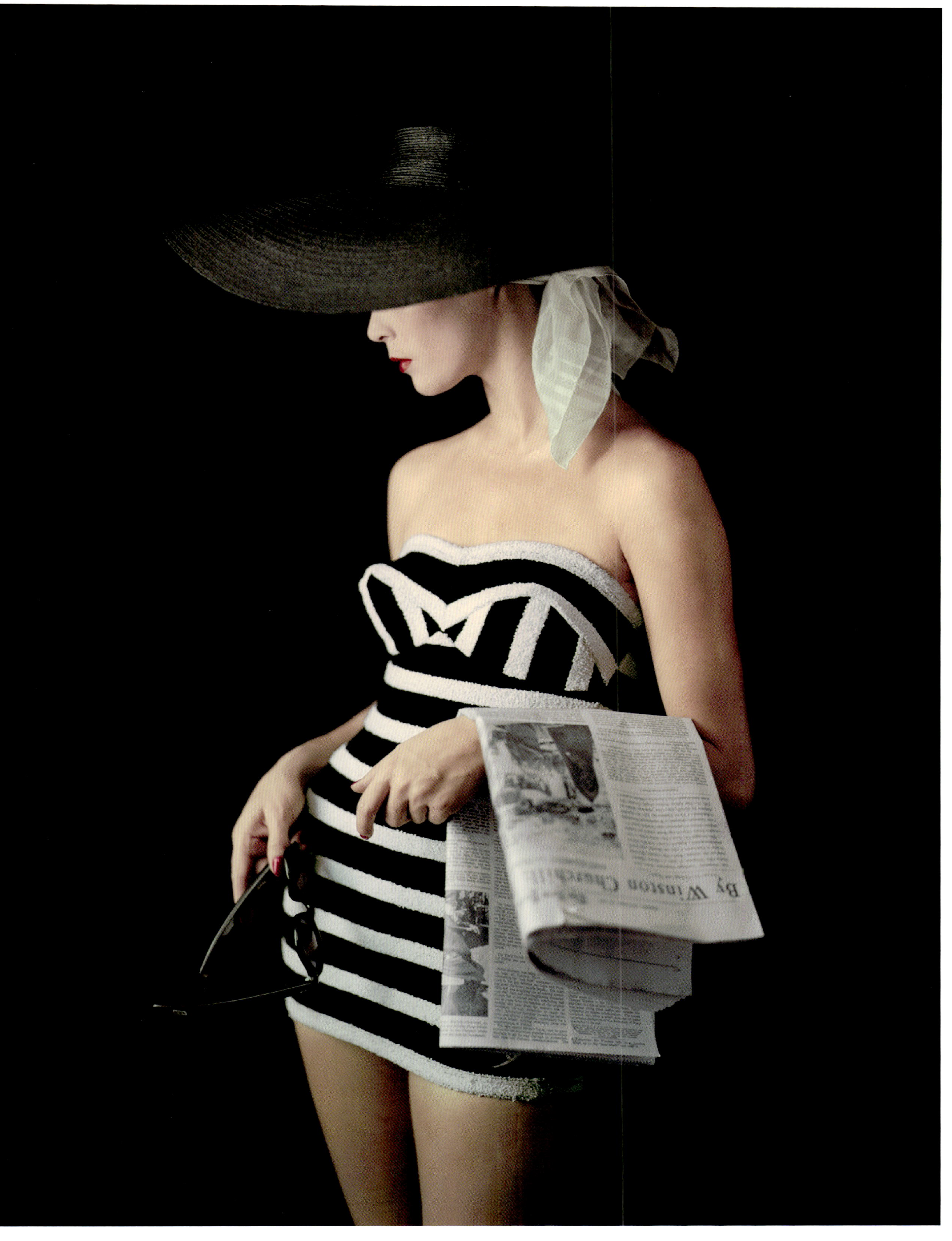
By Winston Churchill

Summer fashion indispensables
Vogue
June 1, 1954
Photograph by Irving Penn

Harper's Bazaar
June 1953
Photograph by
Louise Dahl-Wolfe

Harper's

BAZAAR

June 1953

Incorporating Junior Bazaar

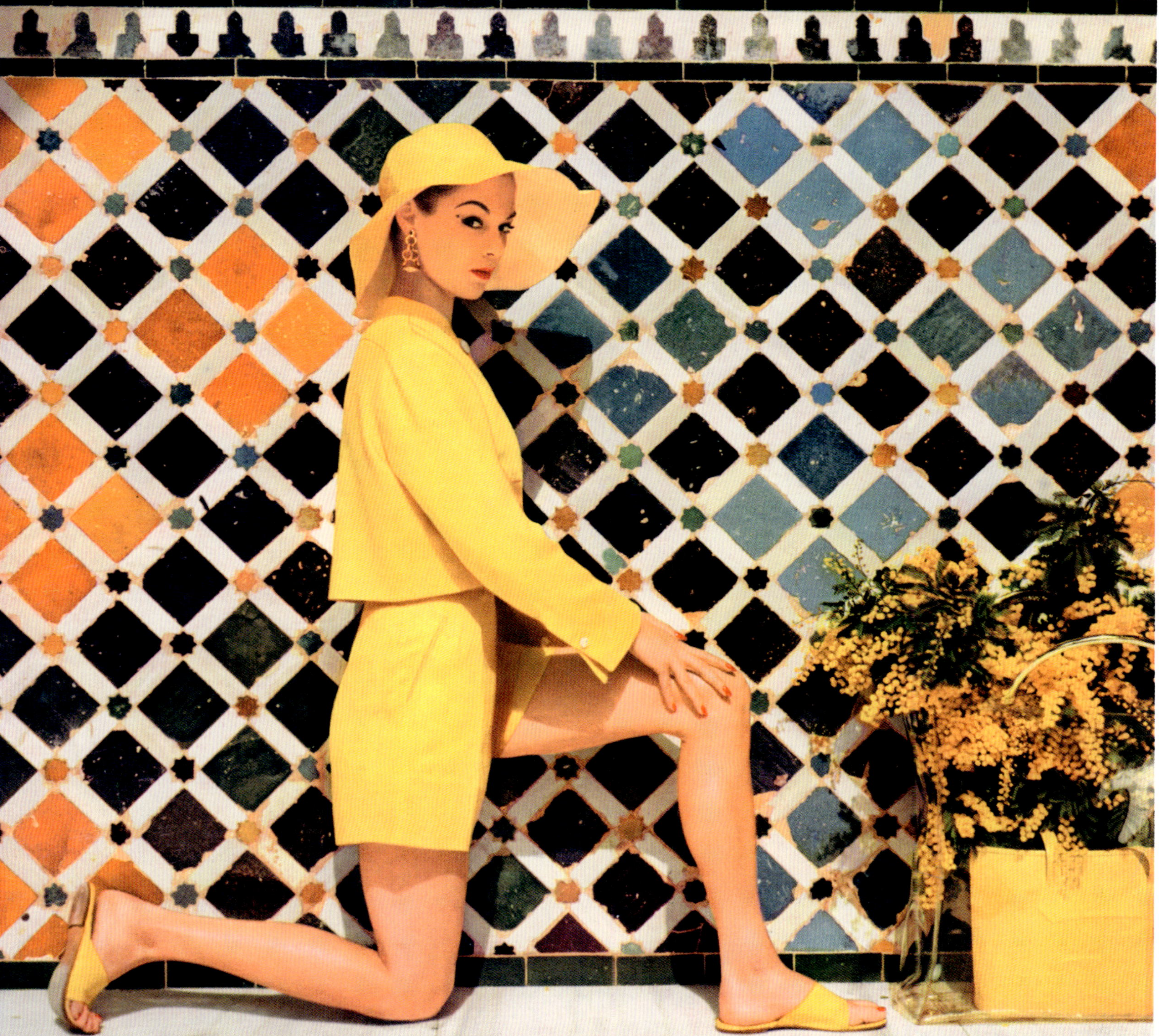

The Clothes for Summer Everywhere · Coronation in England

60 cents

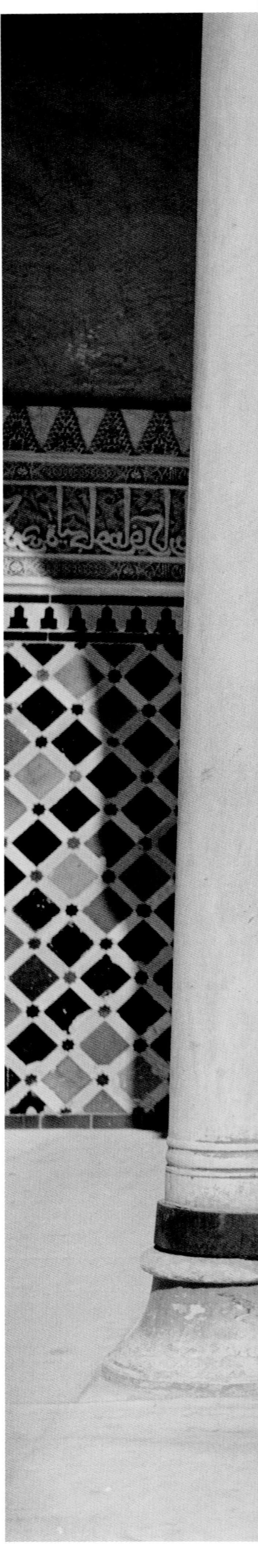

Cloths of 1953 in Granada
Harper's Bazaar
May 1953
Photograph by
Louise Dahl-Wolfe

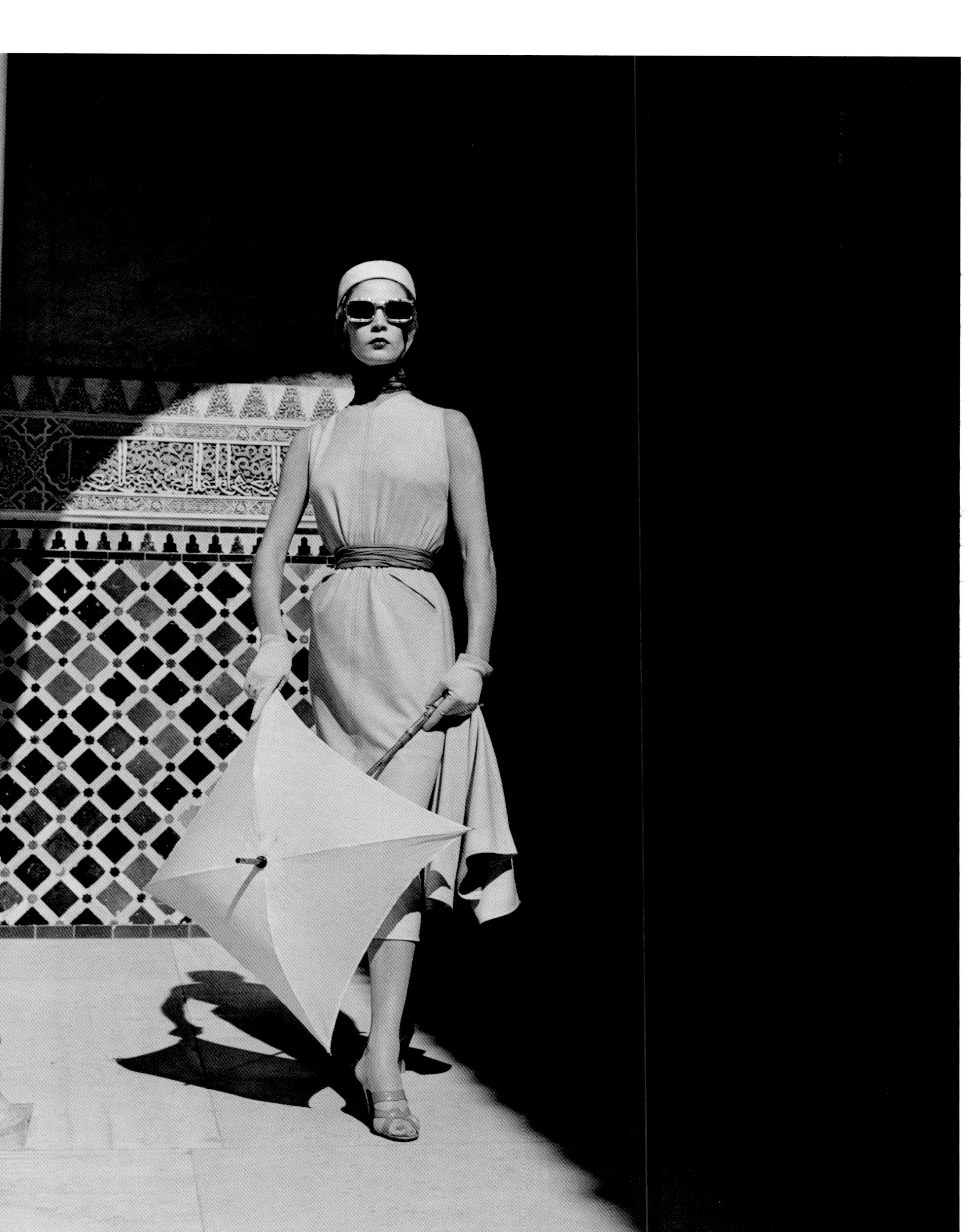

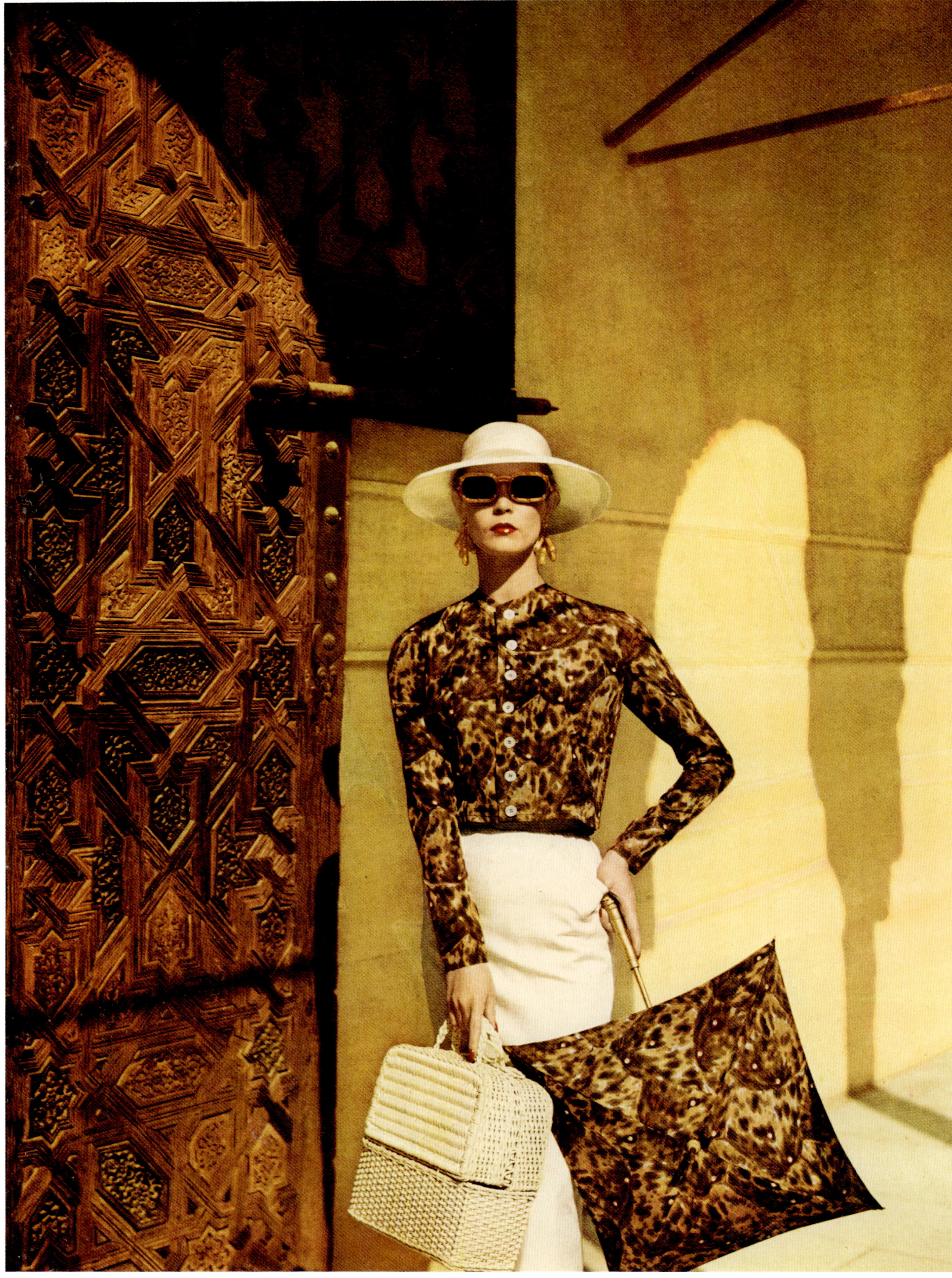

Light-and-Shadow color in Spanish Light
Harper's Bazaar
June 1953
Photograph by
Louise Dahl-Wolfe

Harper's Bazaar
January 1953
Photograph by
Louise Dahl-Wolfe

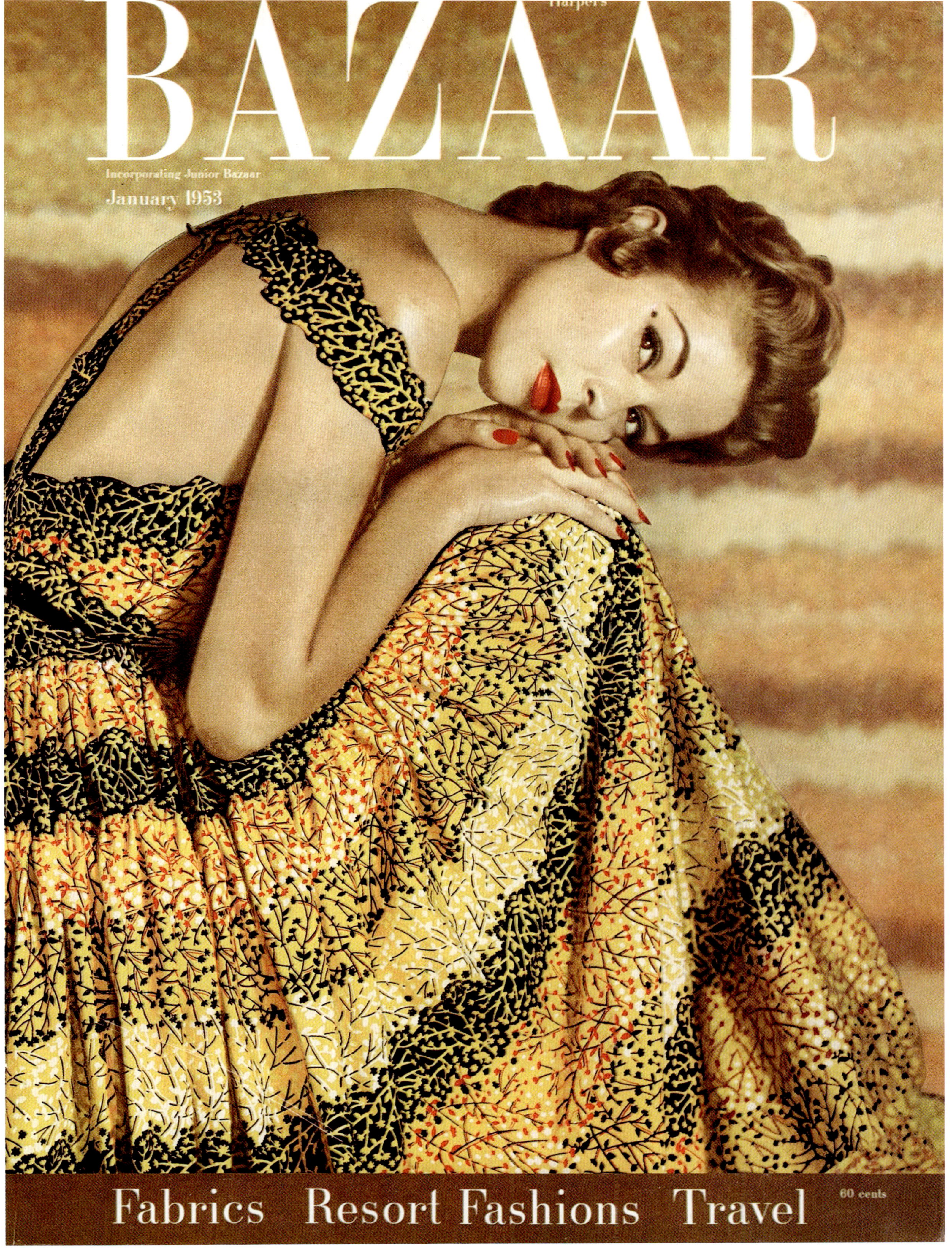
BAZAAR
Incorporating Junior Bazaar
January 1953
Fabrics Resort Fashions Travel
60 cents

Opposite:
American clothes, in the Sun and in the World
Harper's Bazaar
May 1953
Photograph by
Louise Dahl-Wolfe

Following spread, from left:
Summer in Your Glass
Harper's Bazaar
June 1953
Photograph by
Louise Dahl-Wolfe

The heel — Prettier When It's Pink
Harper's Bazaar
January 1953
Photograph by
Louise Dahl-Wolfe

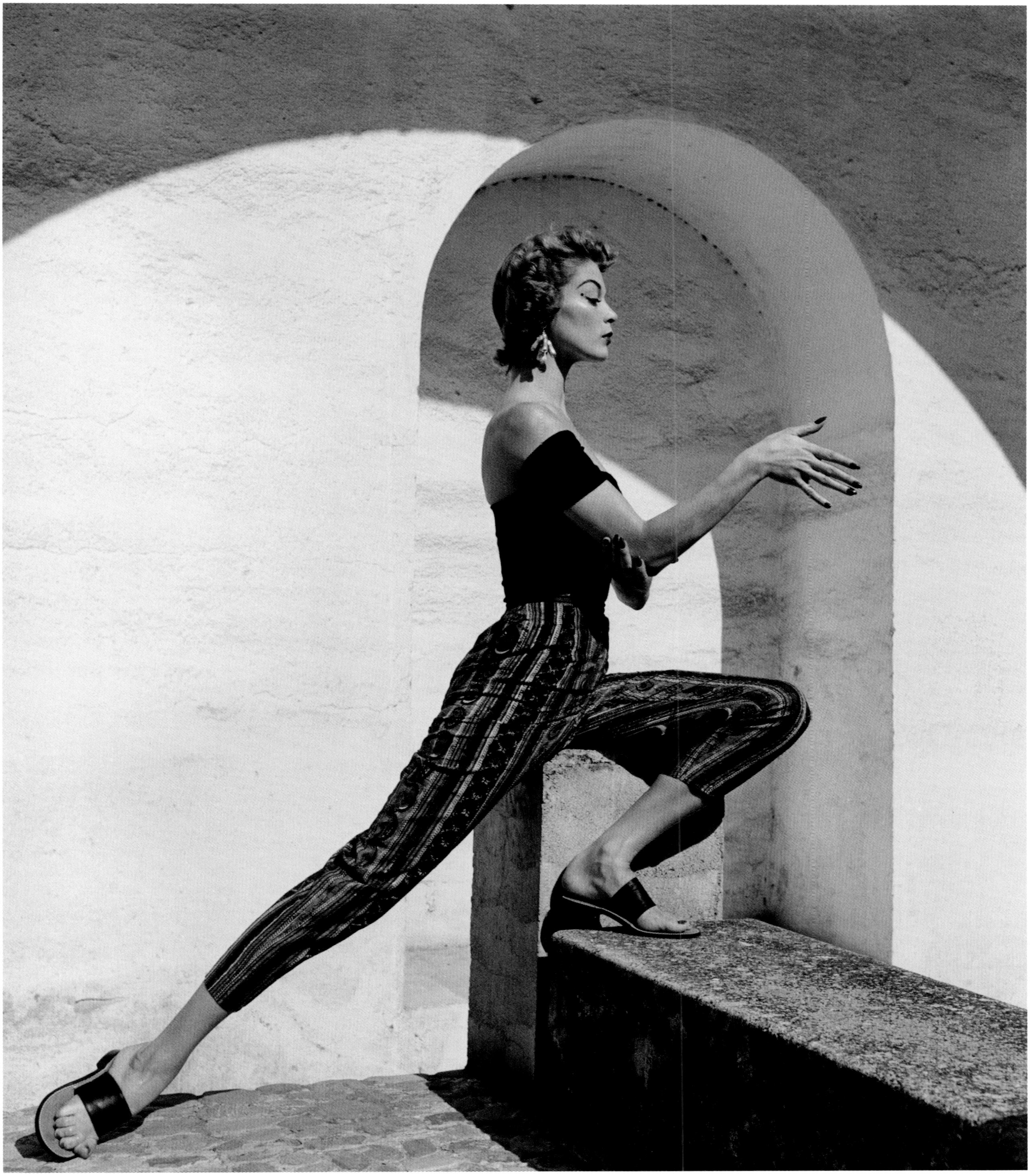

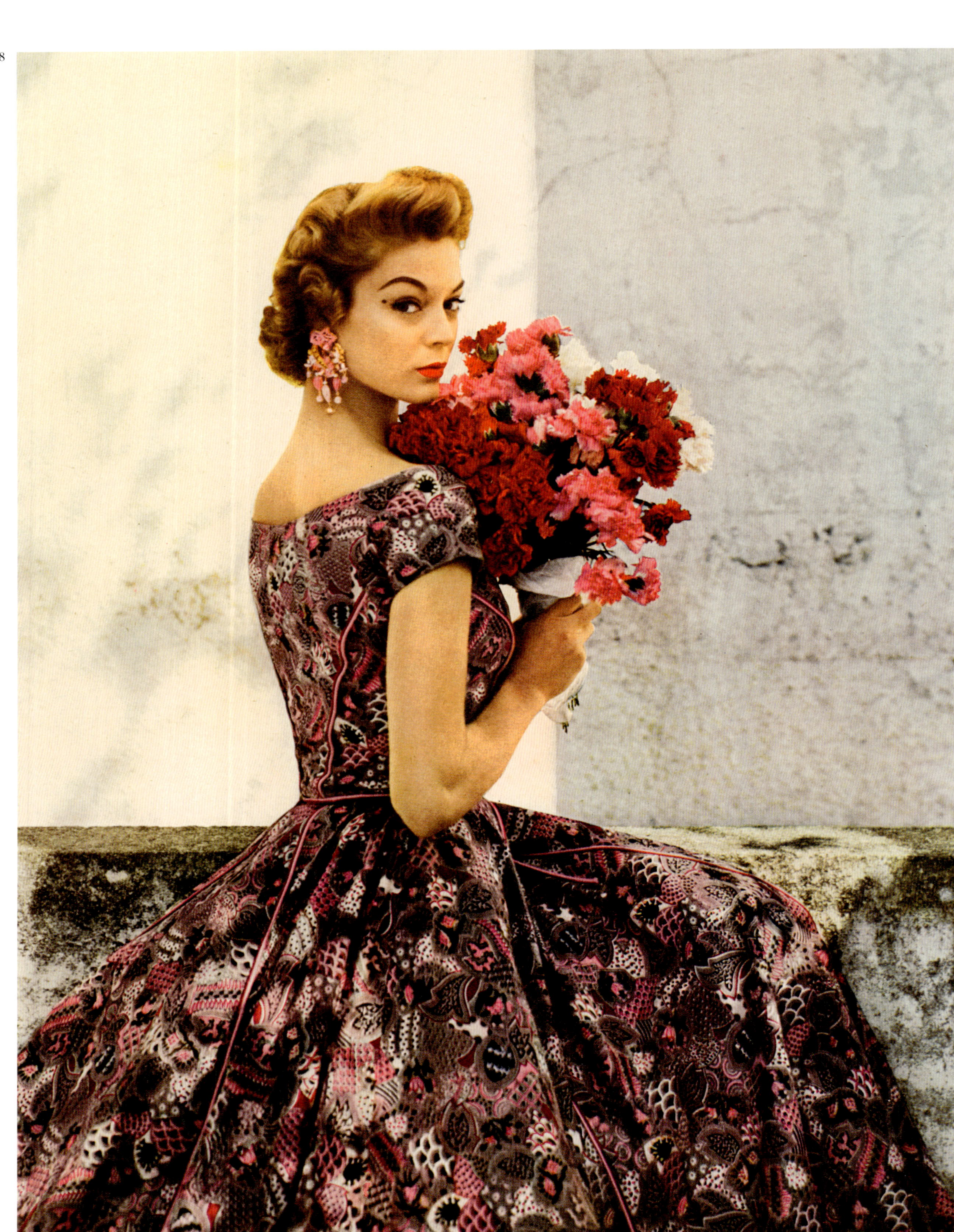

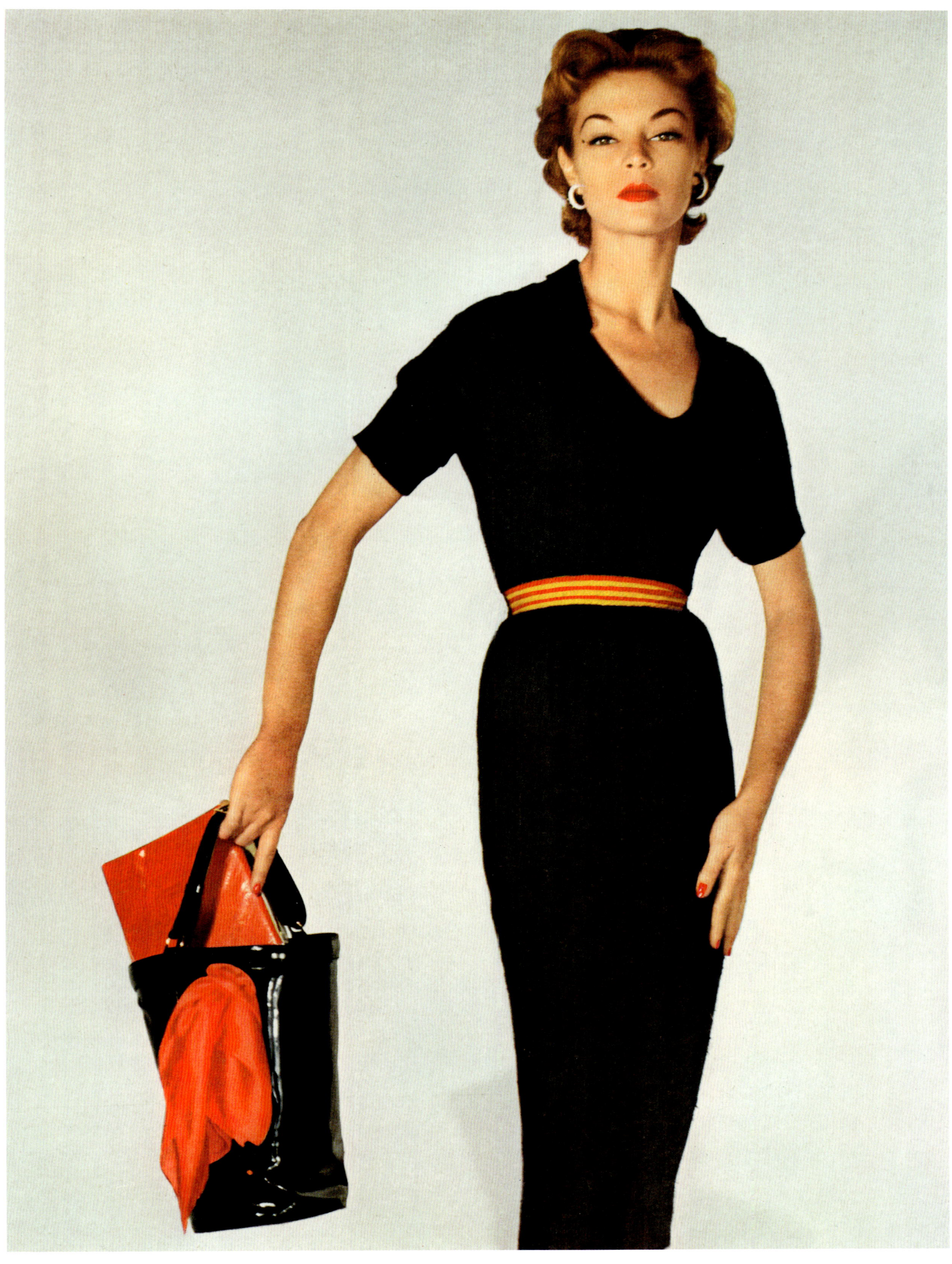

Advertising photograph for
Doyle Dane Bernbach
1954
Photograph by William Helburn

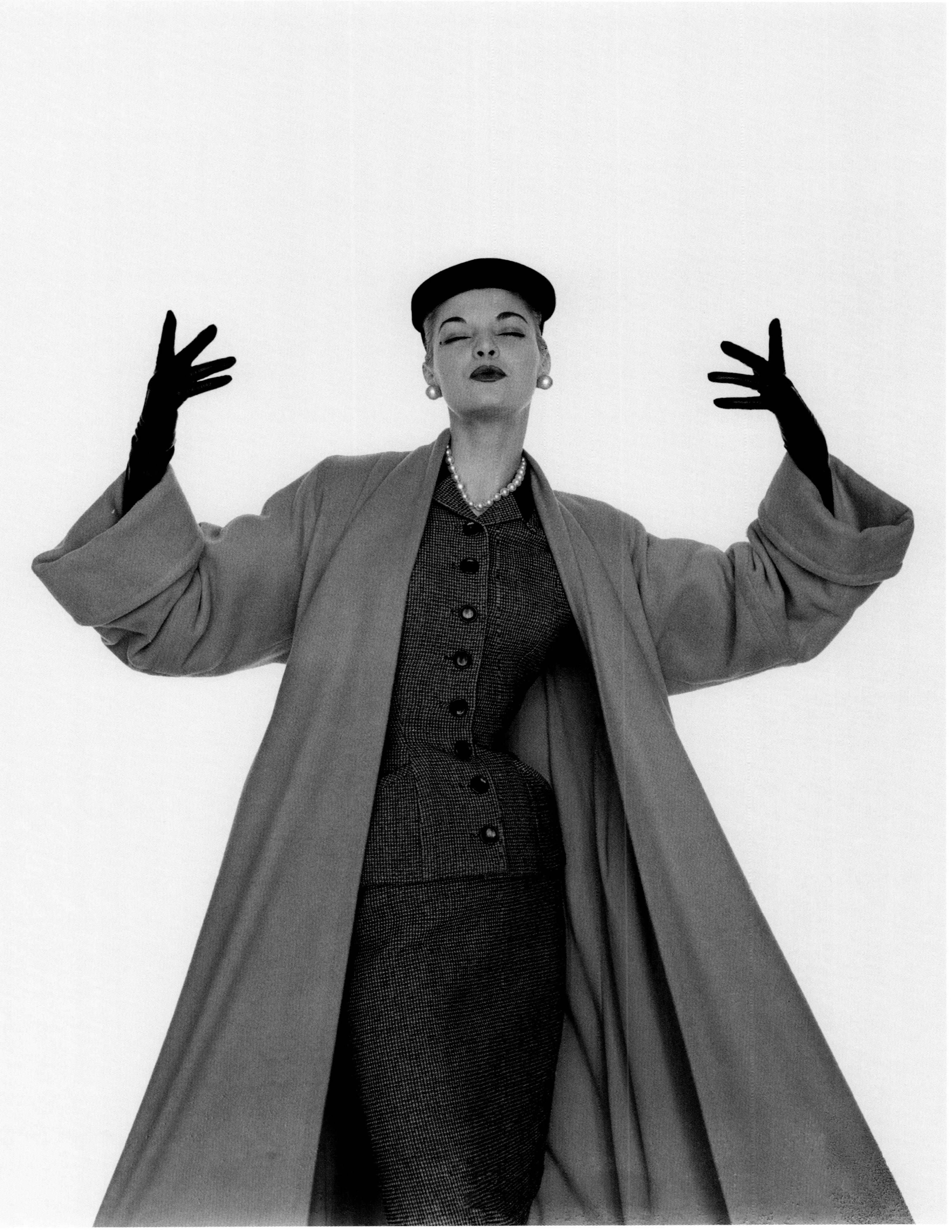

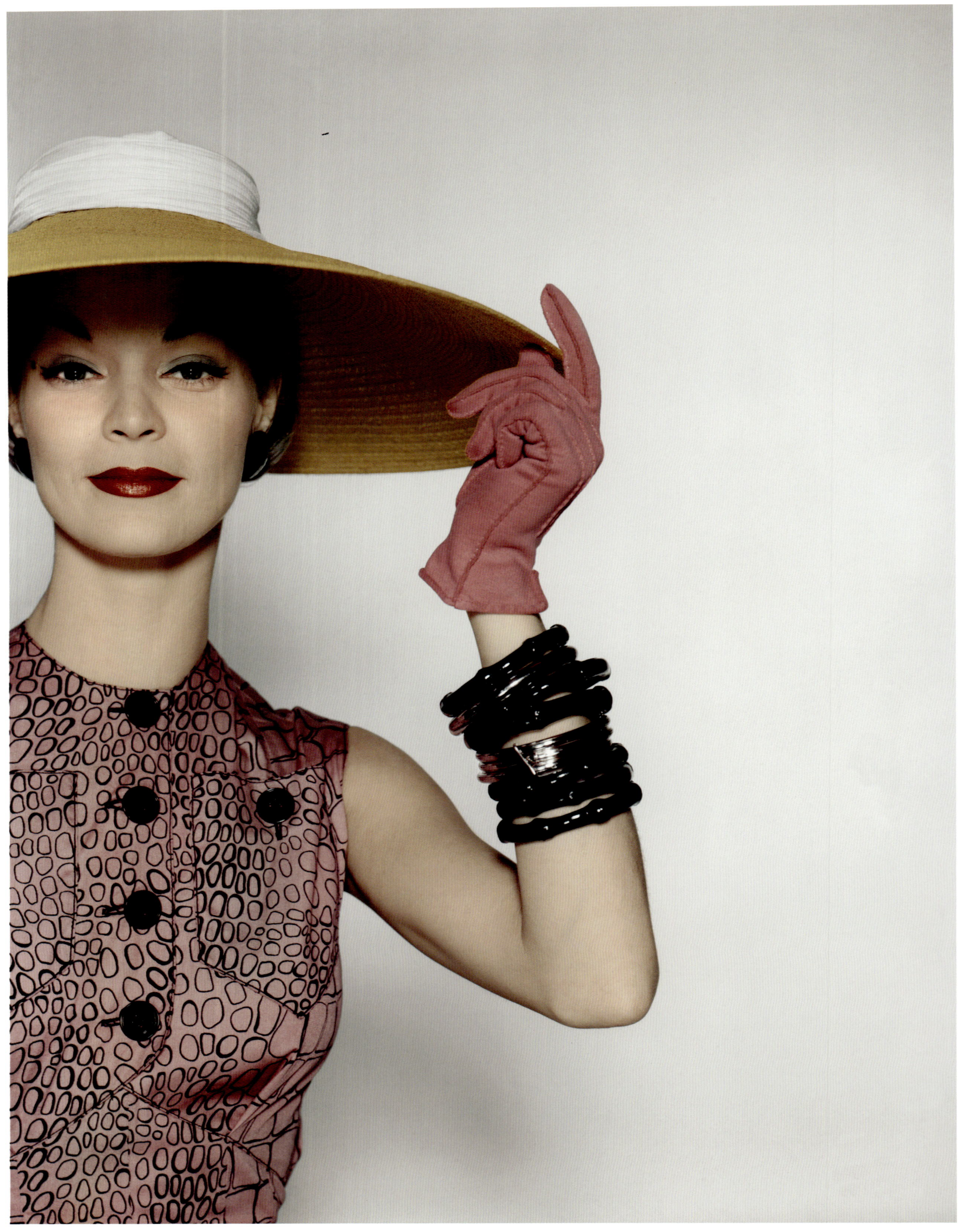

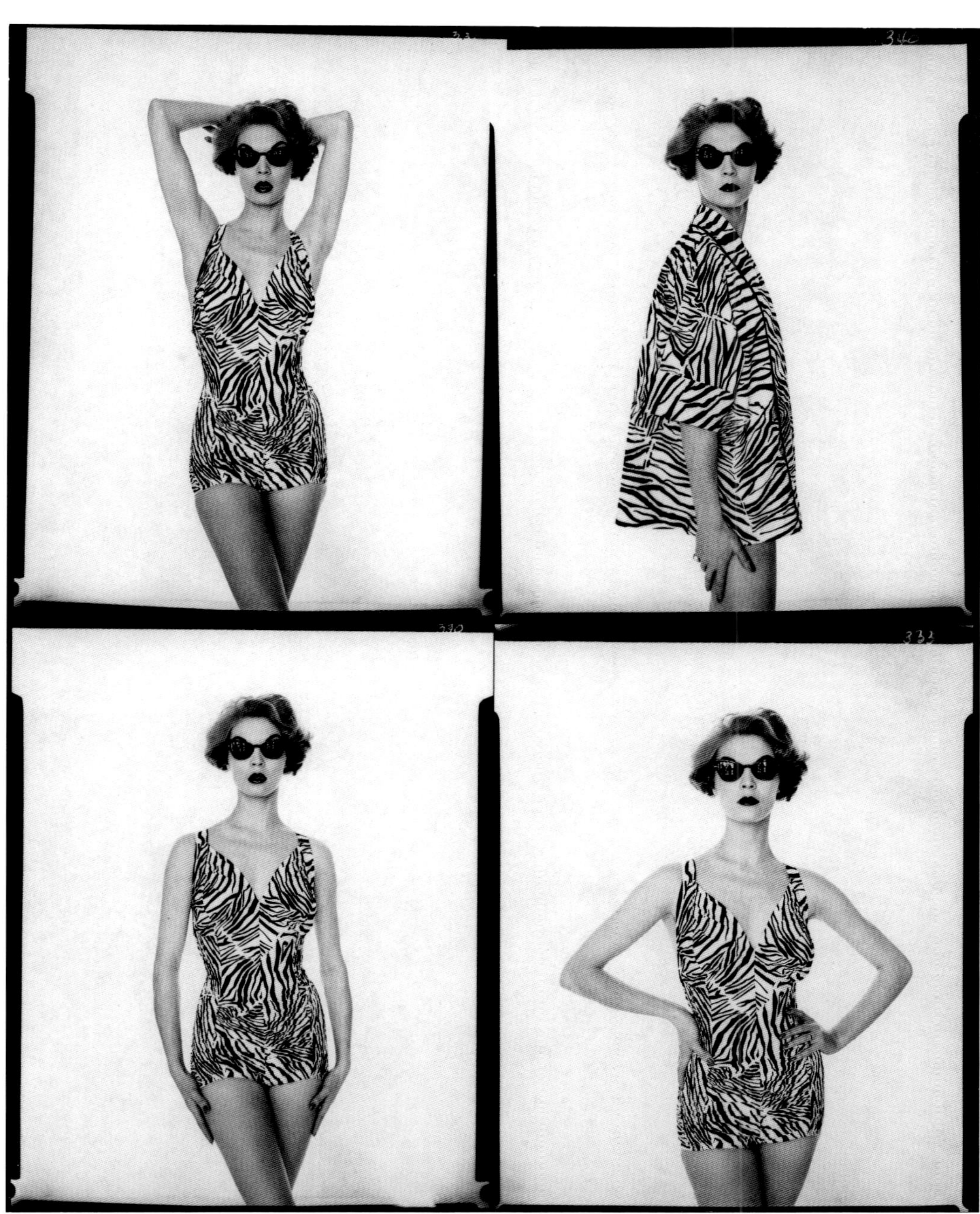

Above:
Advertising photographs for Cole of California
Contact sheet
1954
Photographs by
William Helburn

Opposite:
Vogue
Cover image variant
May 15, 1954
Photograph by
Erwin Blumenfeld

Following spread:
Ad for "Kissing Pink" by Revlon
Vogue
June 1954
Photograph by
Richard Avedon

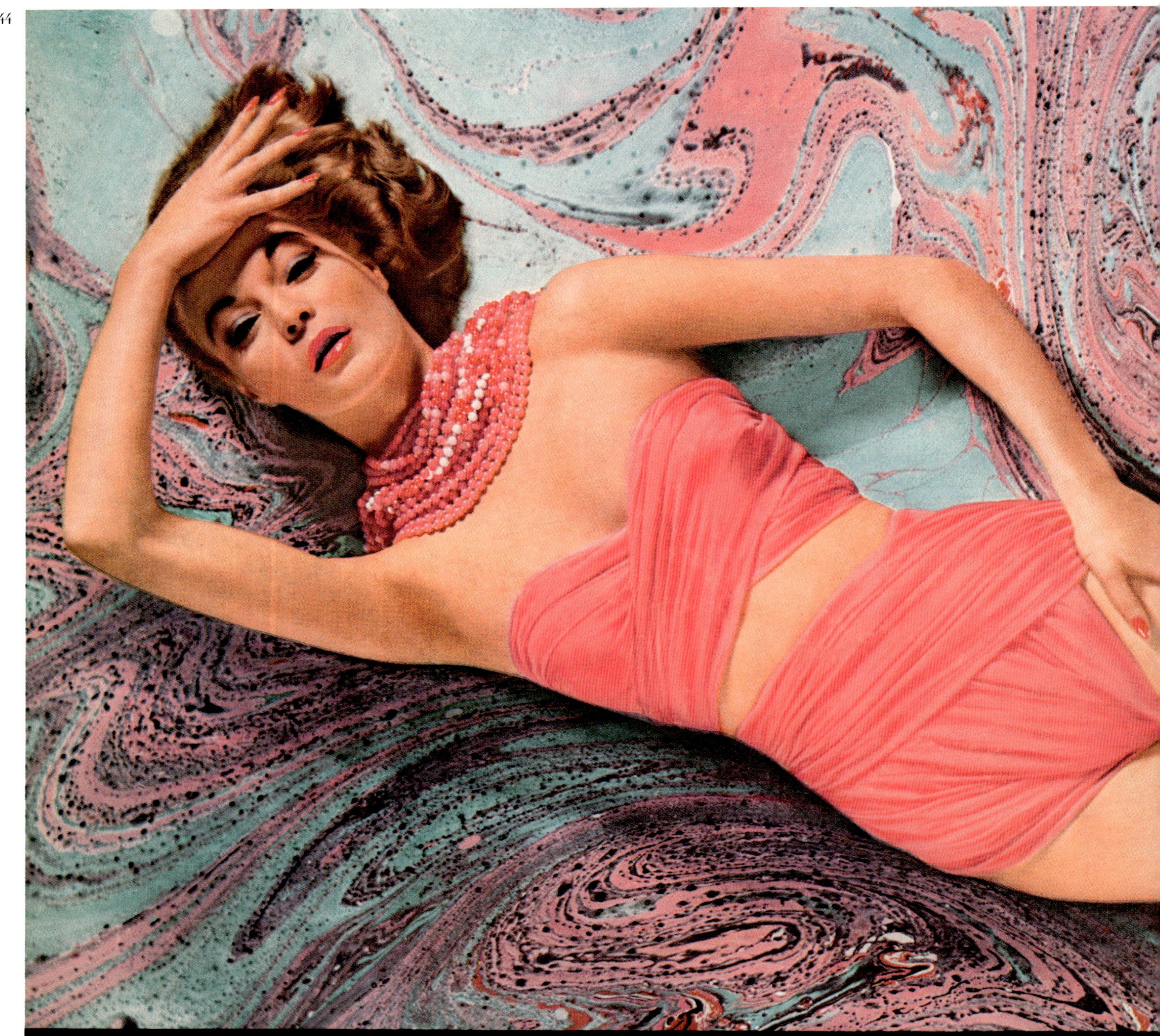

If the kiss of your lifetime were captured in color...
this is the color that kiss would be!

Revlon's *new* 'Kissing Pink'

New color for lips and matching fingertips
in two terrific tones... one for day, one for night!

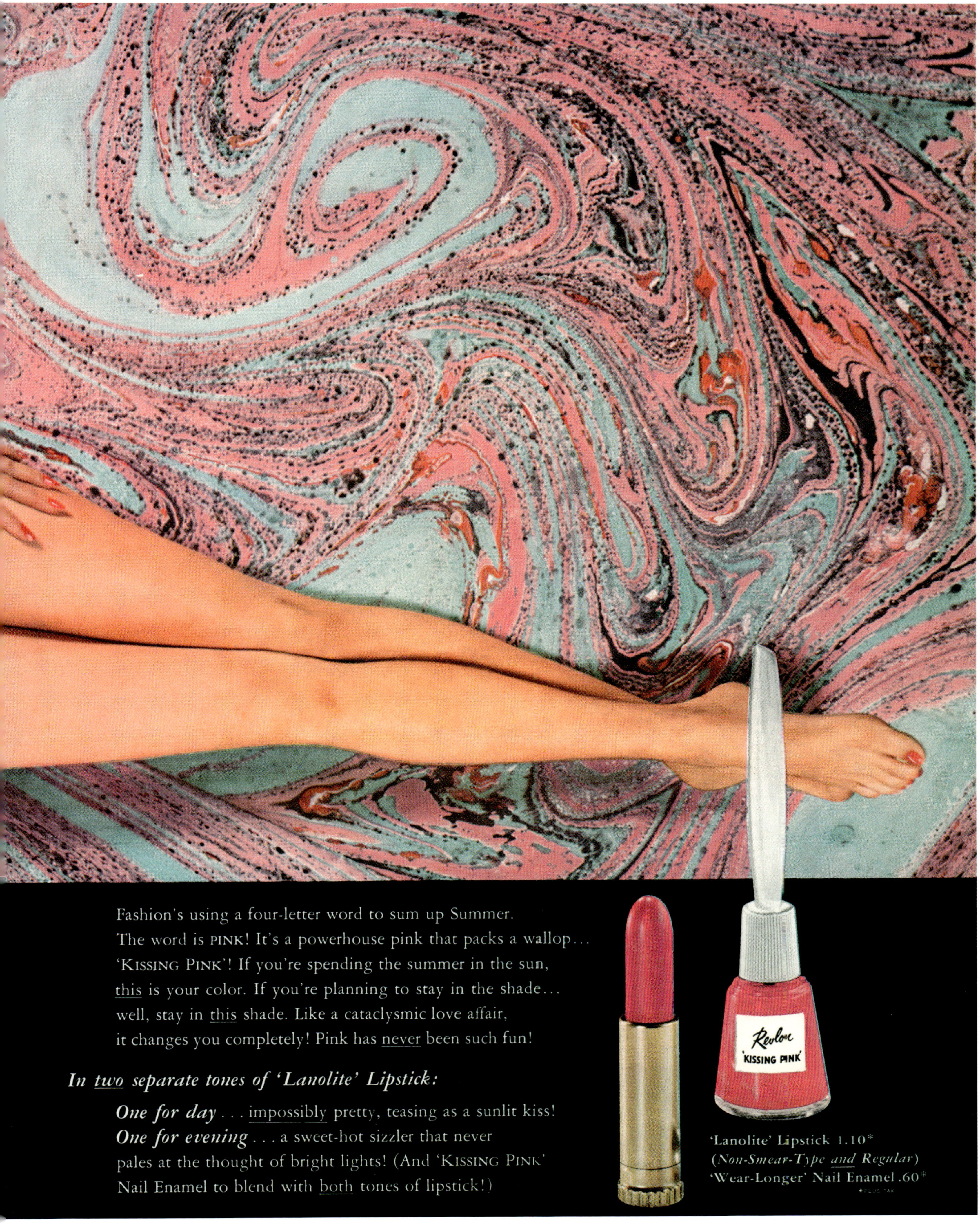

Fashion's using a four-letter word to sum up Summer. The word is PINK! It's a powerhouse pink that packs a wallop... 'KISSING PINK'! If you're spending the summer in the sun, this is your color. If you're planning to stay in the shade... well, stay in this shade. Like a cataclysmic love affair, it changes you completely! Pink has never been such fun!

In two separate tones of 'Lanolite' Lipstick:

One for day . . . impossibly pretty, teasing as a sunlit kiss! ***One for evening*** . . . a sweet-hot sizzler that never pales at the thought of bright lights! (And 'KISSING PINK' Nail Enamel to blend with both tones of lipstick!)

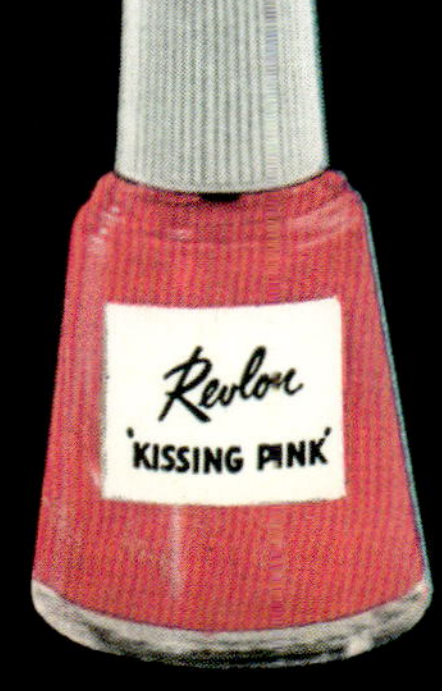

'Lanolite' Lipstick 1.10*
(*Non-Smear-Type and Regular*)
'Wear-Longer' Nail Enamel .60*

*PLUS TAX

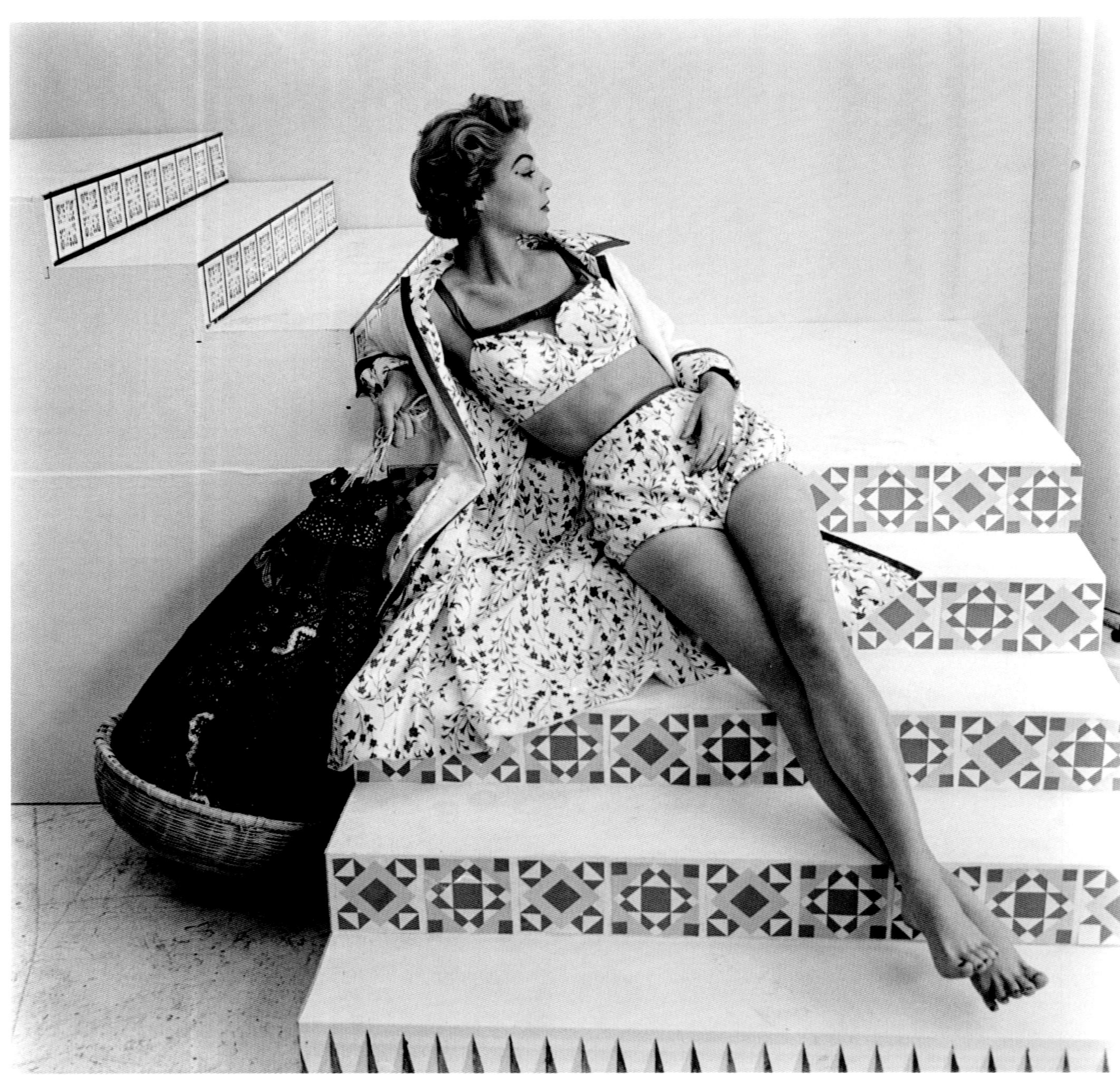

Above:
Making a whole
new impression:
1954 prints
Vogue
January 1954
Coat by Carolyn Schnurer
Photograph by
Frances McLaughlin-Gill

Opposite:
The New World Travelers:
Fibers of 1953
Harper's Bazaar
May 1953
Photograph by
Louise Dahl-Wolfe

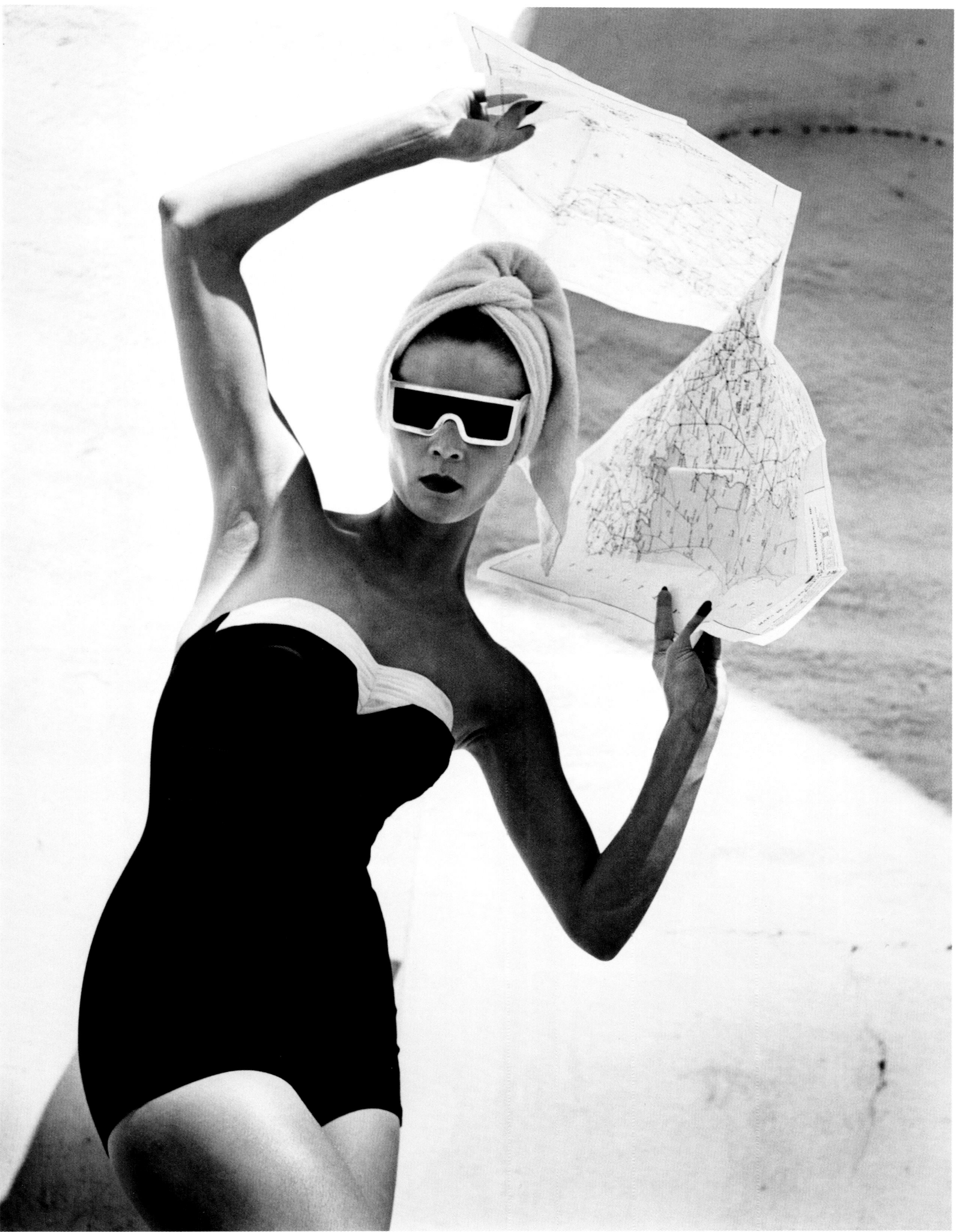

Summer suits and big hats
Vogue
April 15, 1954
Cherry Nelms
and Jean Patchett
Suits by Handmacher,
hats by Emme
Photograph by
Richard Rutledge

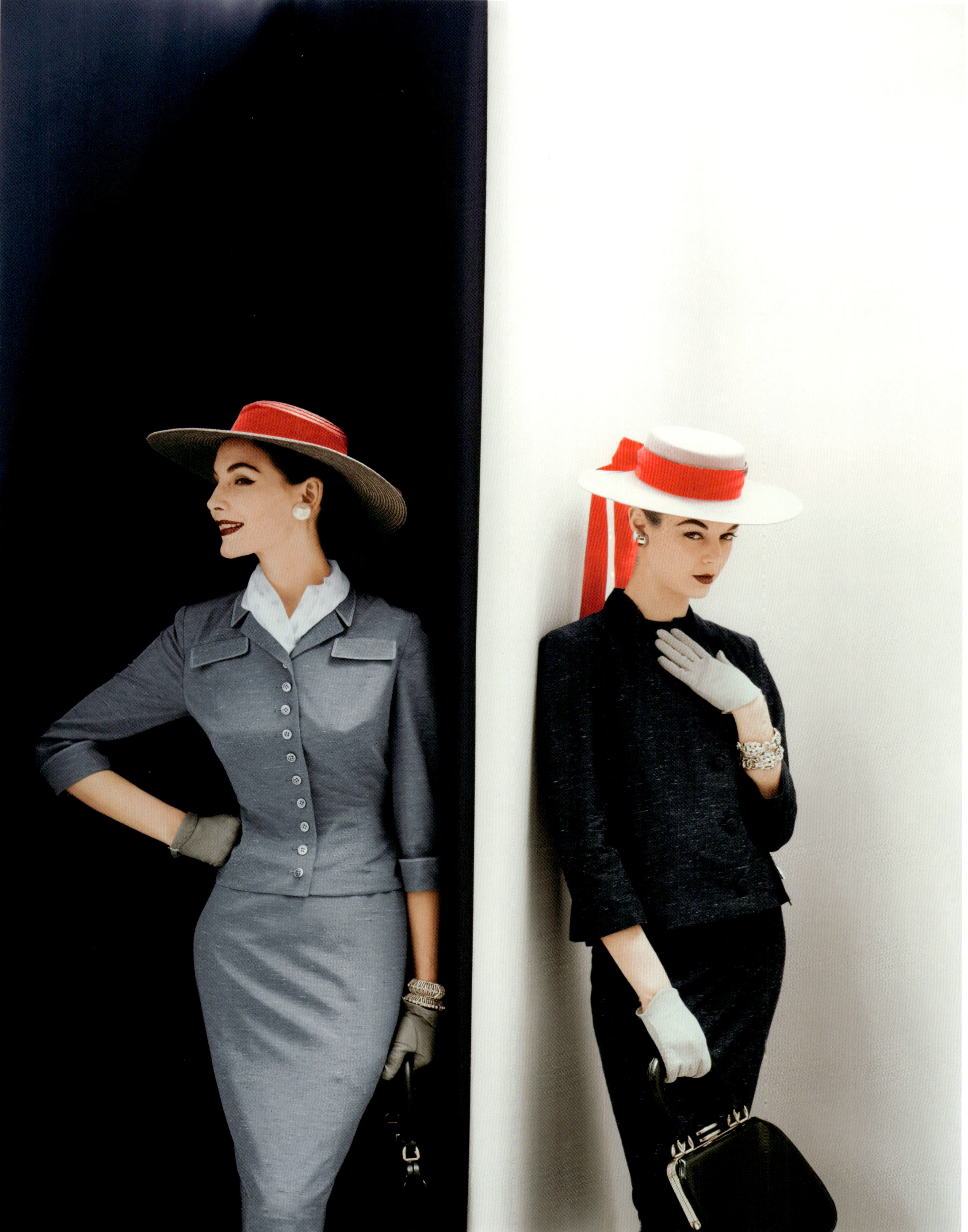

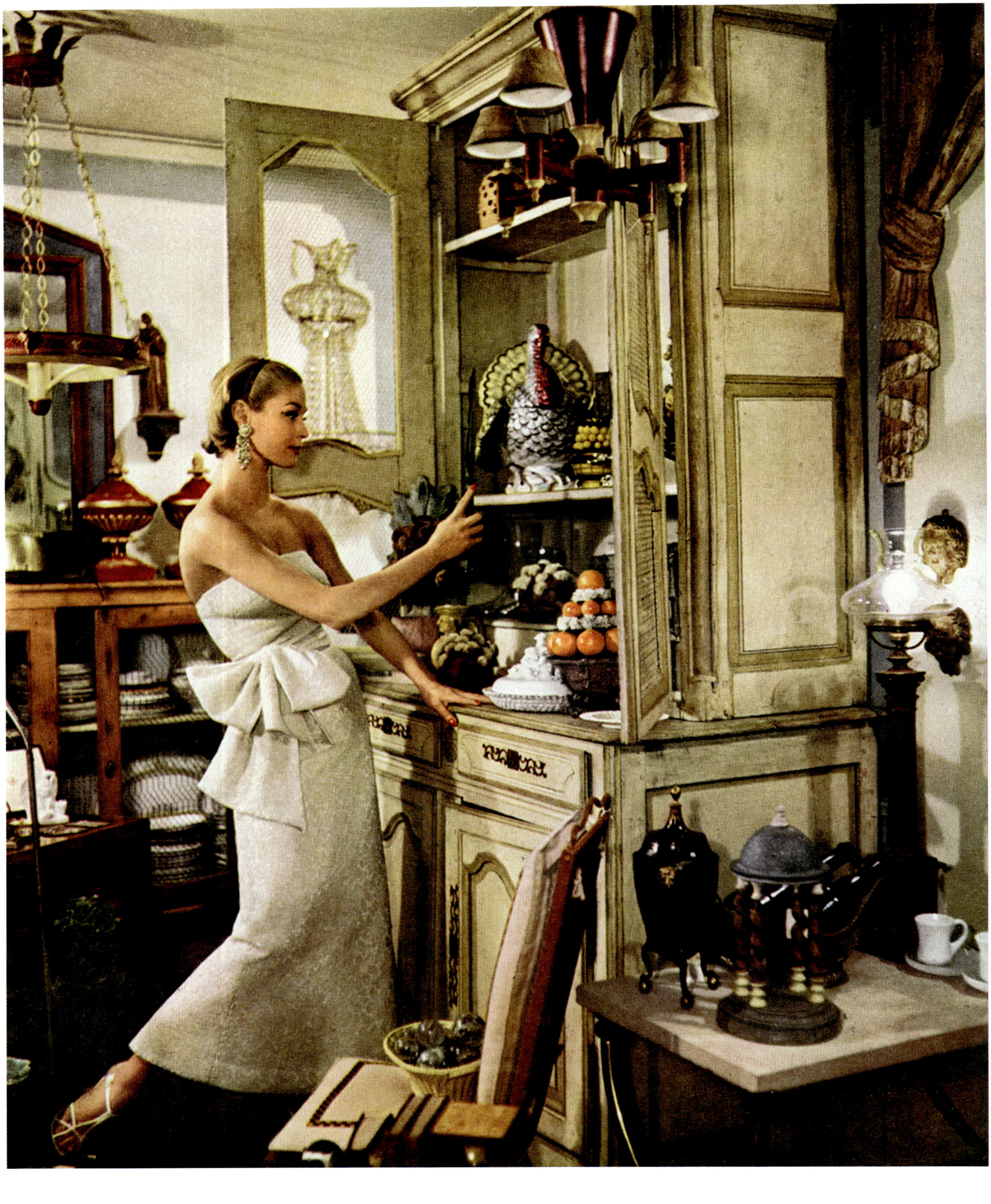

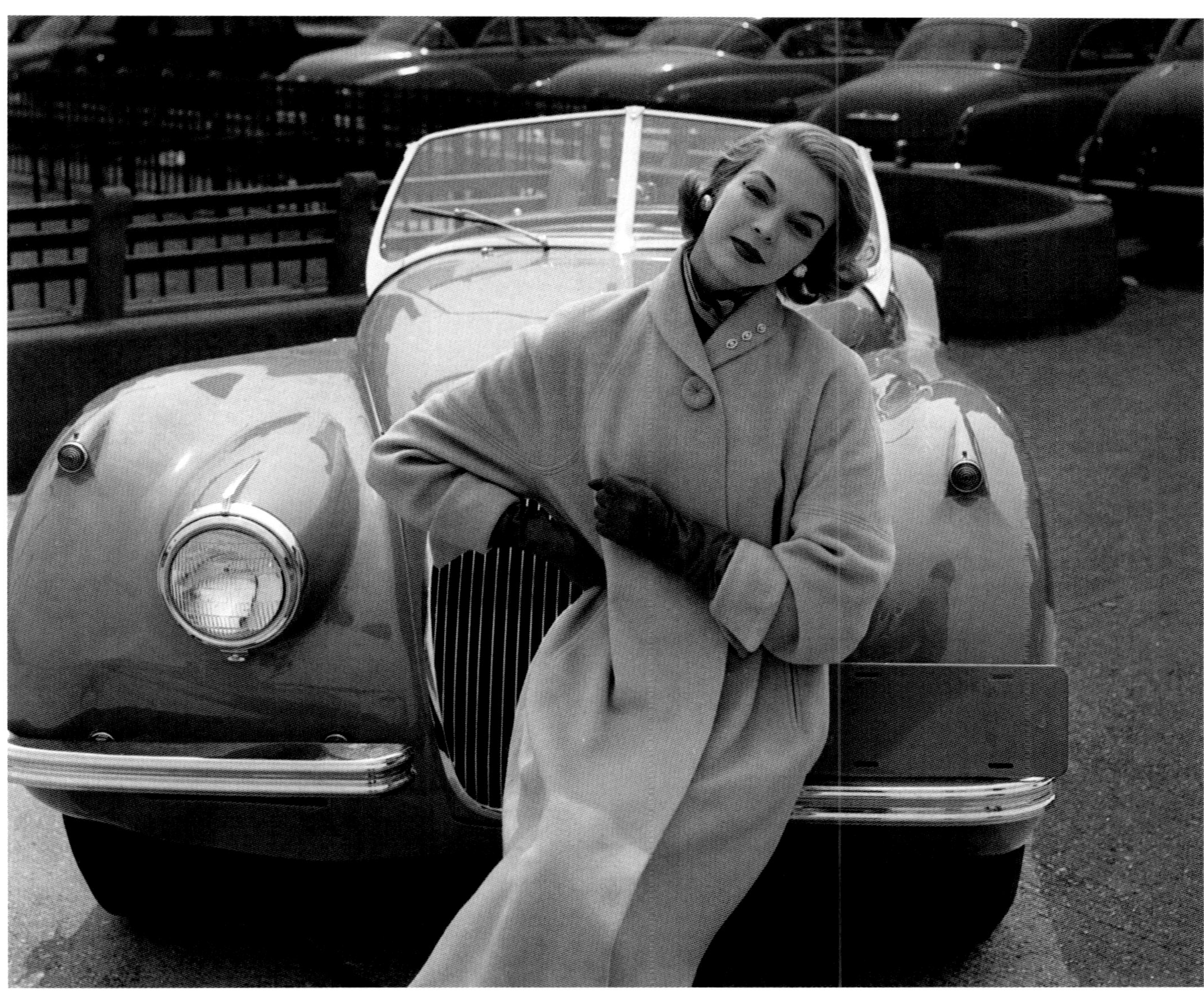

Above:
Advertising photograph for Kashmoor by Country Tweeds by Einiger
Harper's Bazaar
August 1954
Photograph by
William Helburn

Opposite:
Make it from a Pattern—For Evenings All Year
Harper's Bazaar
July 1954
Photograph by
Gleb Derujinsky

Harper's Bazaar
November 1954
Photograph by
Louise Dahl-Wolfe

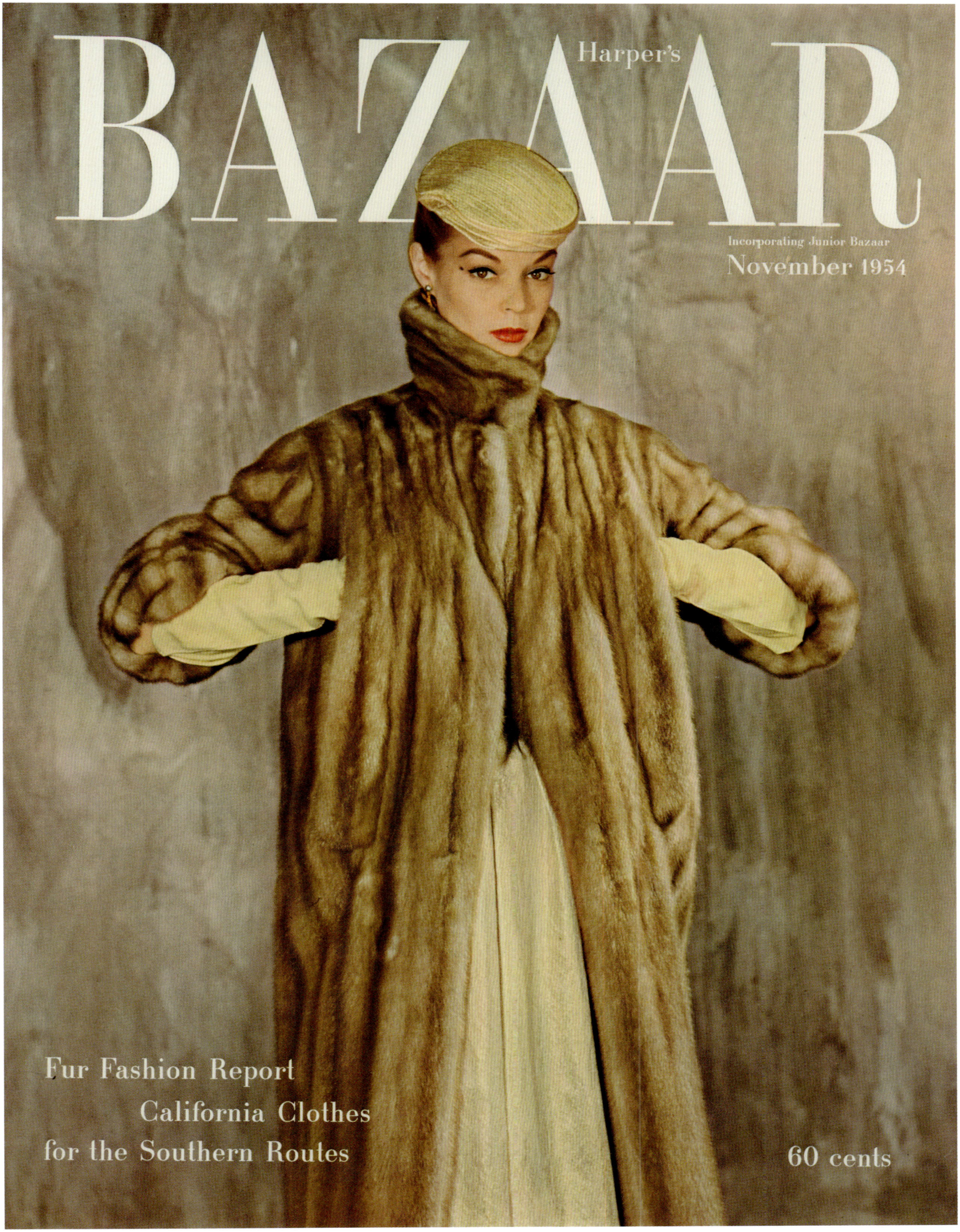

Harper's

BAZAAR

Incorporating Junior Bazaar

November 1954

Fur Fashion Report

California Clothes for the Southern Routes

60 cents

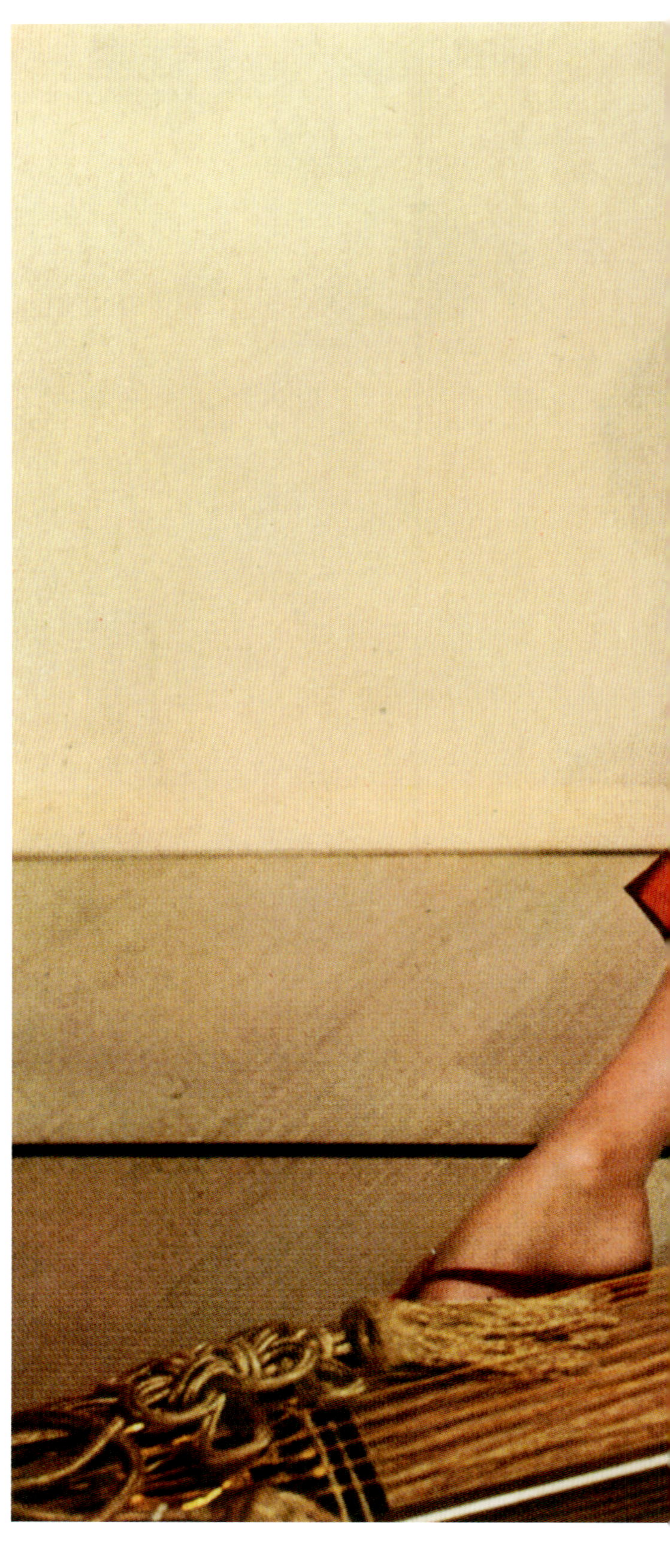

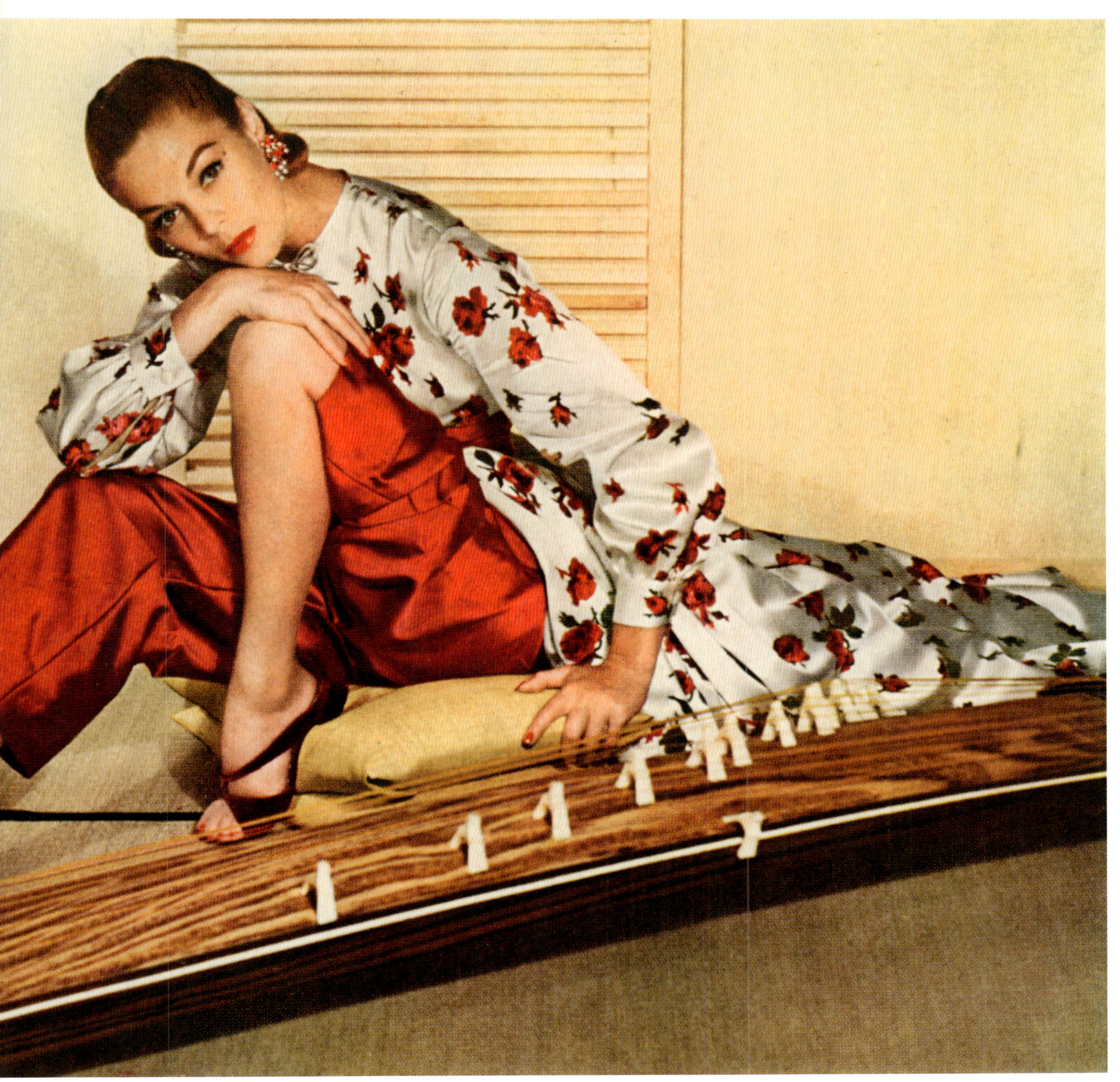

The Observance of Beauty
Harper's Bazaar
October 1954
Photograph by
Louise Dahl-Wolfe

VOGUE

MAY 15

5 Wardrobes for
5 Different Kinds of Week Ends

New Coolness in Men's Clothes

New Reducing Diets,
with Sugar and Bread

Travel Memos – 9 Countries

ADVANCE RETAIL TRADE EDITION

50 CENTS

COPYRIGHT 1954 THE CONDÉ NAST PUBLICATIONS INC.

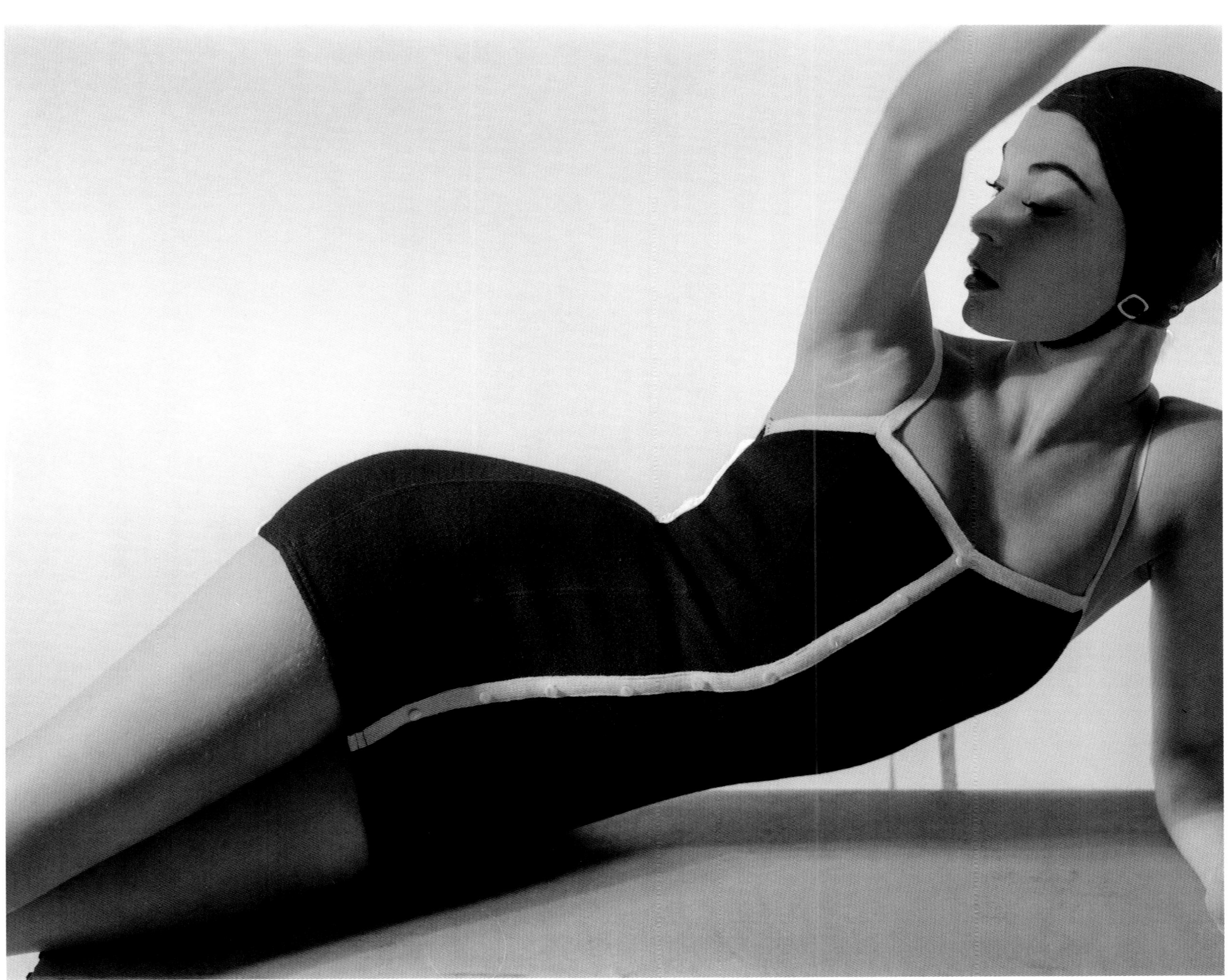

Above:
The one-piece black bathing suit return trip
Vogue
January 1954
Swimsuit by Sacony
Photograph by Horst P. Horst

Opposite:
Vogue
May 15, 1954
Photograph by
Erwin Blumenfeld

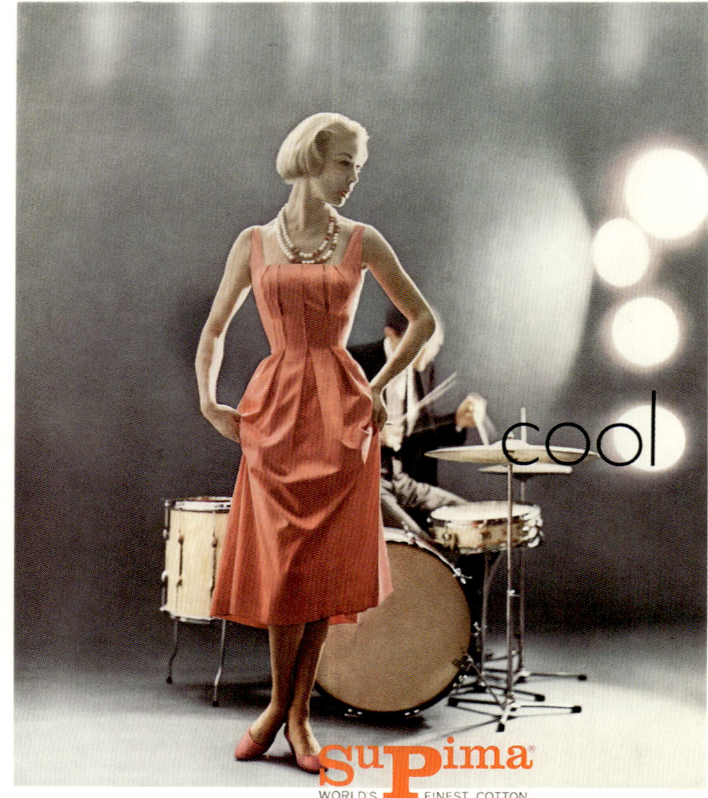

Cool means wonderful. Wonderful means Supima. Supima means the champagne of cottons grown in Arizona, Texas and New Mexico. This new extra-long staple fibre has a lustre, strength and silkiness all its own. See how its color sings in **Tina Leser**'s summer cooler of Fashion-Fair, a **Fuller** broadcloth. Supima Association of America. 112 West 34th Street. New York 1.
Lord & Taylor, all stores • Montaldo's, all stores • Sakowitz, Houston • Joseph Magnin, San Francisco

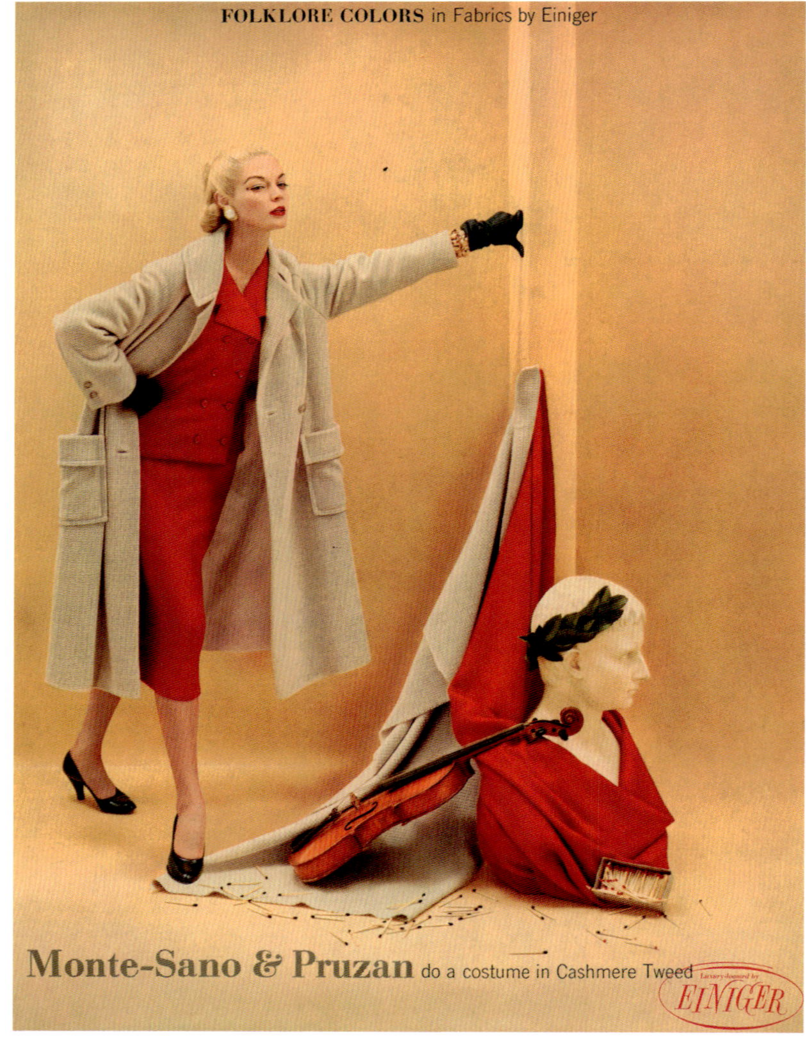

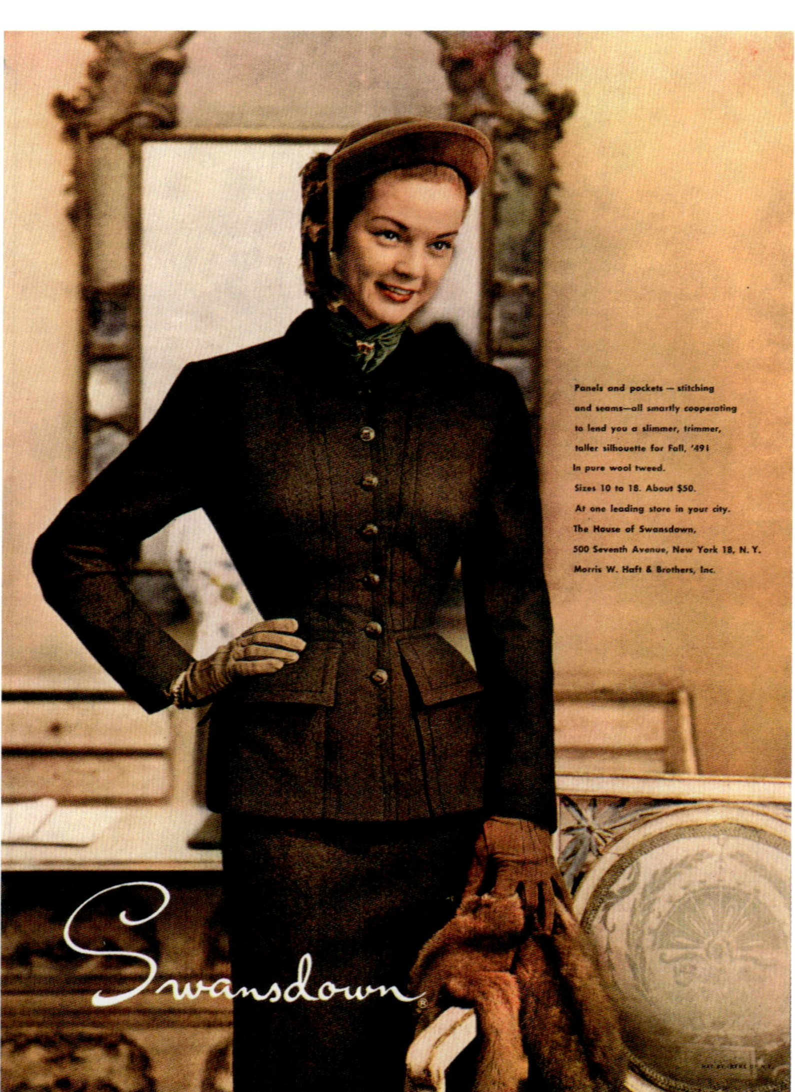

This page, clockwise from top left:
Ad for Supima
1957
Photograph by
William Helburn

Ad for Monte-Sano
& Pruzan for Einiger
1955
Photograph by
William Helburn

Ad for Swansdown
1949

Opposite:
Jean Patchett
and Victor Cutler,
Penn Station, NY
circa 1955
Photograph by
William Helburn

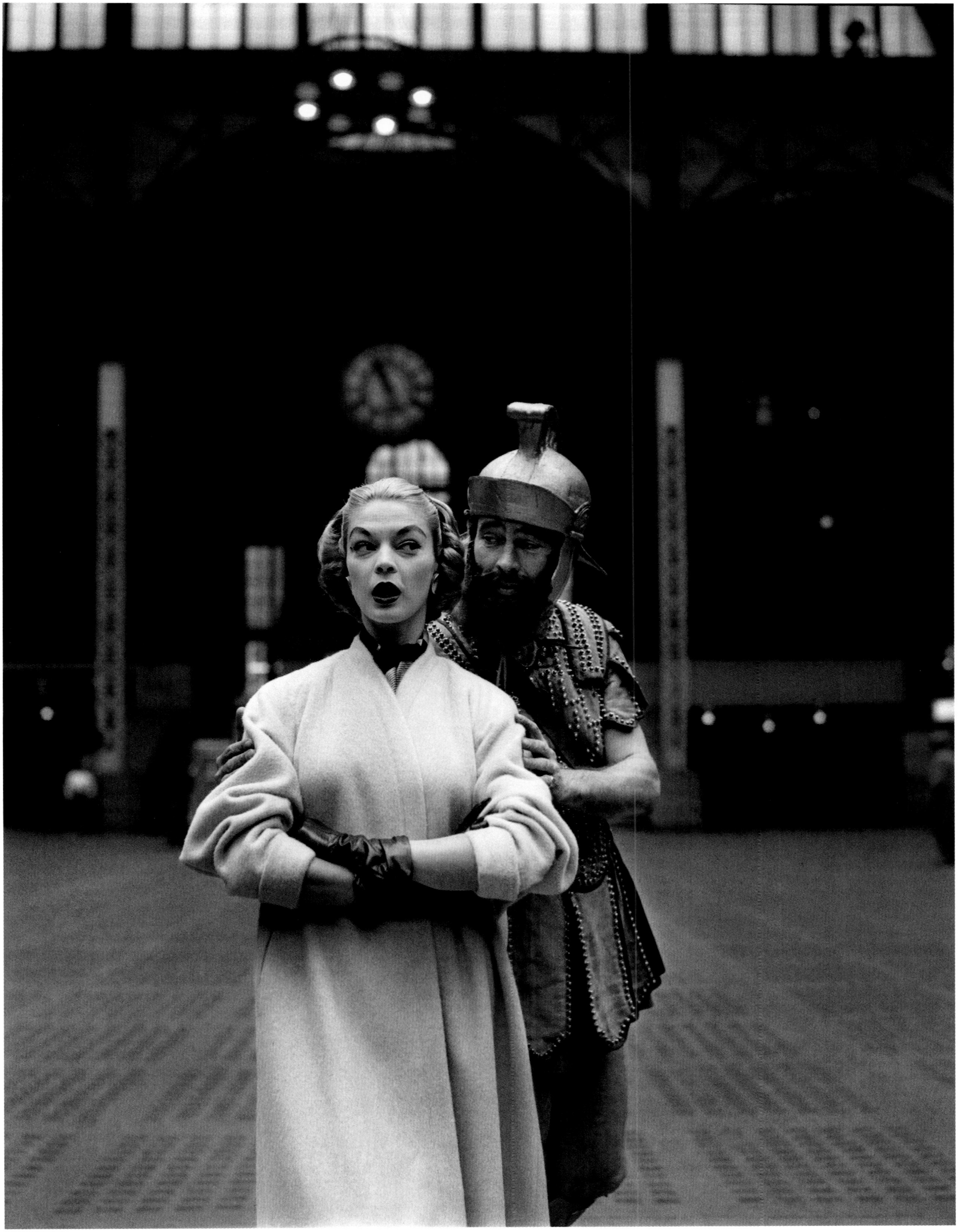

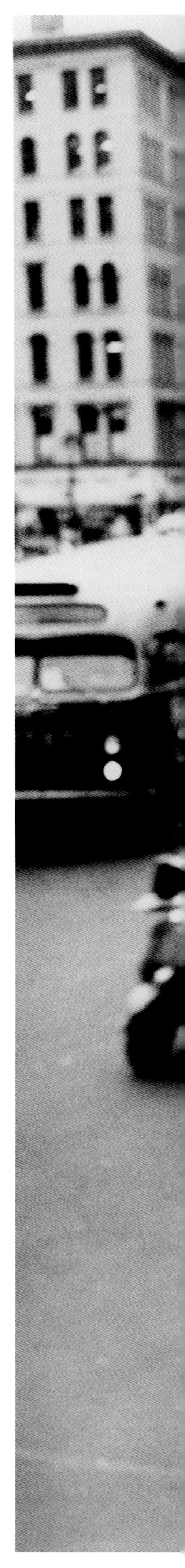

Bus Top
Harper's Bazaar
December 1958
Jean Patchett
and Dovima
Photograph by
William Helburn

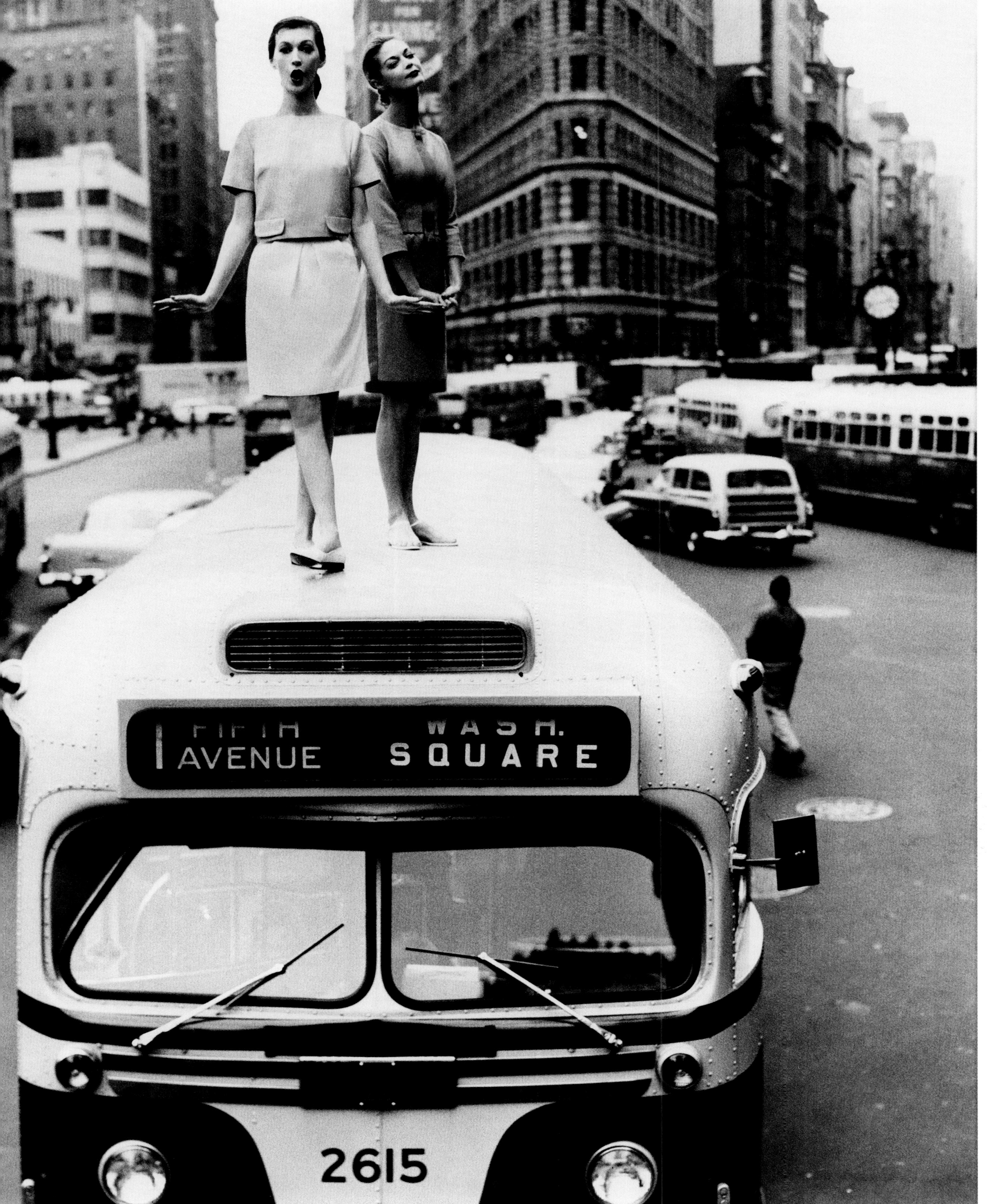
1
AVENUE
WASH.
SQUARE
2615

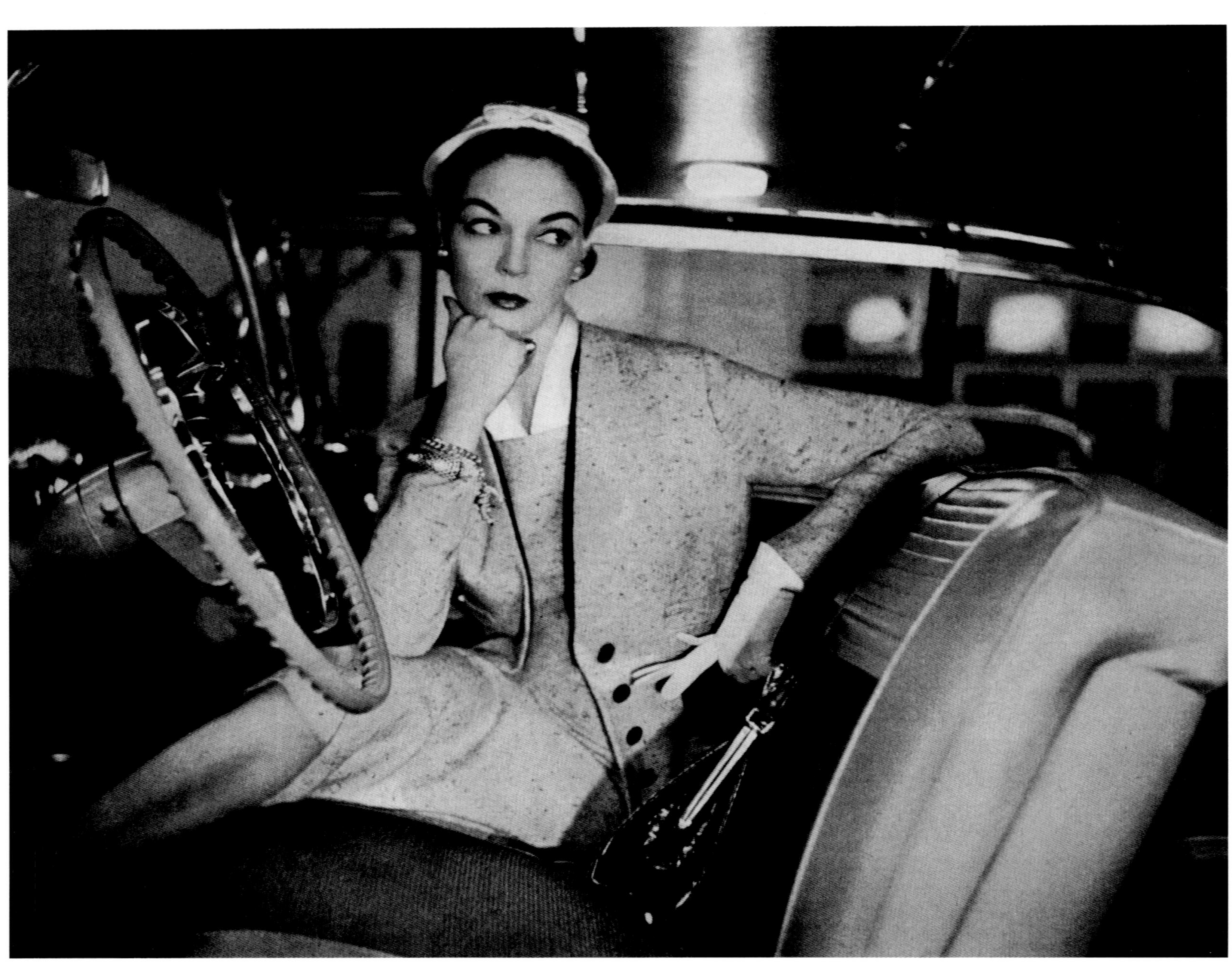

Above:
Americans — dressing for where they're going
Vogue
February 1, 1955
Photograph by Karen Radkai

Opposite:
Eileen Ford and Ford Agency models
McCall's
Cover image (variant)
April 1955
Front row, left to right:
Patsy Shally, Eileen Ford;
Second row: Jean Patchett, Lillian Marcuson, Nan Rees, Leonie Vernet;
Third row: Dorian Leigh, Suzy Parker, Georgia Hamilton, Dolores Hawkins, Kathy Dennis, Mary Jane Russell
Photograph by Mark Shaw

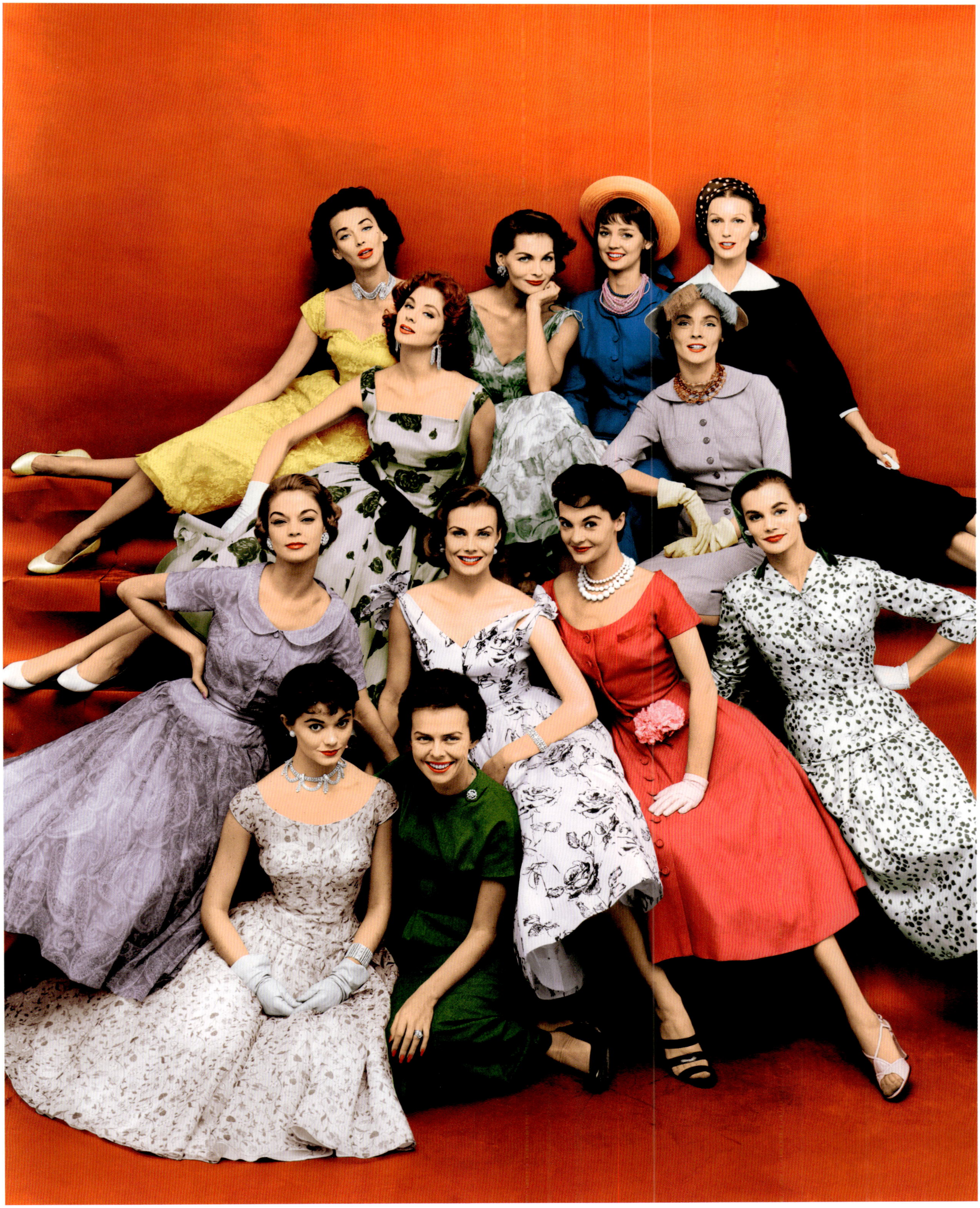

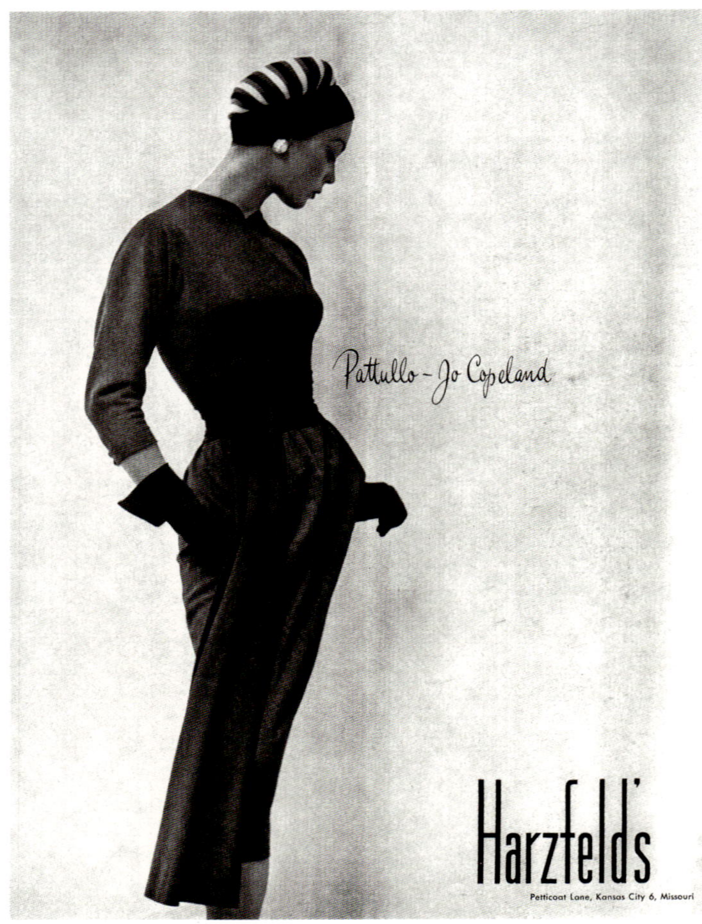

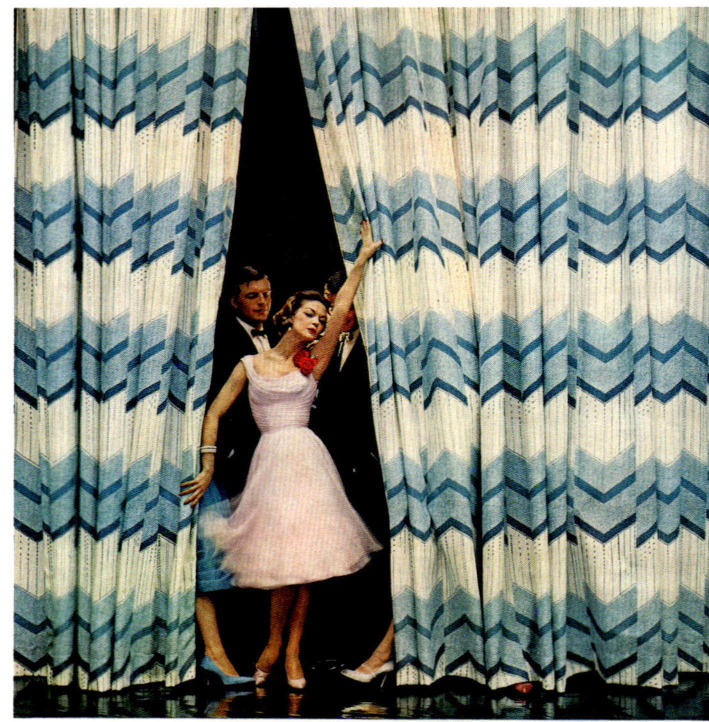

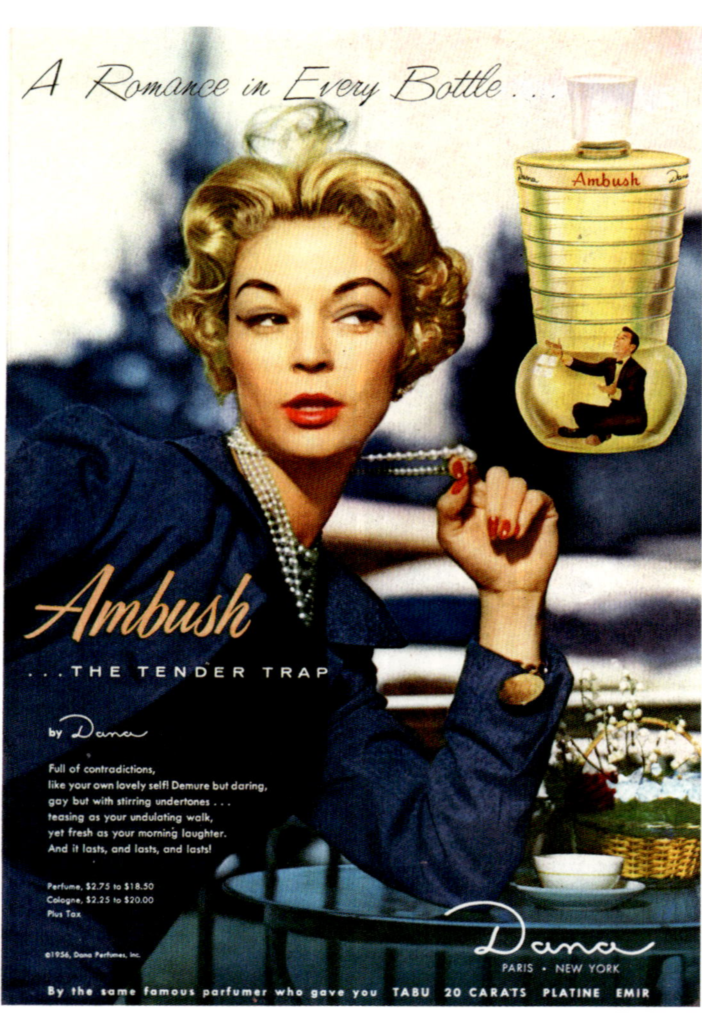

This page, clockwise from top left:

Ad for Pattullo-Jo Copeland for Harzfeld's
1952

Ad for Covington Fabrics for PPG Fiber Glass
1957
Photograph by William Helburn

Ad for Dana perfumes "Ambush"
1957

Opposite:
New blonds — city and country
Vogue
March 1, 1956
Suit by Davidow
Photograph by John Rawlings

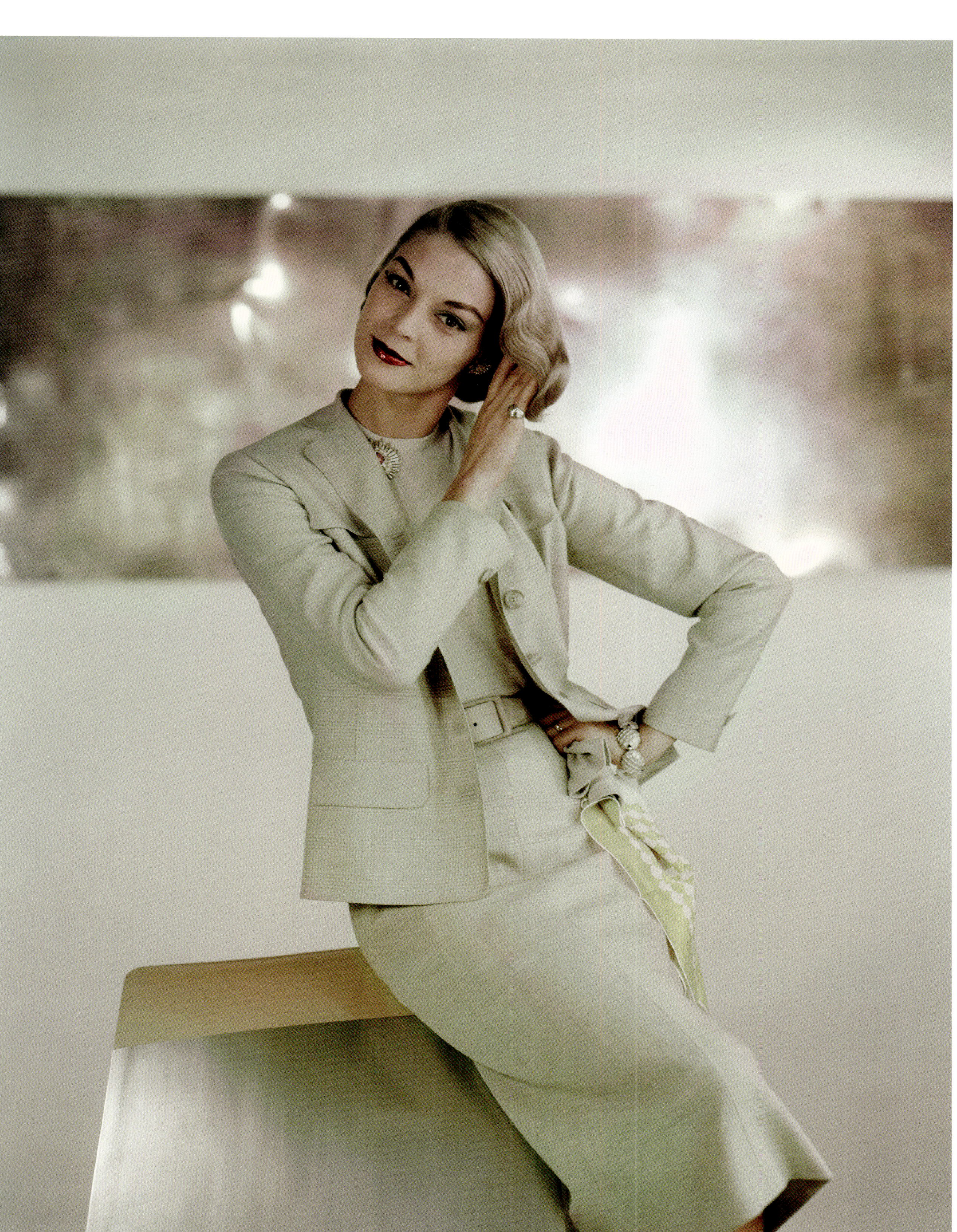

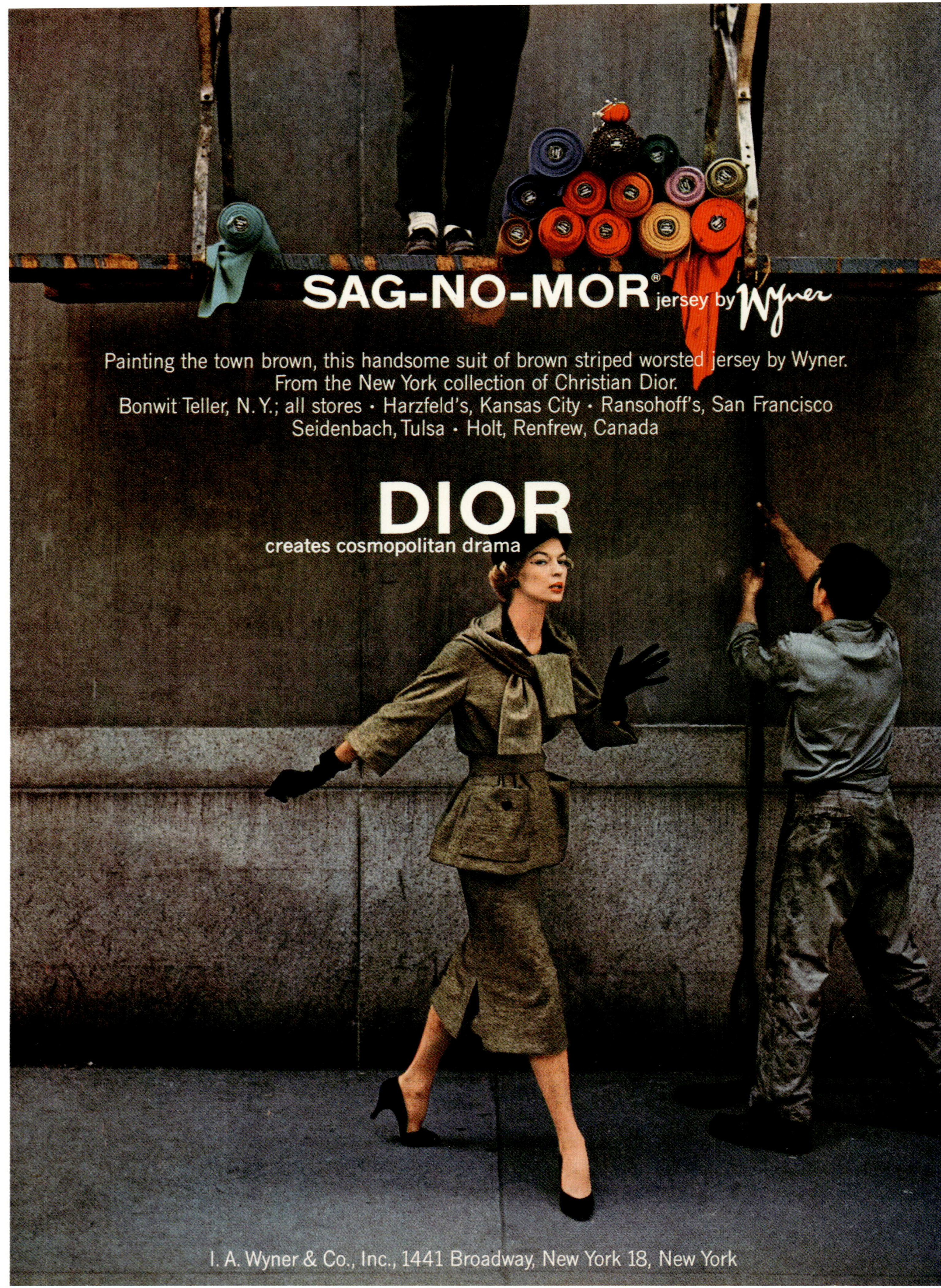
SAG-NO-MOR® jersey by Wyner
Painting the town brown, this handsome suit of brown striped worsted jersey by Wyner.
From the New York collection of Christian Dior.
Bonwit Teller, N. Y.; all stores · Harzfeld's, Kansas City · Ransohoff's, San Francisco
Seidenbach, Tulsa · Holt, Renfrew, Canada
DIOR
creates cosmopolitan drama
I. A. Wyner & Co., Inc., 1441 Broadway, New York 18, New York

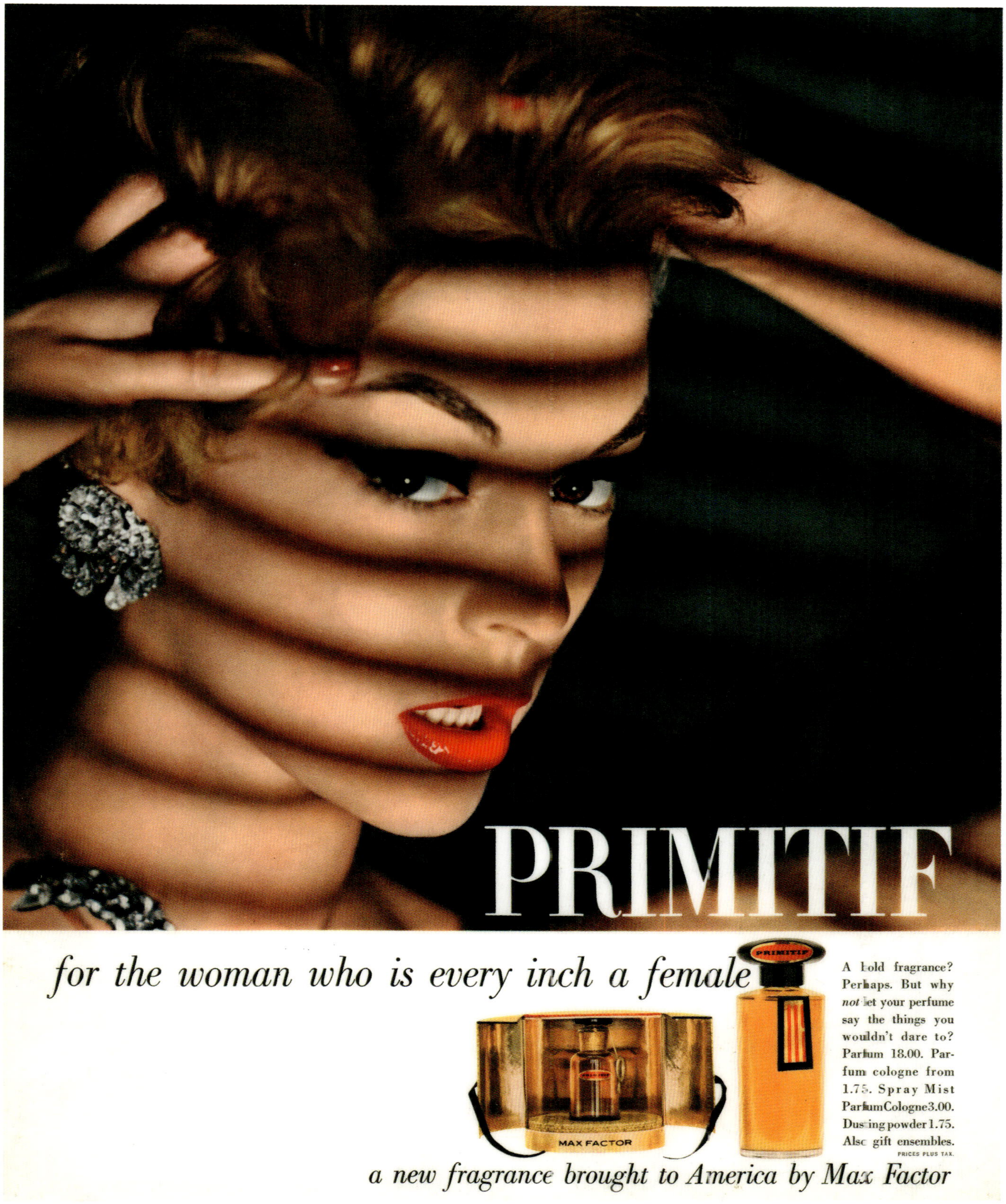

PRIMITIF

for the woman who is every inch a female

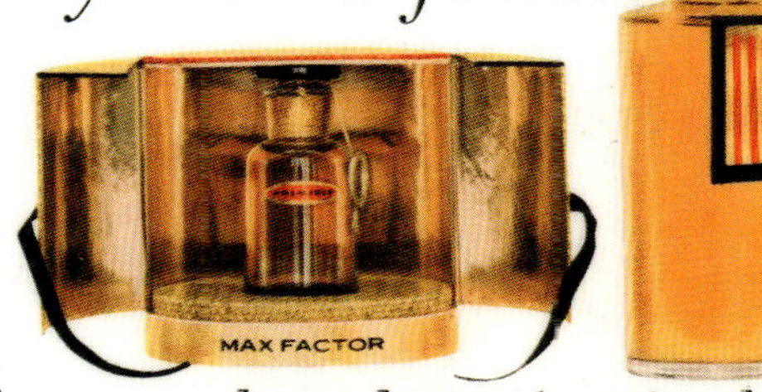

A bold fragrance? Perhaps. But why *not* let your perfume say the things you wouldn't dare to? Parfum 18.00. Parfum cologne from 1.75. Spray Mist Parfum Cologne 3.00. Dusting powder 1.75. Also gift ensembles.

PRICES PLUS TAX.

a new fragrance brought to America by Max Factor

Above:
Ad for Max Factor
"Primitif"
1956
Photograph by
William Helburn

Opposite:
Ad for Sag-no-Mor
by Wyner
1957
Photograph by
William Helburn

Ad for Borg Fabric "Borgana"
1956
Photograph by
William Helburn

Borg Fabric Division, The George W. Borg Corp., Delavan, Wisconsin

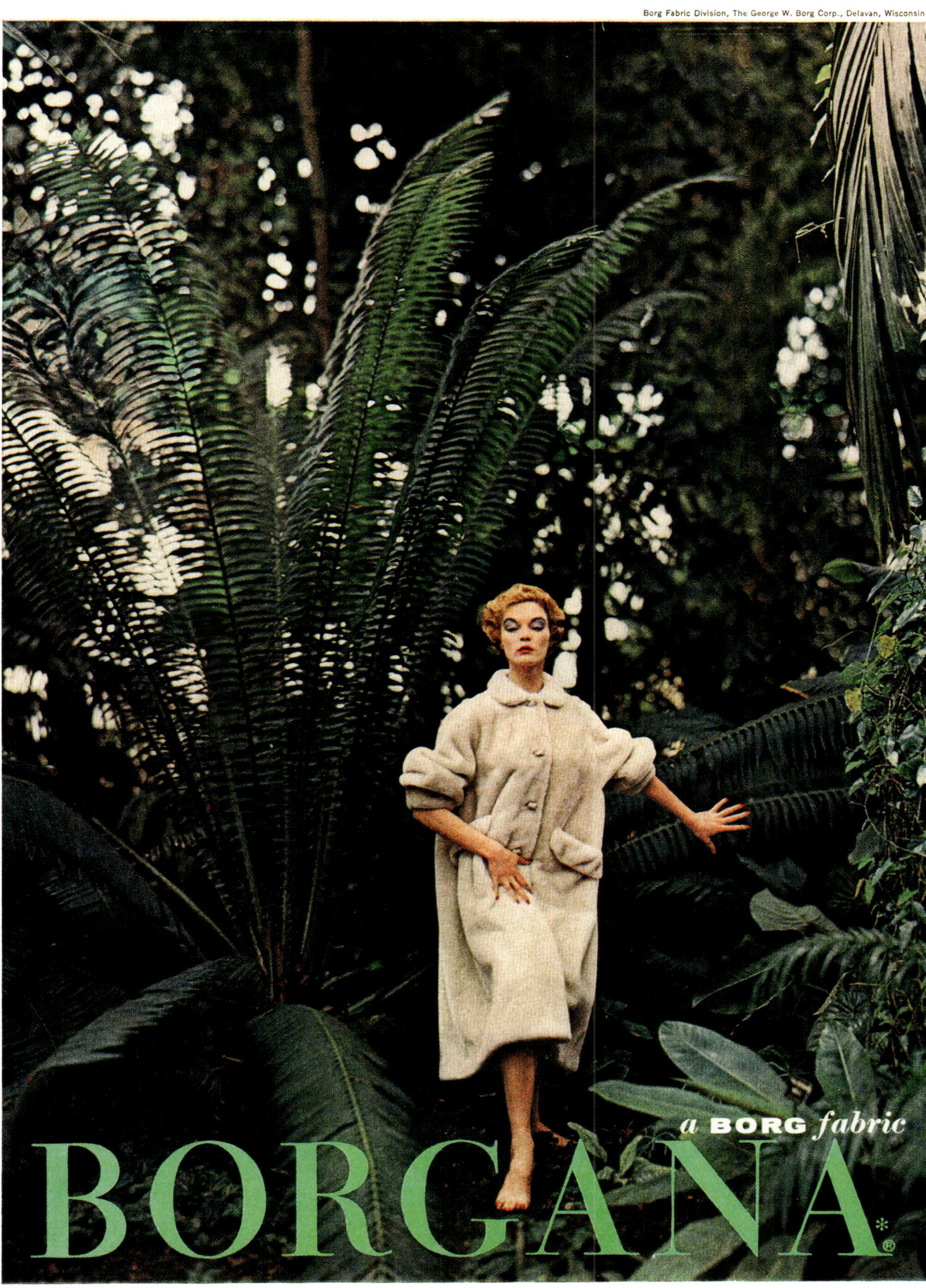

looks more like fur than fur itself

If you saw it in the jungle you'd think it was born there. That's how much Borgana looks like fur. First of the fabrics with a fur face, Borgana is still first—in beauty, in quality, in smartness. Offered this year in Sauterne, Pewter, Brandy, Black, Coca Brown, Charcoal...in misses, junior, petite and children's sizes...superbly fashioned by these fine makers:

Modelia, Inc., 205 W. 39th St., New York
Kraeler-Frasca, 500 Seventh Ave., New York
Albrecht Furs, 21 W. 5th St., St. Paul
Rothmoor Corp., 22 W. Madison St., Chicago
Annis Furs, 130 W. 30th St., New York
Gordon Mfg. Co., Ltd., 423 Mayor St., Montreal, Canada
Linker & Herbert-Junior Aire, 205 W. 39th St., New York
Mode Kiddie Coats, 520 Eighth Ave., New York
Rosenblatt & Kahn (children's coats), 520 Eighth Ave., New York

*Registered Trademark of The George W. Borg Corporation

Borgana* is the original fabric made from a balanced blend of Orlon†/Dynel and manufactured under U.S. Patent No. 2,705,880

†Du Pont Trademark

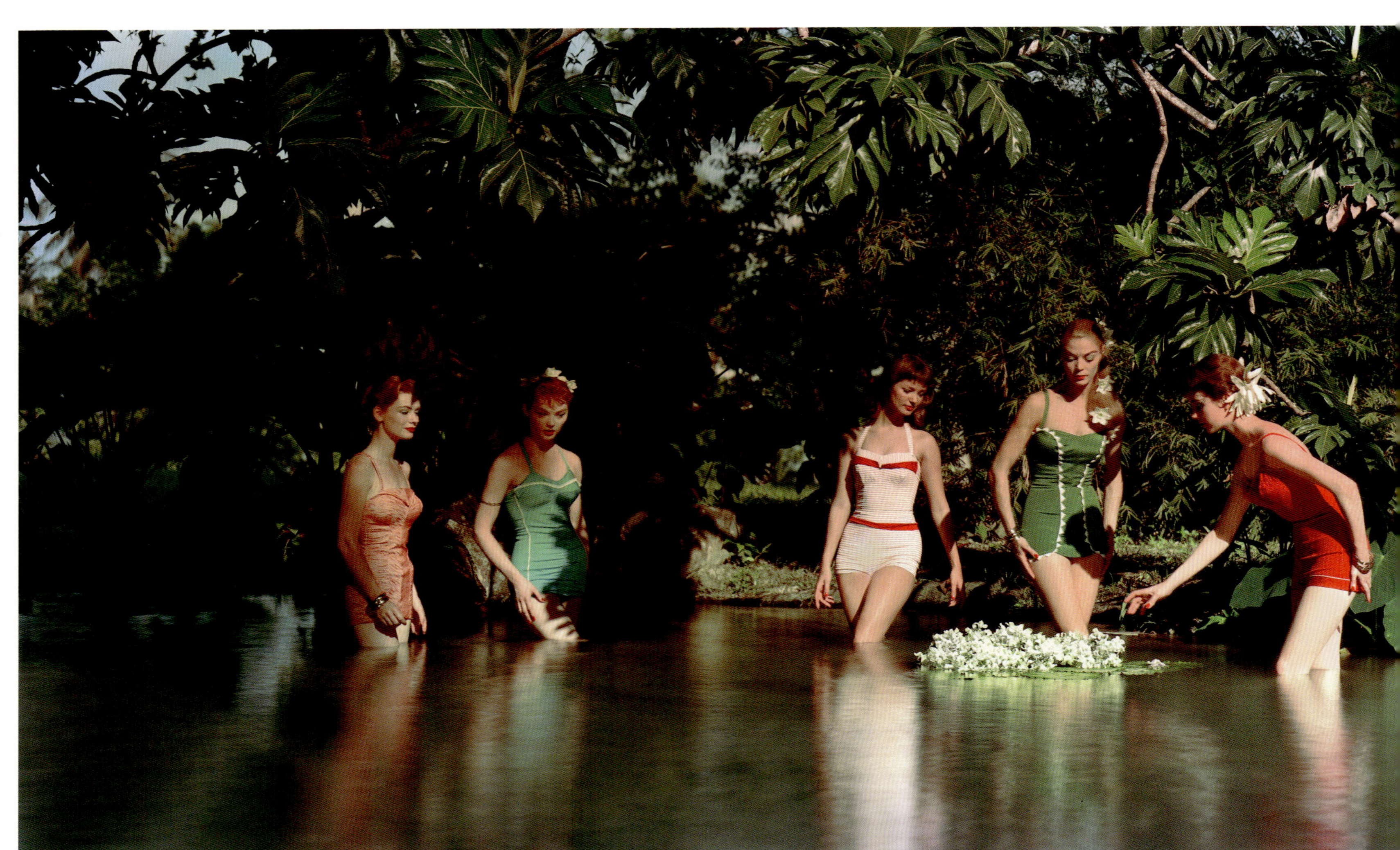

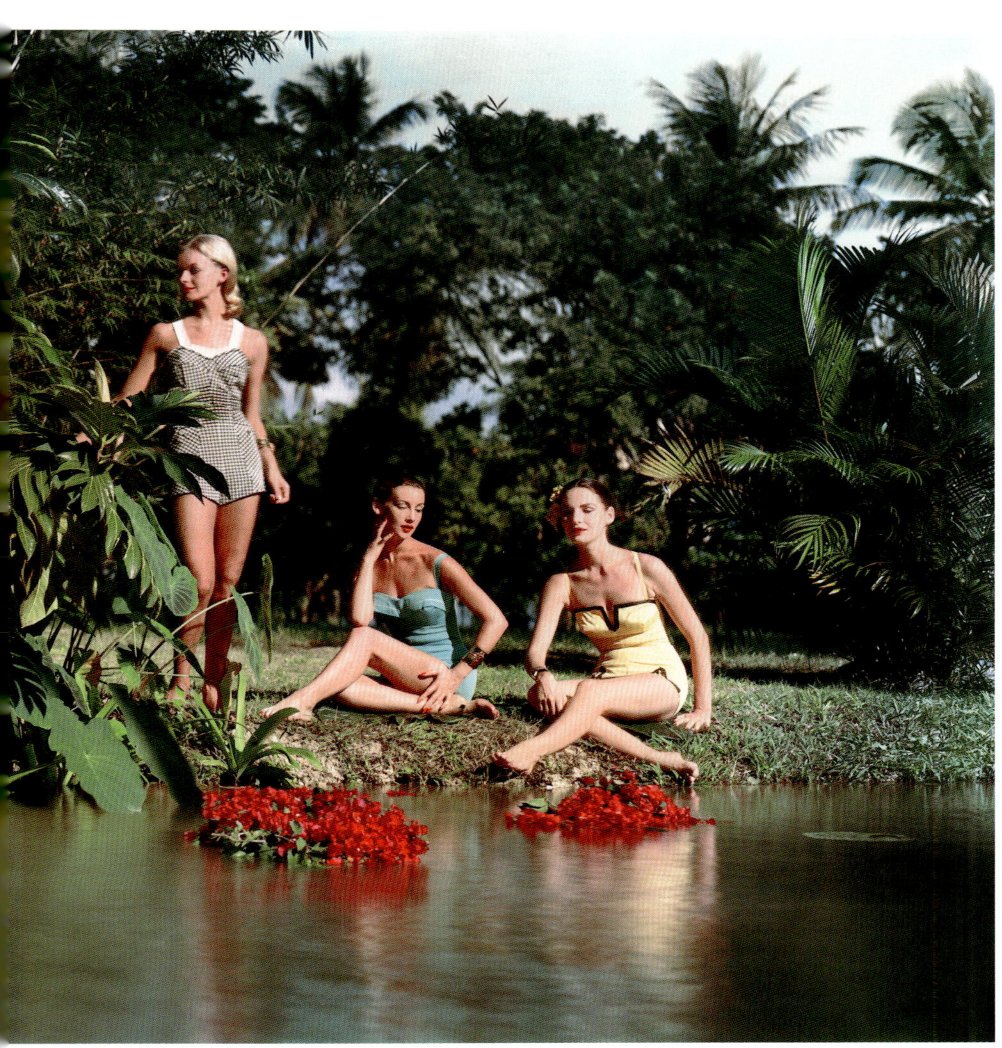

"Chromspun Colorama No. 104"
Shown on Colorama display at New York's
Grand Central Station Concourse
1956
Unidentified models, Jean Patchett,
Claire Griswold, Lois Gunas Wideman,
Ruth Neumann Derujinsky, unidentified model
Photograph by Larry Guetersloh
Courtesy of the George Eastman Museum

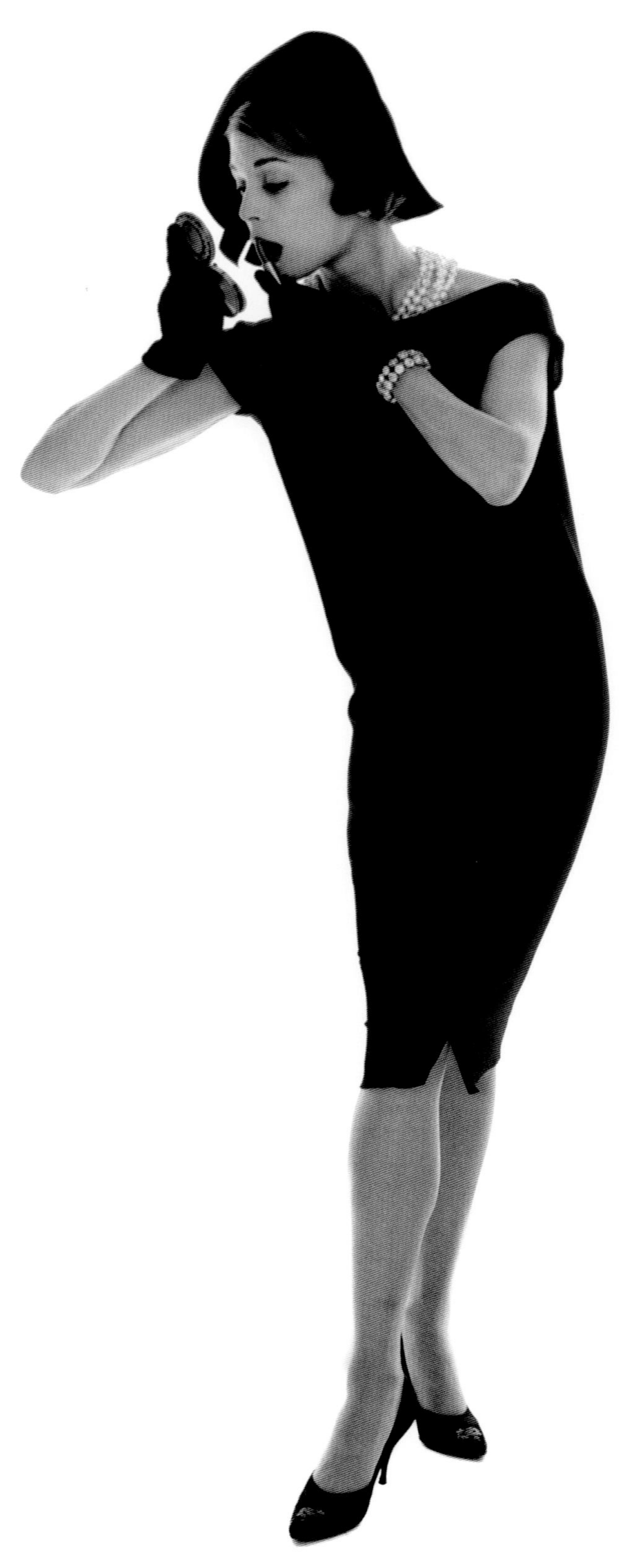

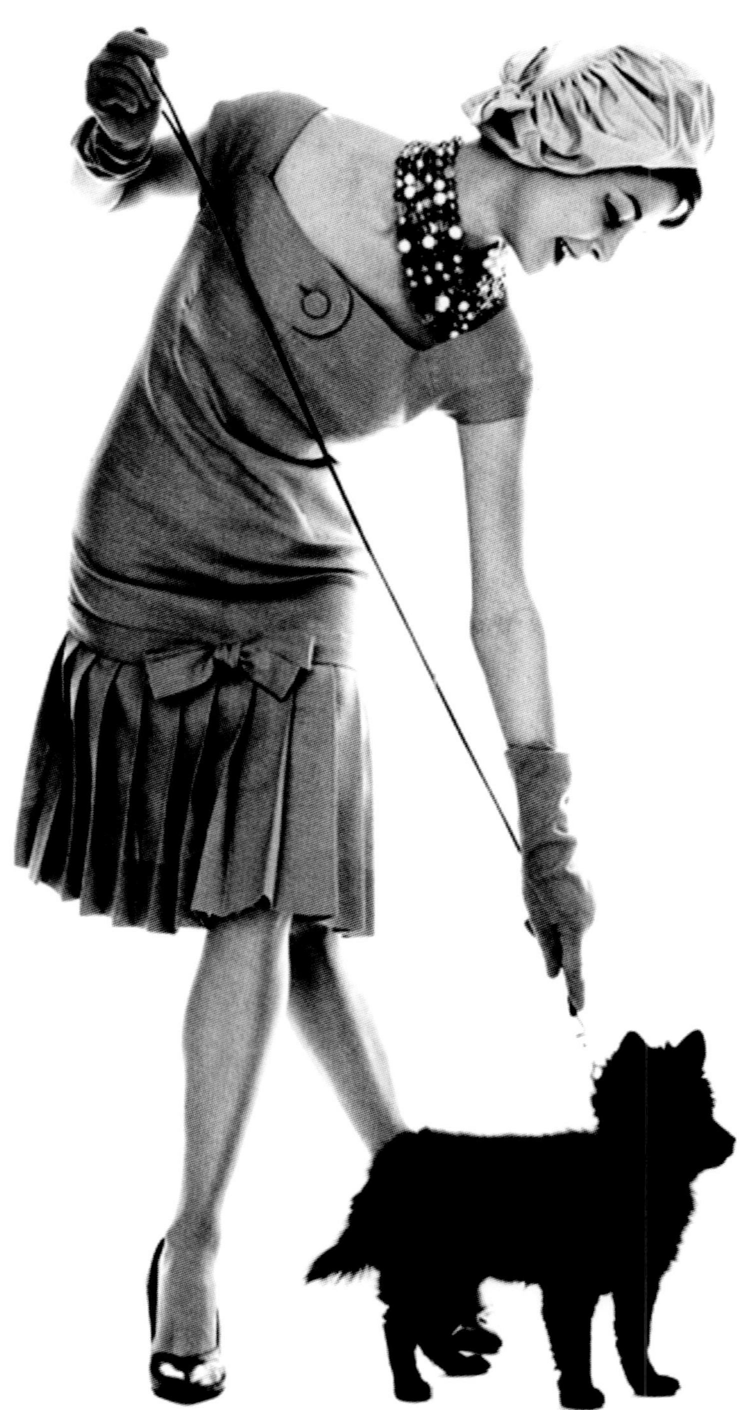

Opposite and previous spread:
Cha Cha Cha Series
Vogue
February 17, 1958
Photographs by
Jerry Schatzberg

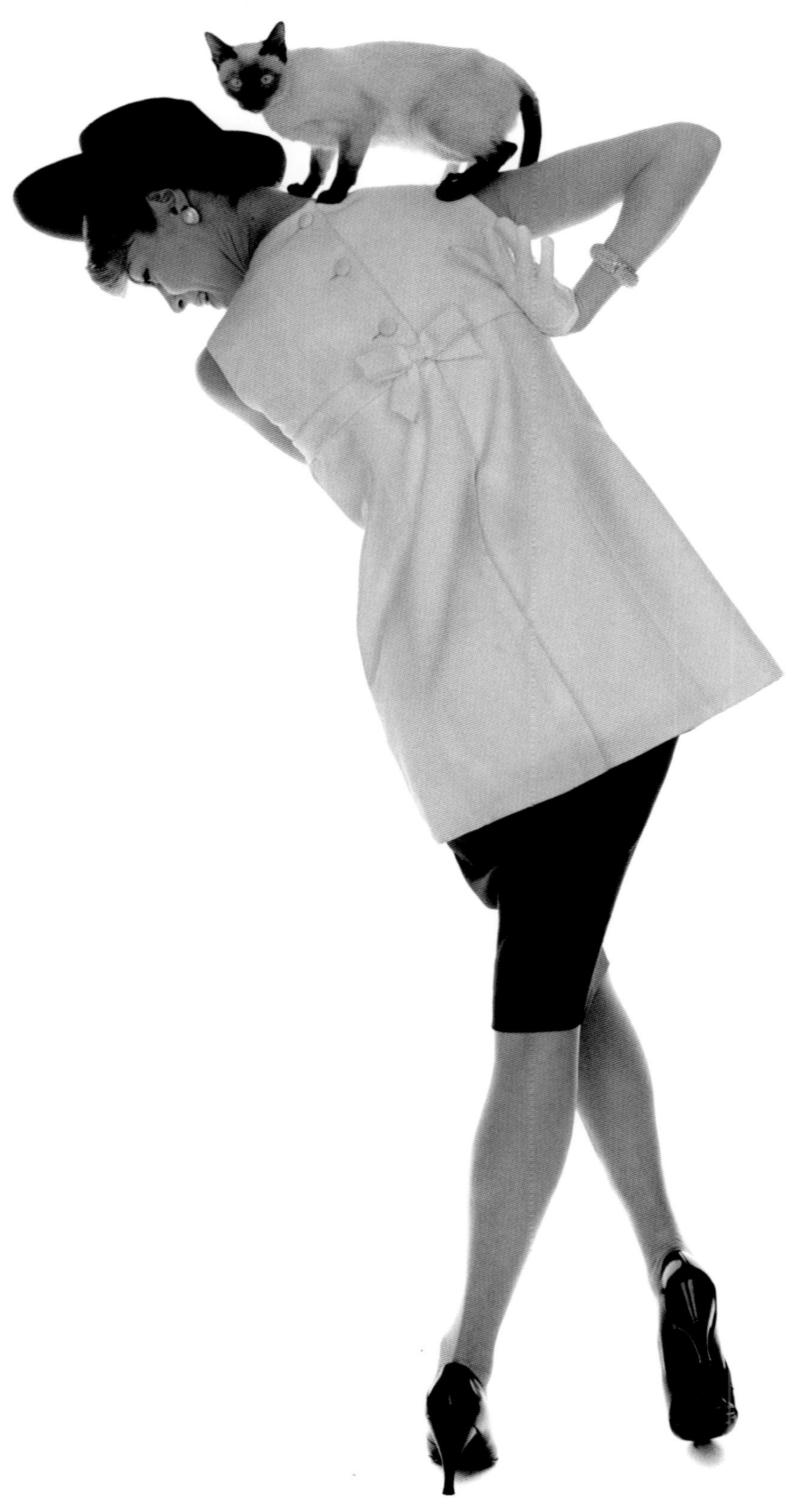

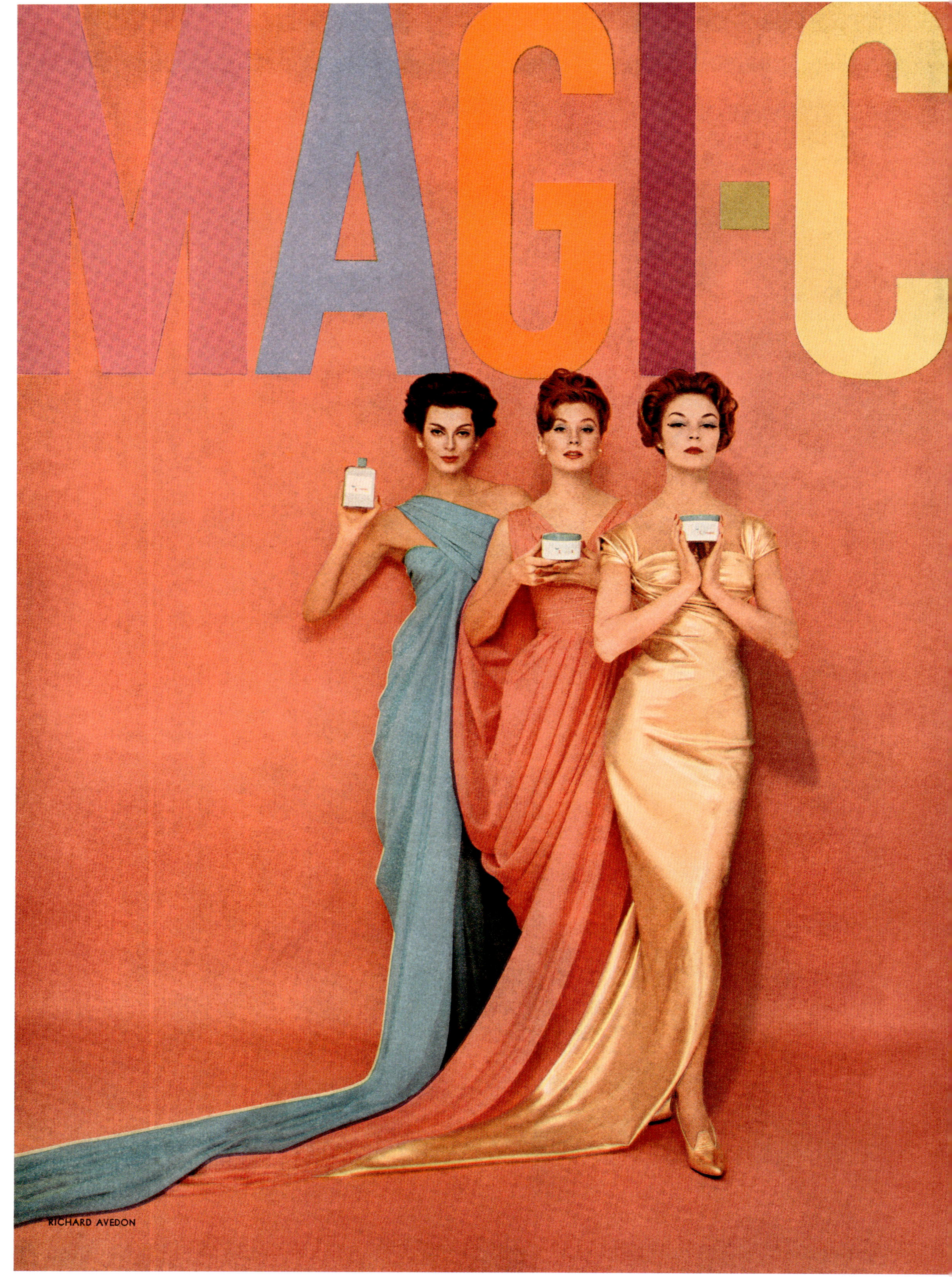
MAGI-C
RICHARD AVEDON

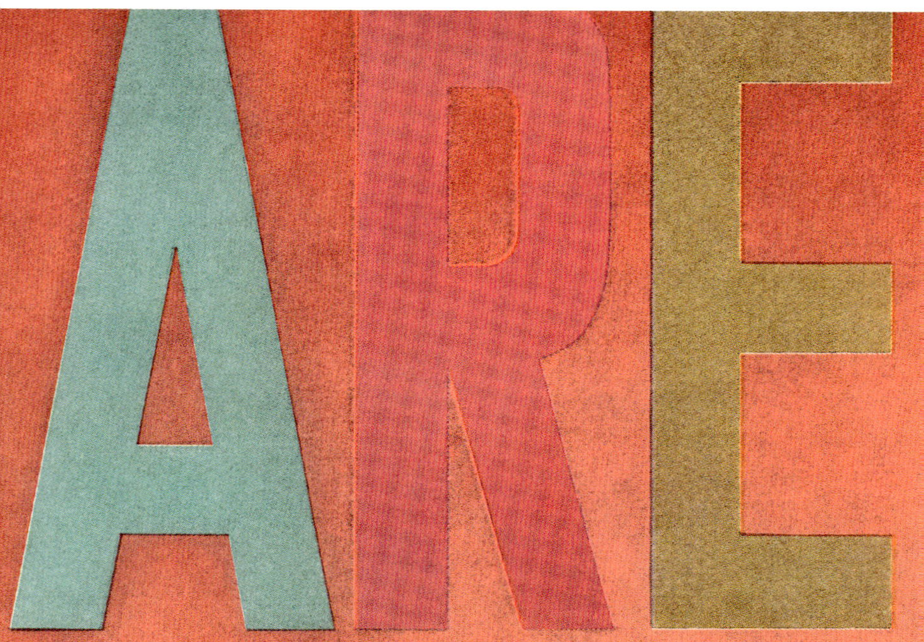

Your skin often reflects the life you lead and the way you care for yourself. This is why the MAGI-CARE three point beauty plan has won the grateful acclaim of women who have achieved dramatic improvement in the appearance of their skin through daily use of the MAGI-CARE Trio of products.

Every skin holds within itself the potential of beauty . . . the ability to maintain a fresh, moist blooming look that gives the illusion of flawless texture. But skin care cannot be a "sometime" thing. It must be planned and pursued regularly with fine products that bring compliments as welcome reward for effort and money spent.

The MAGI-CARE products are: Vita-Flair, a lavish moisturizing lotion; Cool Blush, a stimulating mask; and Femine 20, a triumphant new non-greasy night cream. The Trio is formulated to bring pleasing results when all products are used daily in a continuing cycle of skin care. If the appearance of your skin seems to lack the reflection of an inner glow, shows the results of over-exposure to sun, wind, steam heat, and lack of care—use the MAGI-CARE Trio for truly extraordinary effects.

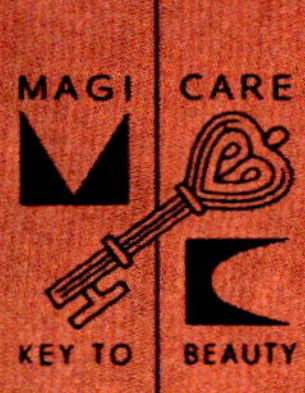

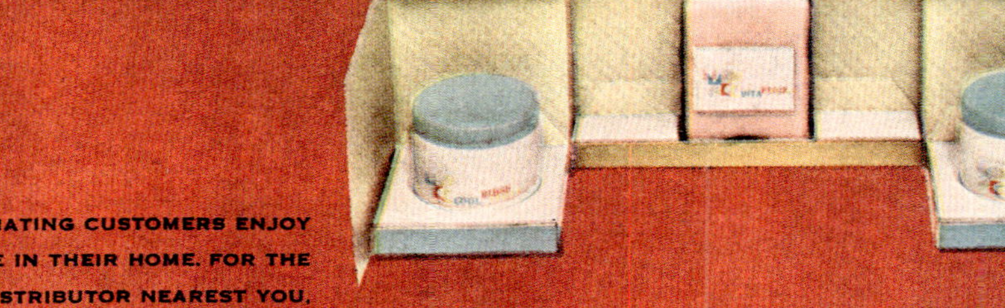

DISCRIMINATING CUSTOMERS ENJOY PERSONAL SERVICE IN THEIR HOME. FOR THE MAGI-CARE DISTRIBUTOR NEAREST YOU, SEE THE FOLLOWING PAGE OR WRITE: MYTINGER & CASSELBERRY, INC., 1700 SANTA FE AVENUE, LONG BEACH, CALIFORNIA

Opposite:
"Dress and Coat by Mainbocher"
Harper's Bazaar
March 14, 1956
Photograph by
Richard Avedon

Previous spread:
Ad for "Magi-Care"
Carmen Dell'Orefice,
Suzy Parker, Jean Patchett
November 21, 1958
Photograph by
Richard Avedon

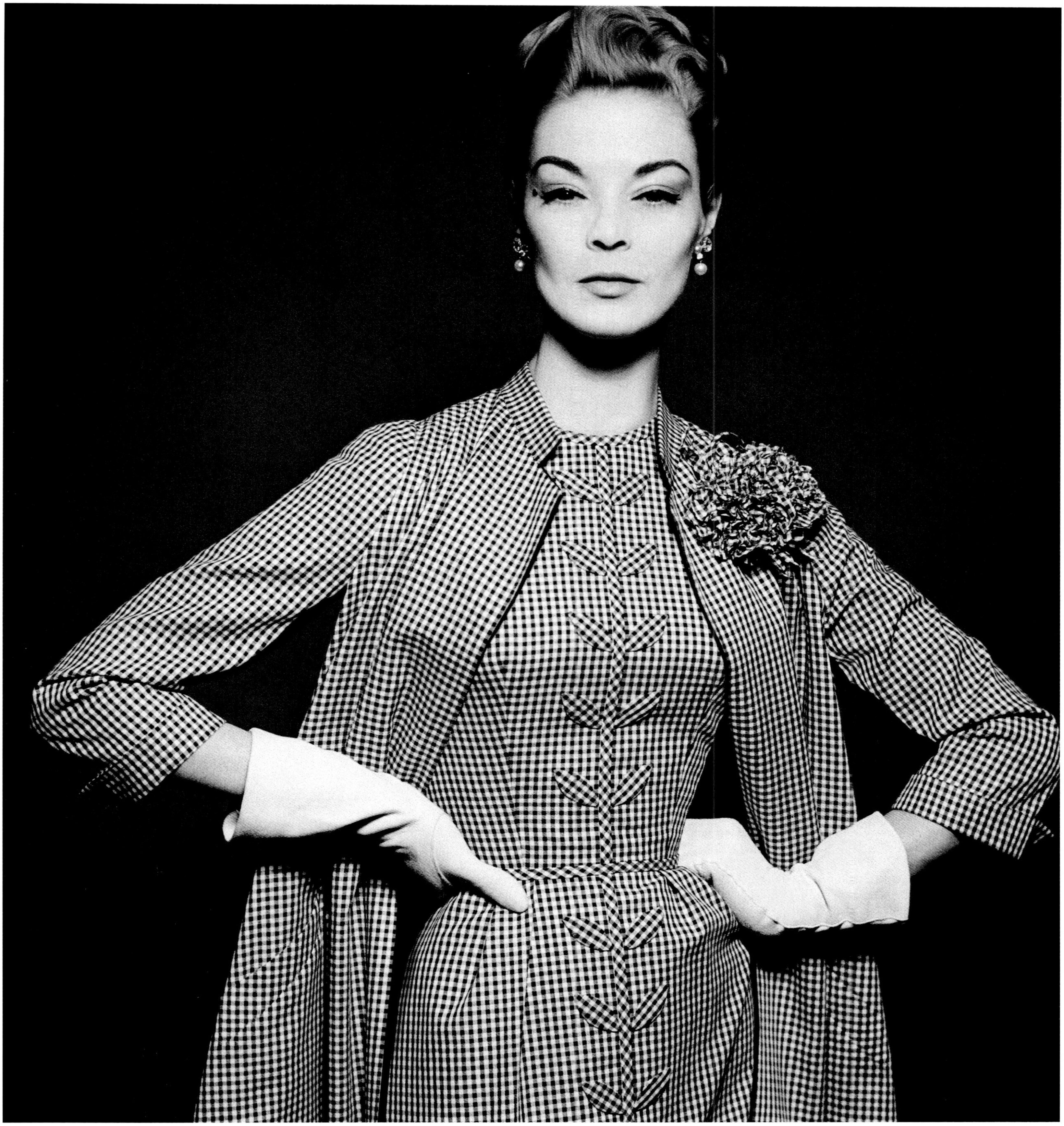

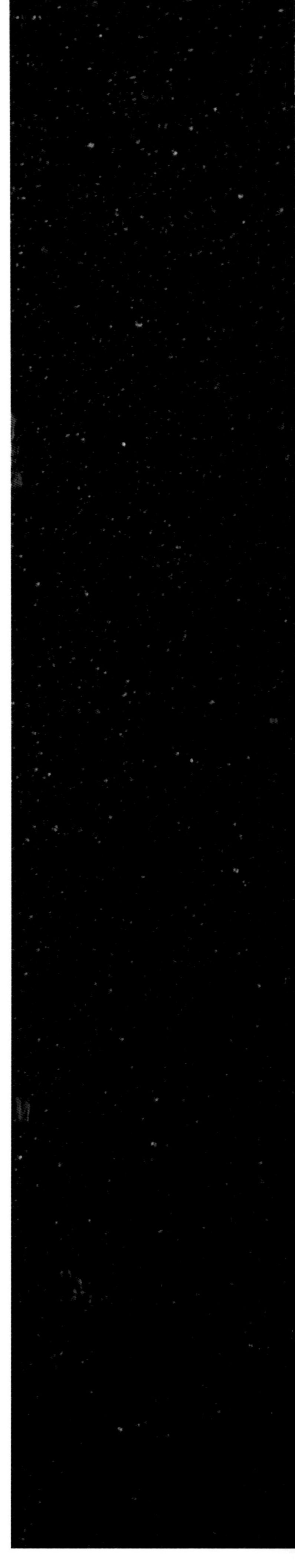

The prettiest girls on the beach this summer will be wearing Precious Little
McCall's
January 13, 1960
Photograph by
Jerry Schatzberg

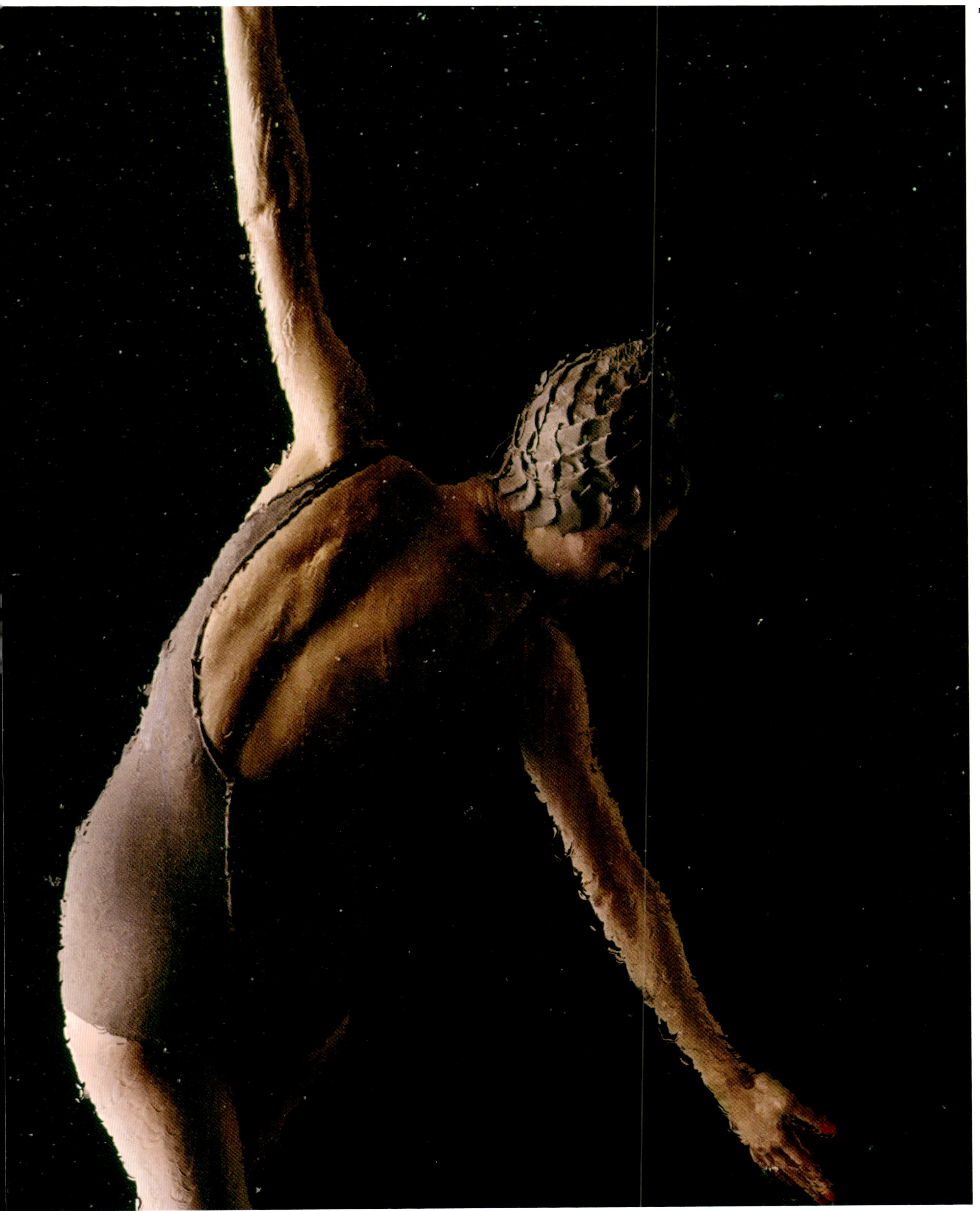

Studio test
March 1, 1961
Photograph by
Jerry Schatzberg

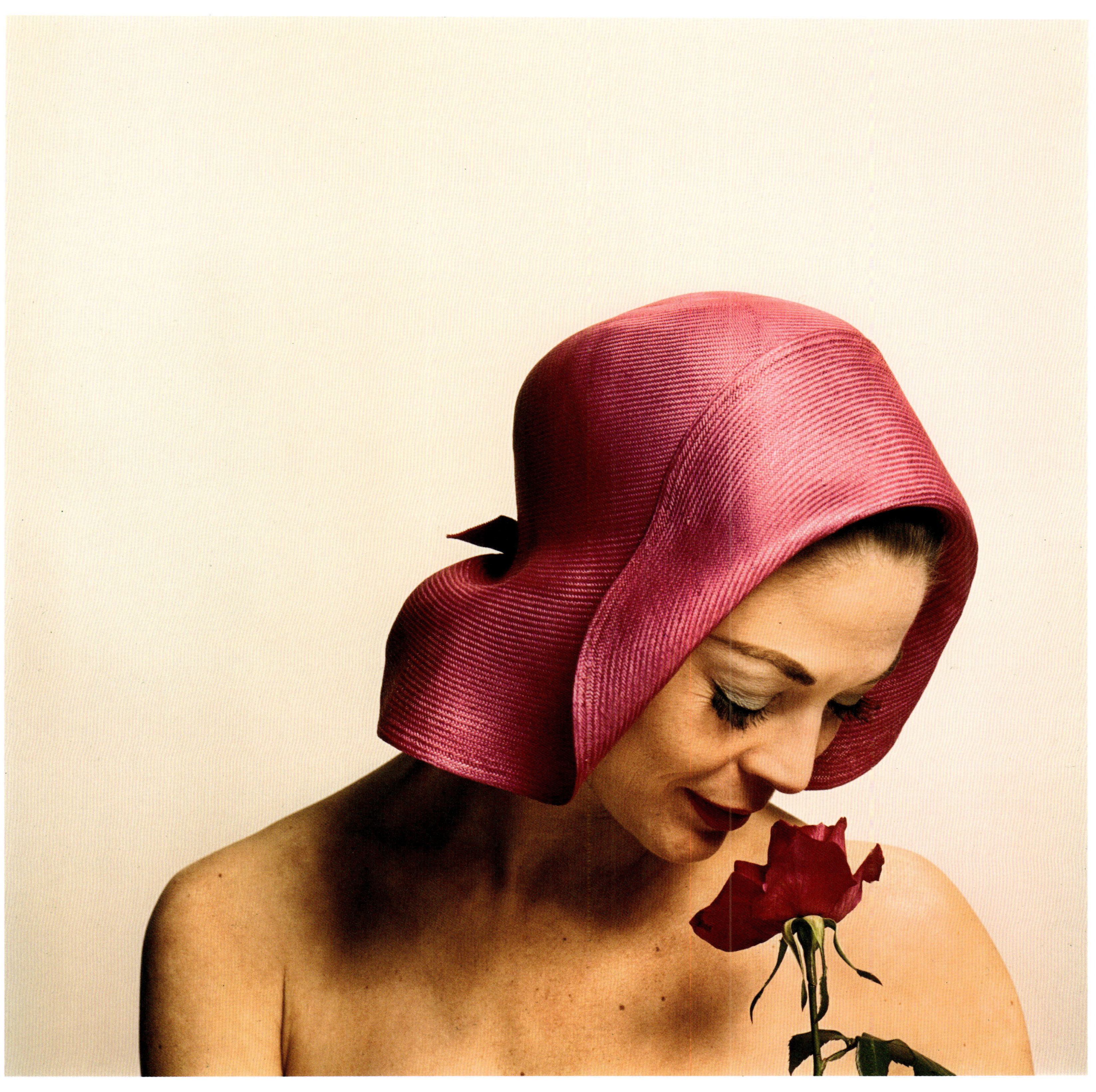

DEDICATION

I dedicate this book to my mother, Jean Patchett Auer.
Her legacy to the modeling industry and fashion photography is undeniable.
This book is a tribute to that legacy. It is a story that deserves to be told.
Much love and respect, Mom. I am still trying to figure out when you slept.
And to my cousin, Daniel C. Patchett. This book would not have happened without him.
He had an idea, a dream—now his passion, dedication, and vison have become a reality.
Cousin—thank you for bringing Mom's legacy to a new generation
and for honoring her, as you have done with all things Jean.

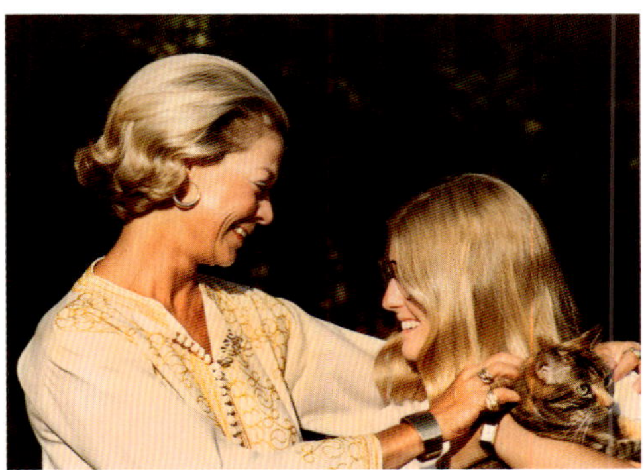

Jean Patchett Auer
and Amy Auer Hensley
Westhampton Beach,
New York, 1976

ACKNOWLEDGMENTS

This is Amy Auer Hensley's book as much as it is ours. Her unflagging commitment and support for this tribute to her mother made it possible.

The same can be said for Daniel Patchett. Without his passion for Jean's career and legacy this book would not have happened. Dan's dedication to all things Jean can be witnessed on his website, jeanpatchett.com.

Special thanks to Patty Sicular of Iconic Focus, who made key contributions and brought the principals together—and to publishing maven, author, and friend Christopher Sweet, who found this book a home.

We are gratified by the generous support of The Irving Penn Foundation and our contact there, Matthew Krejcarek, along with The Richard Avedon Foundation and Erin Harris, Miranda Muscente at Conde Nast, and the ever-helpful Leigh Grissom at the Center for Creative Photography.

Sincere thanks as well to Faith Cooper at the Museum at the Fashion Institute of Technology, Lizzie Himmel, Nadia Blumenfeld Charbit, Ellie Brown and Catherine David at Iconic Images, Laurie Feigenbaum at Hearst, Dan Boland at Getty Images, Andrea Derujinsky, and Joshua Greene.

Thanks to Bill Helburn and Jerry Schatzberg for sharing their memories of Jean and her milieu, to Melvin Sokolsky for his observations, to Barbara Mullen, Dolores Hawkins, Tippi Hedren, and Nyna Giles for reflections on life from the other side of the lens, and to advertising executive Joe Nissen and Jean's cousin Walt Patchett for their memories of Jean.

We are grateful for Maria Morris Hambourg's generosity with her time and knowledge—essential to our efforts to understand Jean's collaboration with Irving Penn. Laird Borelli-Persson shared a perspective without which this book would be bereft; a deep understanding of the fashions Jean modeled and the magazines where her images appeared. Our deepest thanks to Etheleen Staley and Takouhy Wise of the Staley-Wise Gallery for sharing their space, deep knowledge of fashion photography, and their continued support.

The steady hands of Craig Cohen and Will Luckman at powerHouse Books helped steer us throughout the production process. Designer Francesca Richer spun gold with her layout.

Richard Jackson of Hance Partners Inc. lent his painterly touch to some of the finest fashion images ever made.

Getting this book to the publisher would have been a much steeper climb had we not had the multi-talented Raphael Carleton as our all-around assistant, technical advisor, and spreadsheet consultant. Up in Boston, Jason Lilly lent a musical ear and a quick hand to turning our interviews into transcripts.

Thanks again to Susan Camp for her friendship and unrivaled speed and accuracy at identifying many of the models who posed with Jean, to Peter Fetterman, of the Peter Fetterman Gallery, for his mentorship, and to our friends at Supima for their support.

We greatly appreciate the legal guidance of Judith Bass and Doreen Small.

Much of the research for this book was done in the stacks at the Gladys Marcus Library at New York's Fashion Institute of Technology, with side trips to the Public Library in Port Washington, New York. Special thanks also to Megan Ó Connell at the David M. Rubenstein Rare Book & Manuscript Library at Duke University.

Thank you, Jean.

CREDITS

Photographs by RICHARD AVEDON:

© The Richard Avedon Foundation
Pages 50–51, 118–119, 121, 144–145, 176–177, 179

Photograph by SERGE BALKIN:

Serge Balkin/Vogue © Conde Nast
Back cover, page 15

Photographs by PETER BASCH:

Image by Peter Basch © Basch LLC
Pages 69, 83

Photographs by LILLIAN BASSMAN:

© Lillian Bassman/Reprinted with permission of Hearst Magazine Media, Inc.
Pages 52, 53, 103

Photographs by CECIL BEATON:

© Cecil Beaton/Conde Nast Collection/Getty Images
Page 19

Cecil Beaton/Vogue © Conde Nast
Page 90

Photographs by ERWIN BLUMENFELD:

© 2019 The estate of Erwin Blumenfeld
Front cover, pages 21, 95, 142

© Erwin Blumenfeld/Conde Nast Collection/Getty Images
Page 20

Erwin Blumenfeld/Vogue © Conde Nast
Page 156

Photographs by A. AUBREY BODINE:

© Jennifer B. Bodine courtesy of www.aaubreybodine.com
Pages 12, 18

Photographs by CLIFFORD COFFIN:

Clifford Coffin/Vogue © Conde Nast
Pages 40, 44–45, 46, 47, 96–97, 104

Clifford Coffin/Glamour © Conde Nast
Back cover, pages 79, 109

Photographs by LOUISE DAHL-WOLFE:

© Center for Creative Photography, Arizona Board of Regents/Collection: Amy Auer Hensley
Page 54

© Center for Creative Photography, Arizona Board of Regents/Collection: Center for Creative Photography, University of Arizona, Louise Dahl-Wolfe Archive. Posthumous reproduction from original negative
Pages 54–55, 99, 130–131, 137

© Center for Creative Photography, Arizona Board of Regents/Courtesy the Museum at FIT/Reprinted with permission of Hearst Magazine Media, Inc.
Back cover, pages 129, 153

© Center for Creative Photography, Arizona Board of Regents/Courtesy the Museum at FIT
Page 132, 138, 139, 154–155

© Center for Creative Photography, Arizona Board of Regents/Collection: Center for Creative Photography, University of Arizona, Louise Dahl-Wolfe Archive
Page 147

© Center for Creative Photography, Arizona Board of Regents/Reprinted with permission of Hearst Magazine Media, Inc.
Back cover, page 135

Photograph by JERRY DANTZIC:

© Jerry Dantzic Archives, all rights reserved
Page 39

Photograph by GLEB DERUJINSKY:

© Derujinsky
Page 150

Photographs by FRANCES MCLAUGHLIN-GILL:

© Frances McLaughlin-Gill/Vogue © Conde Nast
Pages 100–101, 146

Photographs by MILTON H. GREENE:

Milton H. Greene © 2019 Joshua Greene
www.archiveimages.com
Page 78

Milton H. Greene © 2019 Joshua Greene
www.archiveimages.com/Iconic Images
Page 125

Photographs by WILLIAM HELBURN:

William Helburn/Charm © Conde Nast
Back cover, pages 48, 92

© William Helburn LLC
Pages 41, 93, 141, 143, 151 159, 160–161

Courtesy William Helburn
Pages 122, 158, 164, 166, 167, 169

Photographs courtesy AMY AUER HENSLEY:

Pages 8, 9, 13, 14, 26, 27, 42, 45, 185

Photographs by HORST P. HORST:

Horst P. Horst/Vogue © Conde Nast
Back cover, pages 2, 23, 62, 64, 67, 75, 82, 105, 110, 157

Horst P. Horst/Vogue © Conde Nast Collection/Getty Images
Page 74

Photographs by NINA LEEN:

© Nina Leen/The LIFE Picture Collection/Getty Images
Pages 10, 11

Photograph by LEONARD MCCOMBE:

© Leonard McCombe/The LIFE Picture Collection/Getty Images
Page 22

Photograph by GJON MILI:

© Gjon Mili/The LIFE Picture Collection/Getty Images
Page 111

Photographs by NORMAN PARKINSON:

© Norman Parkinson/Iconic Images
Pages 6, 81, 91, 106–107, 114, 117

Photographs by IRVING PENN:

Irving Penn/Vogue © Conde Nast
Back cover, pages 5, 25, 28, 35, 59, 60–61, 68, 70–71, 72, 86, 89, 126

© The Irving Penn Foundation
Pages 30, 31, 32, 33, 34, 36, 37

Photograph by KAREN RADKAI:

Karen Radkai/Vogue © Conde Nast
Page 162

Photographs by JOHN RAWLINGS:

John Rawlings/Vogue © Conde Nast
Pages, 16, 63, 77, 84–85, 113, 165

Photograph by RICHARD RUTLEDGE:

Richard Rutledge/Vogue © Conde Nast
Page 149

Photographs by JERRY SCHATZBERG:

© Jerry Schatzberg
Pages 57, 172, 173, 175, 180–181, 183

Photograph by MARK SHAW:

© 2000 Mark Shaw, MPTVIMAGES.com
Page 163

© CBS News
Page 42

BIBLIOGRAPHY

Photobiography, Cecil Beaton, Doubleday & Company, 1951

Eye to I: The Autobiography of a Photographer, Erwin Blumenfeld, Thames and Hudson, 1999

Stork Club: America's Most Famous Nightspot and the Lost World of Café Society, Ralph Blumenthal, Little, Brown and Company, 2000

Model Girl, Charles Castle, Chartwell, 1977

The Real Mad Men: The Renegades of Madison Avenue and the Golden Age of Advertising, Andrew Cracknell, Running Press, 2012

The Fashionable Mind: Reflections on Fashion 1970–1981, Kennedy Fraser, Alfred A. Knopf, 1981

Model: The Ugly Business of Beautiful Women, Michael Gross, Harper Perennial, 2003

Focus: The Secret, Sexy, Sometimes Sordid World of Fashion Photographers, Michael Gross, Atria Books, 2016

Irving Penn: Centennial, Maria Morris Hambourg and Jeff L. Rosenheim, Metropolitan Museum of Art, 2017

Earthly Bodies: Irving Penn's Nudes, 1949–50, Maria Morris Hambourg, Bulfinch, 2002

Kilgallen: A Biography of Dorothy Kilgallen, Lee Israel, Delacorte Press, 1979

Alex: The Life of Alexander Liberman, Dodie Kazanjian and Calvin Tomkins, Alfred A. Knopf, 1993

The Model as Muse: Embodying Fashion, Harold Koda and Kohle Yohannan, Metropolitan Museum of Art, 2009

Model Woman: Eileen Ford and the Business of Beauty, Robert Lacey, HarperCollins, 2015

Horst: His Work and His World, Valentine Lawford, Alfred A. Knopf, 1984

William Helburn: Seventh and Madison, Robert Lilly and Lois Allen Lilly, Thames & Hudson, 2014

The Photographer and His Model, John Rawlings, Viking, 1966

Clifford Coffin: Photographs from Vogue 1945 to 1955, Edited by Robin Muir, Stewart, Tabori & Chang, 1997

Lillian Bassman: Women, Deborah Solomon, Abrams, 2009

Avedon: Something Personal, Norma Stevens and Steven M. L. Aronson, Spiegel & Grau, 2017

"Changes in women's labor force participation in the 20th century," Bureau of Labor Statistics, U.S. Department of Labor, February, 2000

On the Edge: Images from 100 Years of Vogue, Vogue editors, Random House, 1992

1950s American Fashion, Jonathan Walford, Shire Publications, 2012

This Year's Model: Fashion, Media, and the Making of Glamour, Elizabeth A. Wissinger, New York University Press, 2015

AMERICAN GODDESS: JEAN PATCHETT

Text © 2019 Robert Lilly and Lois Allen Lilly
All images used with permission and © their respective owners

All rights reserved. No part of this book may be reproduced in any manner in any media, or transmitted by any means whatsoever, electronic or mechanical (including photocopy, film or video recording, internet posting, or any other information storage and retrieval system), without the prior written permission of the publisher.

Published in the United States by powerHouse Books,
a division of powerHouse Cultural Entertainment, Inc.
32 Adams Street, Brooklyn, NY 11201-1021
e-mail: info@powerHouseBooks.com
website: www.powerHouseBooks.com

First edition, 2019

Library of Congress Control Number: 2019941650

ISBN 978-1-57687-927-6

Book design by Francesca Richer

Printed by Artron Art

10 9 8 7 6 5 4 3 2 1

Printed and bound in China